The
Amateur Naturalist

I dedicate this book to the most inspiring and truly beautiful creature that I have ever studied. My wife, Mireya.

The
Amateur Naturalist

Nick Baker

Foreword by Lee Durrell

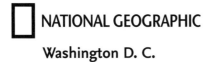

NATIONAL GEOGRAPHIC

Washington D. C.

HarperCollinsPublishers Ltd.
77-85 Fulham Palace Road
London
W6 8JB

Everything clicks at:
www.collins.co.uk

Collins is a registered trademark of
HarperCollinsPublishers Ltd.

First published in 2004

A catalog record for this book is available from the British Library.
ISBN 0 00 715731 2

Edited by Caroline Taggart
Layout by Colin Brown

Color reproduction by Radstock
Printed and bound in Great Britain by Bath Press

Library of Congress Cataloging-in-Publication Data
Baker, Nick
The amateur naturalist / Nick Baker; foreword by Lee Durrell. p.cm.
ISBN 0-7922-9348-7
1. Nature Study. 2. Natural history--Technique. I. Title.
QH51.B244 2005 508--dc22   2004057568

One of the world's largest nonprofit scientific and educational
organizations, the National Geographic Society was founded in 1888
"for the increase and diffusion of geographic knowledge." Fulfilling
this mission, the Society educates and inspires millions every day
through its magazines, books, television programs, videos, maps and
atlases, research grants, the National Geographic Bee, teacher workshops, and
innovative classroom materials. The Society is supported through membership dues,
charitable gifts, and income from the sale of its educational products. This support is
vital to National Geographic's mission to increase global understanding and promote
conservation of our planet through exploration, research, and education.

For more information, please call 1-800-NGS LINE (647-5463)
or write to the following address:

National Geographic Society
1145 17th Street N.W.
Washington, D.C. 20036-4688 U.S.A.

Visit the Society's Web site at www.nationalgeographic.com.

Contents

Foreword

Having spent some of the most enjoyable years of my life researching, writing, and filming *The Amateur Naturalist* with my late husband, Gerald Durrell, I was delighted to be asked to write this foreword for Nick Baker's new *The Amateur Naturalist* and eager to see the finished manuscript. How was Nick going to handle the vast subject of natural history, what exciting new ideas and techniques had he come across, would he have had as much fun as Gerry and I did putting the information together? Did he hope, as we did, that a generation of readers would take the book to their hearts and learn to cherish nature and become part of the movement to protect it?

My keen anticipation was hugely rewarded, and I was enticed into the natural world all over again. The book begins very sensibly with what equipment you need as an amateur naturalist, offering tips as to how to choose and use it, from binoculars and hand lenses to notebooks and clothing. It then leads you logically through the animal and plant kingdoms: mammals, birds, reptiles, amphibians, fish, invertebrates, and plants. You get a solid grounding in what to look for and how to observe it, but Nick also grabs your attention with unusual facts – how to tell a right-handed from a left-handed squirrel, for example – punctuated with the occasional hysterically funny personal reminiscence. The activities he suggests are creative and fun – recognizing bird calls in the dawn chorus, a foolproof recipe for rearing tadpoles, what you do to preserve a spider's web. The projects are all safe and eco-friendly as well.

Nick has a deft style and a quirky sense of humor that brings to life the animals and plants he is writing about. More than anything, he makes you want to spend time outdoors becoming a nature detective. He teaches you how to pick up and interpret signs that reveal an animal's behavior, and to gather clues that will unravel ecological mysteries.

Today it is more important than ever before that humans understand the natural world. We need to know what its components are and how they come together to make operational ecosystems. We must appreciate how the ecosystems in turn influence each other to make the whole planet tick. Otherwise, the rate at which we modify the natural order of things will outpace our ability to correct our environmental mistakes, let alone avoid making them in the first place. We can already see our eco-blunders wherever we look – irreversible loss of soils, severe floods and droughts, actual and imminent extinctions of animals and plants, to name but a few examples of the human "footprint" on the planet. But if decisions which impact on the environment are made by people who understand and cherish the natural world, then our tread will be lighter and the planet a more hospitable place for all its inhabitants.

The more youngsters are encouraged to pursue natural history, the more likely it is that they, as the decision-makers of the future, will make the right choices.

Lee Durrell

Lee Durrell
2 June 2004

Introduction

For as long as I can remember I have been mesmerized by plants and animals, and not just the living, breathing ones. Everything about them — feeding signs and other evidence they leave behind, even their dead bodies — can tell us so much about them. But although I have been an amateur naturalist all my life, to this day I continue to learn how and where to look at the living world. That is really what this book is about — using my experiences and the tricks of the trade that I have amassed over the years to gain more insight into the world we live in.

My interest started as soon as I could crawl, and pretty soon I was putting my mother through situations no mother can be prepared for: giant silk moths in the wardrobe, tarantulas under the bed, and the countless dead animals I would find while out and about and bring home to dismantle at leisure — a form of behavior my family found particularly disturbing! But to me there was very little difference between wishing to see and understand the internal workings of an animal and my brother pulling a lawn mower engine to pieces for the same reason.

Through those dark, misunderstood times, a wonderful book called *The Amateur Naturalist* by Gerald and Lee Durrell became my friend, inspiring me to look, investigate, and satisfy my natural curiosity. That book was a major influence on my becoming a naturalist, and it was very much the inspiration behind this one. I am deeply grateful to Lee Durrell for providing such a generous foreword to this new *Amateur Naturalist*.

Things haven't changed much since those early days, despite the fact that I am now a responsible adult with my own house — it is still stuffed full of natural curios, both living creatures and the inevitable collections of debris, skulls, bones, and feathers. To me this hands-on approach is totally in keeping with the ethos of this book. You will never really understand something by looking at pictures and writing. Just as you need to stroke a feather to comprehend what an extraordinary combination of form and function it is, you also need to turn a skull over in your hands if you really want to appreciate the beauty of this remarkable collection of bones.

Having said that, you will find a lot more about the living than about the dead in these pages. After all, the living, breathing, breeding natural world is all around us, and its influences are felt by all of us, naturalist or not. They are the greenfly in your salad, the sticky stuff that gets on your car in the summer, and the bird song that gives a bounce to your step on the way to work or school on a spring morning. Like it or not, we are part of this natural world — it's just that modern life has allowed us to surround ourselves with a cocoon of comfort that isolates us from it.

At its most basic, being an amateur naturalist is simply about enjoying being in touch with our natural surroundings. It's about the joy of observation and discovery, of learning to understand. Some people are put off by the fear that being a naturalist involves learning a lot of science. This is a complete fallacy; to appreciate the miracle of a butterfly emerging from a chrysalis does not require any specialist knowledge. The experience is all that is needed to change the way you look at insects. No Ph.D. required — in fact, a lot of the best and keenest naturalists I know are kids.

On the other hand, you do need an odd collection of personal qualities. You have to be tough enough to be buffeted by the elements and sensitive enough to appreciate the finer points of a wild pansy. And even I will admit that it takes a different approach to life to see beauty in a fox's feces, not to mention some slick thinking in order to explain yourself to those who catch you looking in the first place!

What I have tried to do in this book is introduce you to the various groups of living things that you are likely to come across in your garden, on country walks, and on holiday, and to give you a bit of information on what they are and how they live their lives. I have described a range of useful skills and investigative techniques and explained projects and tricks of the trade that you can try out in the field and when you take your specimens home.

What I really want you to do is get out there, get down on your hands and knees, get your hands dirty, look, learn, and enjoy.

What's what and who's who: a quick guide to classification

The way the animal and plant kingdoms are organized may seem a bit baffling at first, with all those long scientific names, but knowing just a bit about it will help you understand which animals and plants are related to each other; that in turn will give you clues to their appearance and behavior. The kingdoms are the biggest group; the further down the list, the more closely related members of a group are, with members of the same species normally the only ones that can mate and produce viable offspring.

Kingdom

Phylum

Class

Order

Family

Genus

Species

"King Philip Came Over For Great Sex" is how the Americans remember the order of classification.

Try not to be daunted by this system. Great naturalists from Linnaeus, Darwin, and Wallace until the present day continue to fine-tune, correct, and reclassify plants and animals. It is still very much a work in progress as we learn more and more about the natural world and its sweet little mysteries. Keep in mind that this system is intended to make life easier for biologists; just as books are classified in a library, each animal and plant is grouped with other animals and plants with which they have the most similarities.

The scientific names which you will find scattered through this and many other books on the subject are really nothing more than labels. If you always work in the same locality you can get away with using common names, but when you start talking to people in another country, these often fall down and become next to useless. Say something about woodlice to Americans, and they will nearly always look baffled, as they know them as sow bugs, but mention their scientific name, and you are on your way to a common understanding.

These names come in two parts: The first is the genus, which may contain similar and closely related species and is always given a capital letter; and the second is the specific name, which is unique to this animal and is written with a small letter.

Codes of conduct

As a naturalist, you have a duty to the natural world around you. I will remind you of these rules again and again in the course of the book, but here is a summary of the most important ones.

☀ Keep disturbance to a minimum. Never collect more of anything, whether it is a flower or a batch of frog spawn, than you need for your studies, and always release specimens in the same place as you caught them as soon as you have finished looking at them.

☀ Never handle any living creature unnecessarily. Learn as much as you can from observation alone. If you do have to handle specimens, do it gently and quickly.

☀ Never make sudden movements. A lot of wild creatures are of a nervous disposition, and even the smallest of them can scuttle at great speed. Approach them slowly and quietly, from upwind if possible.

☀ Be extra careful if approaching anything you have reason to believe may be venomous or otherwise harmful to your health. If in doubt, don't do it.

☀ Do your homework in advance. There are many protected species of plant and animal that you are not allowed to pick or keep without a license.

☀ If you are setting traps, bait them with suitable food and water and check them regularly. Many small animals and birds need to eat almost constantly, and you are seriously failing in your obligations if you let them die while they are supposed to be in your care.

☀ Use a buddy system, particularly if you are going anywhere off the beaten track or in water. Take a reliable friend with you, or at least make sure someone knows where you are and what time you are expecting to be back.

☀ Take your litter and detritus home or put it in a proper bin. Never, ever dispose of it at sea.

The essential hardware
equipment

As a naturalist you will spend a lot of time trying to get close to wildlife while that same wildlife is doing its best to run away from you. With almost every creature you are eager to observe ready to run at the merest hint of a rustle, cough, or hiccup, it may seem that the odds are stacked against you. But, as you will find throughout this book, there are a few tricks you can employ to redress the balance. The first is to make yourself as invisible as possible when you are close to a subject, and the second is to keep your distance in the first place. From afar you can observe but not interfere, and that's where a pair of binoculars or a telescope comes into its own.

How to hide a human
the art of not being seen

This is a technique that is most useful when you are watching mammals but applies to most other kinds of wildlife too. Remember that when you are out in the field you could bump into a mammal at any moment, and by following these simple rules you can extend the encounter and learn much more.

Blend into the background: wear dark, quiet clothes so that you make as little visual impact and as little noise as possible (see pp.16–18).

Be aware of every noise your body makes: not only obvious things such as footsteps and cracking twigs, but also clothing noise, catching on vegetation, and even breathing.

Be conscious of the wind direction: if you suddenly stumble into an exciting situation, it is good to know instinctively where to go. Regularly check even the slightest fairy breath of air movement by dropping a feather, chalk dust, or ordinary dust from the ground if the terrain is dry enough. Keep the wind in your face or at least not behind you. For many terrestrial mammals, smell is the most important sense and the one that usually gives you away first. The importance of wind direction cannot be overemphasized; in unfamiliar territory it can literally be a matter of life and death. Sure, it will ruin your day if you come across some deer and the wind direction gives you away, but imagine turning a bush and finding a black rhino already midcharge, because it knew where you were coming from before you even realized it was there! This kind of experience can make for exciting tales, if you survive, but from the point of view of the naturalist who wants to observe without interfering with his subjects, you would have failed. Yes, you would have seen some interesting behavior, but you would have altered it considerably.

More haste, less speed: move deliberately and expect the unexpected, especially as you move through visual barriers or approach spots where you are likely to find your quarry. Try to think like the animals you are after.

On sighting: move very slowly, using natural cover if possible. Reduce your outline by slowly crouching down to the ground. Keeping low means there is less of your body profile to be seen and you present a nonthreatening shape to your quarry.

Never make sudden movements: well, I say this as a general rule, but sometimes I find that, if an animal is distracted for a moment, I can take the opportunity to get into the position I want, quickly. There is a fine line between making yourself comfortable and blowing your chances; only experience will tell you what you can and cannot get away with.

Use your senses: we humans are blessed with better noses, ears, and eyes than we often give ourselves credit for. Most of us walk about looking but not seeing, hearing but not listening, and sniffing but not smelling. Train yourself to use what nature gave you effectively.

Choice of clothing

There is no simple answer to the question of what to wear. It's more of a case of what not to wear, and this depends entirely on what you intend to do while wearing it. But there are a number of "crimes of the cloth" that can be avoided with a little bit of foresight.

Color really doesn't matter as much as you may think. I have seen people dressed up in military camouflage, looking like extras from an Arnold Schwarzenegger film, with all the latest real tree-print jackets, face nets, and gloves, who blow their cover simply by stepping out from behind a bush at the wrong time, moving in the wrong way, breaking cover on the crest of a hill, or sneezing. It's really how you move that is critical.

But why run the risk of attracting unwanted attention to yourself in the first place? Generally the best colors are dowdy ones that wouldn't look out of place in nature. Personally I like black, as it doesn't look out of place in the street either.

Material: you don't want that rustle in the bushes to be you! Hearing is an important sense for some of the more highly strung creatures, acting as an early warning system. So you need to keep noise to a minimum, and that includes your clothes. Waterproof tops or shell layers are the worst culprits. You would be surprised how noisy a pair of nylon trousers or a waterproof jacket can be – they may not be huge on the decibel scale, but they will not only drive you insane as you "swizz, swizz, swizz" along, they will also give away your position to any creature in the vicinity. As an alternative, materials such as Ventile, a superdense cotton weave used to make military immersion suits, may be a bit more expensive but are a worthwhile investment if you are going to spend long hours out of doors. If your budget is small, self-awareness is the key. This isn't a bad discipline for naturalists anyway, so look on it as a kind of training exercise. It is possible to walk quietly in even the noisiest of fabrics, by being aware of what is creating the noise. Usually it is legs rubbing against legs or arms against torso, so try to avoid these movements while you walk.

Zippers or flaps? Zips jingle and rattle with every movement, but can be silenced by sticking down the tag with mastic or duct tape. Space-age technology has given us Velcro, which is great for sealing pockets and zippers, but many a flock of geese or pine marten has been sent flapping or flinging its way into the great yonder by someone diving noisily for a pocketed field guide or Kit Kat. This also brings us to the great Velcro dilemma. Do you tear the surfaces apart quickly and make one short, sharp noise, or slowly, which is a little quieter but with the noise sustained for longer? As always, the situation determines.

Clothing tips

Dress quietly: don't keep loose change in your pockets; the jingle of coins can blow the cover of even the most camouflaged naturalist. Loose Wellington boots are among the worst culprits for making clunking noises. Either get some that fit snugly or wear lace-up boots. Rustly layers are usually waterproof ones. Keep waterproofs tucked away in a bag when you are not using them

If you are working in the cold, you need good gloves. Mittens are the warmest, although you have to take them off for any tasks requiring dexterity. Some fingerless gloves come with mitten covers and are a great "best of both worlds" solution.

For flexibility in varying weather conditions, I usually start with a sweat-wicking underlayer (that means that it carries the sweat away from your body and stops you getting uncomfortably hot). Then I build up with multiple lightweight layers and a fleece. A shell layer can be added on top for waterproofing and windproofing. When working in the wet, I like waterproof socks. Even if your boots let in water, these socks mean you remain dry right to their tops.

Hats are very useful for colder weather or if you are out at night. Beanies are warm but get wet, brimmed hats are useful for keeping water off your head and away from shoulders but still expose your ears. On hot days a brimmed hat also helps keep the sun off your neck. Baseball caps are useful if you are working in and against the sun. Not only do they keep the sun off your face, but they also act as a visor, meaning you don't have to keep raising your hand to your brow to shield your eyes against the glare.

A versatile piece of lightweight clothing that I find indispensable is the "buff." These tubes of materials come in a variety of colors and patterns; some are of a thin and stretchy fabric, others are thick and fleecy for winter wear. They can be worn as a kind of draft excluder around your neck, or as a headband, hat, scarf, or face mask for keeping out cold air or even breaking up the outline of your face in the field.

Pockets are good, but too many pockets can be bad when it comes to finding what you are looking for. Get into the habit of having special places for certain items, and you will spend less time fumbling.

Binoculars
through those looking glasses

Most of a naturalist's skill lies in observation, and by putting distance between yourself and your subject, you are less likely to influence natural behavior. Thanks to a Dutch optician who invented the telescope back in the 1600s, we are able to look farther afield than we could with the naked eye. With binoculars and telescope, we can effectively draw our subjects closer to us, so that we can see the details without interfering.

As a naturalist you can skimp and bodge and make do with most things, but good binoculars are essential. Fortunately the technology boom has brought the birder's badge of status within the price range of many who would previously have had to choose between buying a car and owning a pair of quality German optics. I'm not an equipment snob, but when it comes to binoculars, accept no compromise. In a nutshell, you get what you pay for, and so always buy the best you can afford. Cheap binoculars rarely deliver. In fact the view through some is so restricted and dull that, despite the magnification, I can honestly say that, if you were to forget the binoculars and use the eyes you were born with, you would see more of the subject! Binoculars should be a pleasure to use. They will become an extension of yourself, and a friend for life, and most important, they should be with you and accessible wherever you go.

So many binoculars: which to choose?

Well, it's horses for courses. First of all, decide what you are going to be using them for and how often. Are they to sit in the glove compartment of your car, or are you going to drag them through the wilds of Outer Mongolia, miles from the nearest lens cloth? Are you going to use them once every leap year, or will they become your life companions, never leaving your bosom? Are you going to hand-hold them for birdwatching or set them up on a tripod to watch crepuscular mammals or scan the ocean for sharks?

Once you have answered these questions, the rest is relatively easy: Just keep the following points in mind and remember that you are selecting binoculars for *you*. People are different — what suits one person will not suit another, and, because you can be lured into parting with a lot of cash for top models, the wrong choice can be an expensive one.

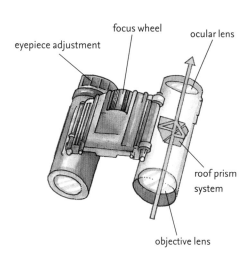

eyepiece adjustment

focus wheel

ocular lens

roof prism system

objective lens

Straight, roof prism binoculars

The price to pay or pay the price: at the risk of preaching, it really is that simple: The more you spend, the better the binoculars, and the better the binoculars, the more you will use them. The better quality the optics, the clearer the image, and because things look great through them, you will use them more often because you want to! They will also be built better, last longer, and become friends for life, even heirlooms. Got the message?

What type? There are two main body styles: porroprism, the traditional "old school" binocular with an angled body; and roof prism, the kind with a straight barrel that is fashionable at present. At the cheaper end of the market, porroprism is better, as there are fewer reflective surfaces for the light to pass through; start spending more than say $450, and the optically corrected roof prisms rule.

Quality on a budget? Go for a secondhand pair. Good binoculars rarely go wrong, they don't rust, and you can tell if they are seriously damaged by simply looking at the lenses and holding them to your eyes – even then a good brand will probably be easy to repair. Once you have worked out exactly what you want, look in the back of local free papers, optical catalogues, and birdwatching magazines. This is what I did, and I still own my first pair of Zeiss dialyts.

Magnification: the properties of binoculars are specified by two numbers, such as 8x32, which will be written on them somewhere. The first indicates the magnification and means that the image you see through the binocular will appear that many times closer to you (i.e. 8 times closer, in this example). Magnification can vary from 4x to 16x, and the most useful for the naturalist is between 8x and 10x. For beginners and for those wanting more depth of field – in other words, more of the scene in focus, which you would need in dense vegetation – 7x and 8x are best; they are also easier to hold steady without technique. For watching raptors and distant birds at sea, 10x are superb. Anything more than this, and tiny movements from your body, your heartbeat and breathing, combined with environmental factors such as the wind, make the image so shaky that the trade-off is not worth it. Also, the higher the magnification, the duller the image.

Generally speaking, the lower the magnification:
* the brighter the image
* the closer the nearest focal point

* the greater the depth of field
* the wider the field of view
* the easier the binoculars are to hold

The higher the magnification:
* the less bright the image
* the narrower the depth of field
* the heavier the binoculars are
* the harder they are to hold still

Stay away from zoom lenses – they are a bit of a gimmick, unless they are built by the higher-end brands, and then they are expensive. Zoom models rarely do what they are supposed to; the quality of the image is inconsistent across the ranges, and so you tend not to use the feature very often; and because the mechanism itself is complicated and fragile, it is more likely to malfunction and need repairing.

Image-stabilizing technology, developed by Canon, allows the use of higher magnification in handheld binoculars without hand shake and is now found in camera lenses, too. Complicated electric-trickery inside the body of the binoculars means steady, high magnifications can be achieved. These binoculars are worth checking out – some people swear by them, though other people complain of a nausea akin to seasickness after extended periods of use.

The letter *B* after the magnification means that they have push-down or rubber eye caps, so that if you wear glasses, you can use them without reducing your field of view.

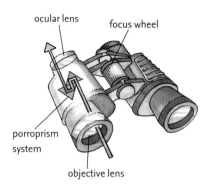

ocular lens   focus wheel

porroprism
system

objective lens

Porroprism binoculars

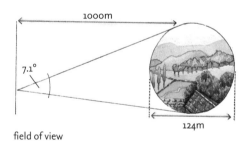

1000m

7.1°

124m

field of view

Brightness: the second number in the pair gives the diameter of the objective lens. This is the lens through which the light enters at the other end of the binocular from the eyepiece. It may not seem as important as magnification, but it has a huge effect on the quality of the image. The bigger the objective lens, the more light enters the binoculars and the brighter the image. This brightness is important, as it determines the detail seen. The size of the binoculars is governed by this second number, not by magnification.

Focus: a maximum of two revolutions of the focus wheel should cover the focus range of the binocular.

Optics: high-density glass (HD) or BAK-4 rather than BK-7 borosilicate glass may seem an insignificant detail but is the major difference between a dull gray blob and a bird with feathers and identity. It's also the main factor in determining price.

Exit pupil: this is the bright hole you see when you look into the eyepiece from a distance – it represents the light entering the binoculars. The exit pupil is given by dividing the size of the objective lens by the magnification. So for a pair of 8x42 binoculars, the exit pupil is 5.2 mm (42/8). Anything above 3.75 mm should cover most naturalists' needs.

Field of view: aim for approximately 120 m at 1,000 m. The wider the field of view, the easier it is to find your subject. Sometimes the field of view is quoted in degrees, and this refers to the field of view at 1,000 m (about 1,100 yd). So if the field of view is quoted as 1°, you will be able to see a range of 17 m at a distance of 1,000 m.

Glass and prism coatings: go for those that are multicoated and, in the case of roof prisms, those that have correctional coatings, too.

Quality of build: good-quality binoculars are fairly robust; they may be metal-bodied or even have rubber armor. The initials "GA" or "RA" show that there is some kind of armor or protective coating. But build quality can come with a price other than the obvious financial one. The question of weight comes into play, and nobody enjoys hanging a brick around their neck on a piece of string.

Comfort and feel: these are personal things – if the most desirable optics in the world feel wrong in your hand, don't balance well, are a nuisance to use, or are just too heavy, they won't work for you. When buying, try different styles, brands, and magnifications until you find the pair that feels right for you. Choose a weight that will be comfortable hanging around your neck, possibly for hours on end, and a size that will fit your hands but allow your index finger to fall on the focus wheel without stretching.

Indestructibility: another very good reason, in fact the best reason, to splash out. This one word should be used in every binocular catalog and by every binocular sales rep. A good pair of binoculars is one that you don't have to worry about, that is robust enough to cope with being dragged through bushes and falling off rocks or out of trees. A more expensive pair is also likely to be gas-sealed, which makes it both waterproof and dustproof. Believe me, this gives you such peace of mind. There is nothing worse than being caught in a downpour and having to worry about your optics getting wet. Mine regularly get a soaking and so far have survived being dropped off a boat into the sea and tangled in the muddy coils of an anaconda.

Tender loving care: another plus for waterproof binoculars is that if they get dusty, sandy, or muddy – regular hazards and the kiss of death to the workings and lenses of cheaper designs – you can simply rinse them off under the tap or wash them in mild soapy water and let them dry on the drainer before polishing the lenses with a lens cloth.

Try them out: take your time selecting the binoculars for you. Do not allow yourself to be swayed by any sales rep. Try as many pairs as you like. Field centers, observatories, and even optical suppliers have open days or will allow you to hold and use their products before you part with your cash. If they don't, go elsewhere – they don't deserve your money.

Protection: once you have selected the exotic optics of your dreams, persuaded the bank to give you that second mortgage, and got the pair home, the first thing you should do is get rid of the lens caps. They will be a hassle and a hindrance when you spring for your binoculars in haste to try to identify that bird that's about to dive. In fact, other than for travel, when you need to protect them, your binoculars should never be put away in a case.

Other ways to use binoculars

A pair that focus close up can be very handy for watching and identifying larger insects, such as butterflies and dragonflies. Close-focus binoculars allow you to focus on near objects more easily. They can also be used as a magnifying apparatus, enabling you to look at tiny details.

Setting up your binoculars

I am frequently horrified when I borrow someone else's binoculars at how badly they are set up or when I mention the adjustment of the diopter and nobody knows what I'm talking about. So here are the two key points to personalizing your binoculars and getting the best view on the world.

Get your IPD correct: interpupillary distance is the distance between your eyes. Everyone is different, which is why binoculars come with a hinge. Look at a distant object with the barrels far apart and then move them together until the image is represented by a nice clean circle. Some binoculars have a scale on them for this. If you are in the habit of lending yours, mark your own setting with a pen or a scratch so that you can restore it easily when you get them back.

Adjust your diopter: for most people there is a difference between the focus of the right and left eye. Most binoculars have a function that accommodates this, and getting it right is a beautiful thing, as everything looks much sharper. It feels more relaxing for the eyes, too.

Different designs have different ways of doing this. If your binoculars have a central focusing wheel, shut your right eye and use the wheel to focus the image you see. Then set the right-eye diopter by shutting your left eye and rotating the barrel of the right eyepiece. Make a note or a mark in case you knock it out of alignment. Once your diopter is set, the focus wheel will focus both eyes.

Some brands have a locking diopter ring on the central focusing barrel; it works in much the same way, but is less easily knocked out of position. A few makes have diopter adjustments on both eyepieces – these have to be reset if you change the distance of the object you are viewing.

The field guide
birding with a bible

The two most important bits of equipment a birdwatcher can have are a good pair of binoculars and a good field guide. For me, top American birdwatching advocate Pete Dunne sums up their importance beautifully: "One confers supernatural intimacy, the other a blueprint to discovery. Together they buy a person passage on a lifelong treasure hunt."

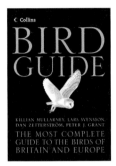
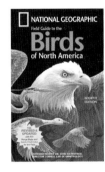

Two birdwatcher's bibles. Nearly every region of the world now has a fine field guide that you can slip into your pocket.

A field guide has to do exactly what it says on the cover: guide you through the process of distinguishing the species you are looking at from all other possibilities and be practical to use in the field. By this I mean that it has to be easily transportable, preferably small enough to fit in a pocket. For some of the recent works of art that cover countries with a huge diversity of birds, it may be worth considering a pouch or bag designed to fit around your waist by being attached to your belt – a much more comfortable way of carrying a large-format book around than the traditional method of jamming it down the back of your trousers. The latter practice should be restricted to smaller guides and to occasions when you do not have to wear a backpack and when the weather is not so hot that your sweat turns even the more robust publications into papier-maché!

Choosing a field guide is really a matter of personal taste. There is no single one that does everything well – they each have their flaws, biases, and layout issues – but you will soon develop your favorites.

To get an idea of some of the best available, check out the *Collins Bird Guide* (Britain and Europe) or, for North America, *The National Geographic Field Guide to the Birds of North America*. Having said that, I have heard pros and cons about both from birders around the world! What it boils down to, and the thing to take home, is *whatever works for you*. A good book is one that allows *you* to identify the birds that *you* see, and, as with all these things, every publisher is always striving to improve, and so even your own favorites may change over time.

A good field guide is organized to enable you to find the bird you want easily – this normally means either in a standard taxonomic order or by visual similarities. To my mind, the most important features are good illustrations that point out noteworthy characteristics and separate a given species from others, especially those species over which confusion often arises in the field. They should also make you aware of any difference between the sexes, or in appearance in flight, and any other plumage variations such as juvenile, breeding, or winter feathers that may throw you off the scent. I avoid photographic guides because I have yet to see one done well. Photographs are restricted in what they can show, and even though a camera doesn't lie, it doesn't always have the flexibility to show all you want to see in the small space allocated to each bird.

I also like a distribution map, ideally on the same page as the identification plates. This is really handy when you are birding in a new and unfamiliar place and have to start from scratch. I will never forget my first trip to Guyana, where I awoke to a dawn chorus unlike any I had ever heard before. As soon as I peered out of the hotel window, it was as if I were five years old again. My birding skills were reduced to excited shouts of, "Oh look, there's a blue one, and a yellow one, and here come five red and green ones!" I had absolutely no idea what I was looking at. Once I had calmed down a bit, my field guide became part of my body, my best friend and an essential organ without which I felt I would perish. Even though there are many pleasures in just looking and watching, the conscious decision to look something up in a book is the beginning of a learning process. To have invested even the tiniest bit of effort in turning a few pages means that the experience somehow sticks better in your head. You become aware of other look-alikes, and you embark on the journey of enlightenment.

One other thing to remember about field guides is not to get too precious about them. Even if the monetary outlay required you to sell your beloved dog, if you are scared to use it in case it gets grubby, dog-eared, or damp, then it isn't working as a field guide. If you are that worried, buy two! Keep one at home all nice and shiny on the bookshelf, and in the other, make notes, draw, tick and add your own observations in the margin. I have seen some birders totally deface their books by tearing out and laminating the color identification plates to carry around, leaving the text part of the book (the heavy words) behind at home to be checked out later. Others add their own keys and stick on color references – it really doesn't matter.

A favorite field guide will become a friend for life, but remember that books are frozen in time while science changes, and so keep your eye on the latest publications and don't be afraid to try others.

Topping it with a telescope

The telescope – the best thing since binoculars! You may think that this is a real luxury in the naturalist's armory, just representing more "stuff" to cart around, but a good telescope revolutionizes the optical experience and, if you have the resources and are serious about your observations, is a very worthwhile investment. If you are worried about size and weight, the new generation of mini spotting scopes is so good that I rarely use my "Goliath" model any more and opt for the little "David" version that I can fit into my waist pack.

Buying a telescope requires a certain amount of knowledge, as they come in component form – the body, the eyepiece, and the support – and each has some bearing on the other. When choosing a telescope, the same overall rules as for binoculars apply, with just a few exceptions:

Magnification: because you are dealing with much higher magnifications than with binoculars – from 15x to 60x – any instability in your support will be noticeable. In telescopes with a fixed eyepiece, a range of between 15x and 30x is normal. But most now come with interchangeable eyepieces, and so if you have any doubts, you can always buy more than one. For general work, between 20x and 30x is good, but for more distant viewing, you can up the magnification to 40x or even 50x, and though they are not a good idea with binoculars, zoom eyepieces work well with the larger objective lens bodies.

Weight: because of the larger bodies and higher magnification, most telescopes require a larger objective lens. This makes for a heavier machine and is the biggest contributor to the telescope being left at home. Smaller, more compact models are a good compromise – try one with a 60 mm objective lens and a 20x eyepiece.

Color fringing can be a problem with telescopes. It means that objects appear to be outlined in a colored halo, especially at higher magnifications. The higher-end models often use extra-low dispersion (ED) glass, which eliminates this. Watch out for this disconcerting effect when trying out telescopes.

What type of scope? There are two different body designs to choose from, straight and angled, and both have their uses. The straight body makes it easier to locate your subject – you simply sight it up along the barrel. Some even have a gun-style sight on the outside to help with

Use a rock to stabilize a tripod in the wind

this. The straight design is better when you are sitting down in hides, assuming you can get behind them (some hides now have fixed benches and seats, which can make getting behind your scope difficult) and it tends to be a little cheaper. Angled (with an eyepiece at 45 degrees to the main body) is easier to use if you are tall or if you are viewing birds in trees or in flight, as the angle reduces neck ache. The best feature of this design, though, is that you do not have to have your tripod so high and so it is a more stable setup.

Supports: obviously telescopes can be pricey, especially if you buy more than one eyepiece, but do not skimp when it comes to support. Whether you go for a monopod, tripod, or some kind of clamp arrangement, the world's best scope may as well be a cardboard toilet roll tube for all the use it will be with a cheap support.

Photography: if you intend to use your telescope with a camera attachment, it is worth remembering that it was not primarily designed for this function and the quality will be far removed from what you would experience looking through a camera lens of equivalent focal length. Having said that, there is a new generation of digi-scoping technology which utilizes the recent advances in digital cameras, with the removal of film and the "mystery" about what you have managed to take a picture of. This can clarify any doubts about identification and be a handy addition to your field notes, too.

Using your telescope

Other than knowing which end to look through (it's usually the little end, by the way), the only loosely technical thing is the support the scope sits on. There are an enormous number of different heads and grips, all with different mechanisms. Try out lots of options and choose the one that fits your budget and feels right. With a lower magnification, say 15x–20x, you can use a monopod or lie on your back with your feet in the air and support the scope between your knees – both ways of reducing the amount of weight you cart around with you. But if you can afford it, the perfect combination is a compact scope of the highest quality and a sturdy carbon-fiber tripod – it's what I use all the time.

Seeing in the dark
the world of image intensification

I remember going badger-watching on a night as black as pitch, hearing the movements of badgers all around me and knowing that the moment I turned on my flashlight I would get a snapshot of badger life before these highly secretive and jumpy mammals bolted in multiple directions, shattering the moment for all of us. These occasional glimpses were very special in themselves, but the more I did it, the more I would fantasize about how wonderful it would be to have a superhuman ability to see in the dark.

image intensifier

image intensifier with goggles

On a moonlit night, when your eyes have become accustomed to the dark, it is possible to see quite well, though details are still a little sketchy. But while I was playing my wishing games the world's military and certain nocturnal hunters were, unbeknownst to me, already using the first versions of a technology that could make all my nocturnal dreams come true. Image intensifiers were just around the corner.

The first one I ever looked through was borrowed from my mammalogy lecturer at university. It was huge, like a bazooka, and seemed just as heavy, like a big, bulky Russian piece of downpipe, with a screw-on screen and a gun grip. Using it or even moving it around late at night made me look like some paramilitary nutcase on nocturnal maneuvers – something I had a bit of trouble explaining to the police on several occasions!

But whatever the knock-on social and practical difficulties, the moment I turned it on was magic. I may as well have been watching fairies, as I was bathed in the eerie green glow that emanated from the eyepiece and the view of everything in the darkest woodland burned on my retinas. I have hankered after owning my own ever since.

Image intensifiers work by gathering ambient light such as moonlight and starlight through the front lens. These packets of light energy, called photons, then enter a photocathode that changes light to electrical energy. The energy is amplified by chemical and electrical processes and hurled back through a phosphorus screen that turns the electrical signals back into visible – albeit green – light.

Night-vision devices come as first, second, third, and fourth generation, a term that refers to the type of light-intensifier tube used. First generation are the most widely available; they also tend to be the cheapest and vary a lot in quality. Some give a reasonable image for the price, but at this level, the technology comes with a whining noise and a variable amount of distortion. The quality increases through the

How an image intensifier works

generations, with fourth generation being fantastic but well beyond the budget of most naturalists. Night-vision devices of all kinds are rated on two criteria: system light gain – how many times the tube amplifies the available light – and system resolution – how sharp the amplified image appears.

If you decide to buy one of these tubes of magic, many of the rules of choosing binoculars and telescopes apply. But, as the nature of night-vision devices means that it needs to be dark before you can use them, trying them out before you buy can be difficult. But do your best to test some different makes and qualities before you remortgage your house in order to afford one! What is most comfortable for you to use is a particularly relevant question, as image intensifiers come in such a variety of sizes and designs, from those that resemble telescopes and binoculars to devices that strap on to your head like a big pair of funky glasses.

One last piece of advice is stay clear of high-street shops selling these products. In my experience they only have them as novelty products and do not know what they are talking about. Always go to a specialist supplier.

I spy with my micro-eye
microscopes

As with binoculars and telescopes, a good microscope is not cheap, but if you are serious about studying the Lilliputian world, you should consider it an investment. It will last for a long time and has very few moving parts to go wrong. So if you have the cash, splash it. Whether you want to examine the internal workings of plants, microscopic animals, the structure of feathers, mammal hairs, or even whole insects, microscopes are incredibly useful. I've used one to turn a group of uninterested kids into avid monster spotters! Who would have thought a droplet of greenish pond water with a few dots in it could keep the imagination and sense of discovery going among the PlayStation generation for a couple of hours or more? If you are not convinced, see if you can have a go on one in a laboratory somewhere, and I guarantee you will be converted.

Unless you are a multibillionaire, microscopes come in two forms: binocular and light.

If you plan to work with whole animals such as invertebrates, you want the binocular version. As the name suggests it has two eyepieces, enabling you to view your subject in three dimensions. It is designed to enable you to manipulate your specimen, either by hand or with tools, while focusing on it through the eyepieces – hence its other name of dissecting microscope. Because it is used with relatively large, solid subjects, the magnification is not huge, but most models have either interchangeable eyepieces or lenses of different magnifications mounted on a revolving carousel that give some flexibility, usually between 10x and 60x magnification. Some have platforms with

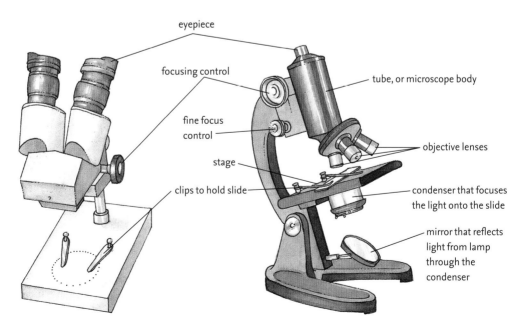

eyepiece

focusing control

tube, or microscope body

fine focus control

objective lenses

stage

clips to hold slide

condenser that focuses the light onto the slide

mirror that reflects light from lamp through the condenser

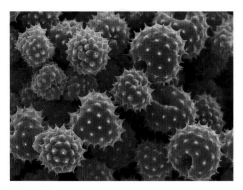

Daisy pollen as seen under the microscope

built-in back lights; others have mounted lights that illuminate from above; while with others, you have to provide light from an extra bench-mounted source. If the latter is the case, be aware that regular lights are also a source of heat, which your living subjects may not enjoy. The cold light of a fiber-optic lamp is much better, but of course comes at a price. Just keep the health and comfort of your subjects in mind at all times and expose them to bright light for as short a time as possible.

The light microscope works at much higher magnifications – up to 500x, which is enough to see the internal workings of cells. It is also great for investigating life forms that are normally invisible to the human eye. Stare down a light microscope at a droplet of water from any pond or puddle, even a blob of estuarine mud, and you will be transported into a weird and fantastical world filled with one-eyed aliens, pulsating shape-shifters, and odd plants resembling hollow spheres and spaceships.

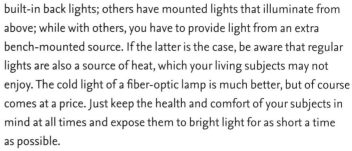

labels

forceps

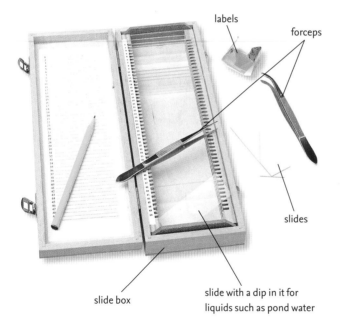

slides

slide box

slide with a dip in it for liquids such as pond water

Because of the nature of these microscopes they require more light and the subjects have to be semitransparent to reveal themselves clearly. So prepare your specimens beforehand: Slice plants on a microtome (the scientist's equivalent of the deli-counter bacon slicer) to study their structure; squash or restrain other subjects on a microscope slide; and "clear" others by treating them in a solution of potassium hydroxide, which dissolves the soft tissues, allowing the light to shine through. Staining can be very useful here – it is done with special biological dyes containing pigments that bond to some compounds in the specimen but not to others, making certain features stand out.

To keep specimens and preparations, wash them well in water and then, using a slide with a cavity, position the specimen plus a drop of gum chloral in the cavity. Seal with a coverslip, wipe away any excess gum, and leave to dry. Larger preserved specimens can be positioned on a bed of tiny glass beads.

Magnifying lenses, glasses and loupes

"Indispensable" is the word to describe this small piece of naturalist's kit, whether you are counting the hairs in a cockroach's armpit, scrutinizing the meanderings of a red spider mite, or counting the stamens in a flower head. The two choices you need to make are what kind and what magnification. And the answers to both these questions very much depend on where and for what you will be using it.

The most basic type of magnifying lens, the type Sherlock Holmes used to use, is not very powerful, but its large field of view makes it handy in the field for observing subjects such as a feeding insect or a nest of ants. Back at base, a similar lens attached to a flexible stem or even a **bench lens** is useful for examining stationary objects, leaving both hands free to manipulate the subject, take notes, or draw. Such lenses usually have a magnification of 2x or 3x, not huge but enough to view certain finer details without straining your eyes.

A **watchmaker's lens** is another way of freeing both hands, and with a little practice can be gripped in your eye socket for close work – though some people find it takes a bit of getting used to, and your "eyebrow muscle" may feel tired at the end of an intense session!

By far the most popular and useful hand lens for the naturalist is the **loupe lens**. It is small, folds up into a self-protecting arrangement, and is available in a variety of magnifications between 5x and 20x. Anything less than 8x is of little use to the naturalist, whereas only the most specialist scrutinizer working with the tiniest of details or organisms will ever need more than 15x. If you really cannot decide, you can buy a pocket loupe with multiple lenses. There are many cheap versions out there, but the higher the price, the better it will be. Maintenance is no more than a quick rub with a lens cloth or clean tissue from time to time.

It's good to have your lens handy at all times, and so tie a piece of string around it and hang it round your neck. Keep it in its protective case to avoid it being scratched. If you have the choice, buy the kind with an adjustable screw-type pivot, but remember to tighten it regularly – I have had many excellent lenses fall to pieces because I have forgotten to do this.

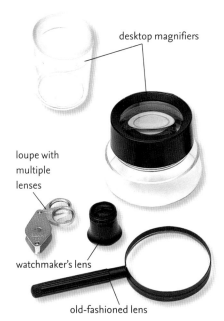

desktop magnifiers

loupe with multiple lenses

watchmaker's lens

old-fashioned lens

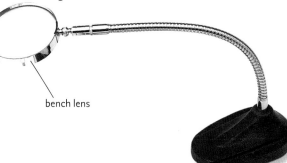

bench lens

Notebook and notes

I have to be honest with you on this one: I find it hard to write notes when I'm in the field. The moment with a bird or insect is often so fleeting that I get caught up in its magic and forget about jotting down any kind of observation.

Getting into this habit is, however, really, really useful. I cannot emphasize enough how much I have learned from the few notes I have actually written down. It is very easy to gaze in mindless wonder at the mysterious brown warbler that has just popped out of the bush for the briefest of moments, and not observe anything at all, as your memory will testify when you recall the moment later on.

The sort of awkward questions field guides ask you when you try to identify what you have just seen – like "What color were its legs?" "How long was its supercilium?" and "Did it have any amount of streaking on its breast?" – become so much easier to answer if you get into the discipline of running through the likely points of note while the bird is sitting in front of you, memorizing them and jotting them down as soon as you get the chance. It becomes easier with experience, as you get to know the groups of animals you are studying and learn, based on previous difficulties, which points of ID will be most useful to you.

This is something I discovered recently while snorkeling off a coral reef in East Africa. I would see a stunning triggerfish, but on getting out the field guide, I would be confronted with a page containing at least 15 candidates for what I had just observed, all of which could be separated by features much more subtle than those I had noted. Next day, armed with this knowledge, I managed to narrow it down to eight possibles! This continued for several days more until I finally managed to acquire an underwater slate and could take notes on the spot. Then bingo! I nailed it. It took me four days to work out which triggerfish was which, but using a little resourcefulness, I got there in the end.

Uses for notebooks

All the great naturalists have made copious notes. It was in the books of such names as Darwin, Bates, and Wallace that species were identified and theories on subjects as diverse as speciation, mimicry, and evolution came together. Darwin spent most of his life writing up and extrapolating many theories from the notes he made on just a handful of field excursions. Those notebooks still exist and are shedding new light on the biological sciences as we speak. This is one

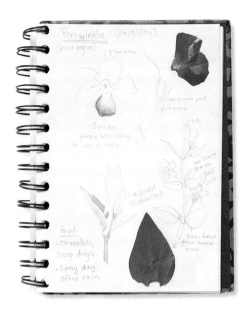

Trees and other plants: note the overall shape and proportions, try to collect leaves and bark rubbings. With flowers, make a note of the number of stems, flower heads and how the leaves attach to the plant.

of the greatest uses of notebooks – not only will they be relevant to you as a tool and an exercise to becoming a better and more observant naturalist, but those scruffy scrawlings and scribbles will also provide you with reference and comparisons long after you made them. Just the other day I was referring to a map of a local badger sett I drew when I was 11 years old. Now, 20 years later, I can stand in the same spot and see the changes: Some holes have long been filled in, trees have fallen down and changed the layout of others, some are brand new, and others remain as if no time had passed at all.

Top tips for note-taking

Pencils are better than pens for note-taking: Ink can freeze and will run and become illegible if it gets wet on paper. Attaching your pencil to the notebook with a piece of string saves valuable minutes of fumbling in the depths of your pocket or hunting around in the grass for the pencil you "just put down for a second."

Buy a reasonably robust notebook, ideally with a waterproof cover and strong binding. For convenience I also use little reporter-type notebooks, the 10 x 6 cm (4 x 2 ½ in) sort with a ring binding at the top, and a piece of elastic to hold the pages in place. Having said that, the smaller the notebook the better. The best book for taking notes is the one you have with you in your pocket, not the one with more pages than the *Encyclopedia Britannica* that you left in the car because you hadn't brought your wheelbarrow with you to transport it!

Keep field notes to a minimum: Use your own code and abbreviations to get the information down quickly. Sketches do not need to be something you would want to hang in the Tate Modern, they need only be useful to you. Keeping your lists and notes brief reduces the chances of note-taking becoming an obsessive chore.

Make your notes as soon as you can: The sooner you write it all down, the more you will remember. Regurgitate details such as time, date, weather, wind direction, numbers of flower heads, calls or noises, dimensions, colors, behavior, and anything else you think may be significant. Use drawings, too. They say so much more than words, so much more quickly. Birds, winged insects, and some mammals simply do not stay still long enough to do a masterpiece, but a few pointers of shape and color will usually suffice for a positive ID.

Birds can be reduced to a couple of oval shapes, a small one for the head and a larger one for the body. You can then join these up with roughly correct proportions of neck, tail, bill, and wing. Add and embellish with any other features, markings, and colors. Use annotations if it helps. For all animals: Do not forget to note any movements, behavioral patterns, and flight paths, as these can be useful in retrospect.

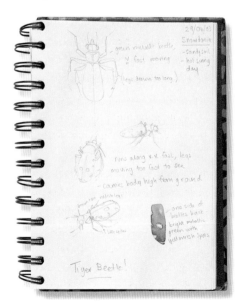

Invertebrates: insects have three body parts, spiders two. Record the proportions of these, then add legs, wings, antennae, hair, and markings.

Do not worry about scruffiness. The whole point of a field notebook is that it is a tool. If you care about presentation, you can always transfer the information to a master notebook later on. Stick in your original notes if you wish, expand on them, add identifications, etc. You can also embellish your "master" notebook with specimen items (assuming you are not dealing with a protected species and that collecting is not against the law in any way) such as hairs, leaves, flowers, fruits, seeds, and bark rubbings.

Keep your book dry: if you are working in the wet, keep it in a Ziploc bag or even purchase a large bag that you can get your hands into and write in relative shelter. Outdoor, field, and forestry stores sell specially designed baffle-type book tents. If this sounds a little tiresome, you can buy waterproof "write in the rain" books from field and forestry suppliers on the internet. They are more expensive but worth it, as good notes are priceless.

Go digital: if you are technologically minded, you can forsake conventional notes by taking a sound-recording device and a digital camera into the field. You need to be careful not to get these things wet and remember to take spare batteries, Memory Sticks, and sound-recording media with you, but there is definitely room for the techno-naturalist to use new technology to his or her advantage.

Using a dictaphone

Another alternative to written notes is the use of a sound-recording device. This can be anything from a cheap Dictaphone with a limited amount of recording time to more advanced and flexible media such as mini-discs, which can be kept and the information transferred to a computer. Speaking into a microphone is a time-efficient way of recording events and a good option if what you are trying to record is unfolding quickly and in a complex manner or if you don't have a lot of time to write up your notes. Another plus is that you can get a great feel for an environment from the noises it creates; and with certain animal calls, recording them and playing them back instantly can instigate an interesting bit of behavior.

Digital cameras

I am a complete convert to digital photography. It is becoming cheaper and cheaper and cameras are getting smaller and smaller, and though for serious photography, only the biggest, most expensive, top-of-the-range stuff is so far really an accepted replacement for film, the technology is not far away.

Digital camera

Camera trap

For the naturalist the possibilities of digital photography combined with portable computer technology are limitless. One of the biggest advantages is that, because there is no film, there is less to go wrong mechanically and you do not need to have spare canisters lying around in the bottom of your field bag, getting hot and dusty.

With digital photography comes instant gratification, and because the pictures are free and editable, you can take a picture simply to help you with identification. If you find a mystery butterfly laying eggs on a mystery plant, you can snap the process itself, then the plant and the eggs, and still keep up with the insect, perhaps recording the number of times it stops to lay. The amount of information and the efficiency with which you gather it are greatly increased and you have an accurate and potentially permanent record. Take the pictures home at the end of the day, identify your subject, and then decide whether or not you want to keep the information as part of your digital journal.

I have even seen a digital camera used as a magnifying device. I was conducting a field course, part of which involved emptying and recording the species of moth that were being pulled out of a light trap. I was getting in a right fuddle: Moths were escaping and I was talking to my students at the same time as I was trying to record the species in my notebook. While I was juggling these tasks, one of my students, a more mature gentleman, was rapidly photographing every moth in sight. I thought no more than that he was taking a very enthusiastic interest in the insects, but later in the evening I found him sitting with his camera, a huge pile of moth books, and a notebook. When I asked what he was doing, he showed me a comprehensive list of the moths we had seen. He had queries over a few points of identification, and the photographs made it possible to go over this again and even to zoom in close enough to tell the sex of some of the insects. It turned out that this moth enthusiast had bad eyesight and had left his glasses behind, and so rather than slow everyone down in the field, he was snapping away as quickly as he could so that he could identify the insects later and enjoy their details in private.

Nets

Most naturalists will find themselves in need of a net at some point – there are some things that you simply can't catch using your hands and arms. Having said that, I believe their use should be kept to a minimum – your eyes are your most important tool, and you should do as much observation as you can without interfering with your subjects. Keep the net for flighty creatures that tend to disappear before you can say "Camberwell beauty," for those that live too high up to be seen properly, or for trawling through long grass, ponds, or rivers.

sweep net

water net

folding net

Different nets do different jobs – a strong white net with a heavy frame is good for sweeping through vegetation; a lightweight black mesh is better for flying insects; a thick, strong net with big holes for drainage is best for pond work; while putting a jam jar at the bottom of a net will enable you to catch tiny pond animals and plankton. All these are available from specialist shops but are also fun and easy to make yourself.

With butterflies and other flying insects, use the net gently, picking them from vegetation or from behind in flight if possible, and try to avoid hitting your subject with the net rim. Avoid swiping with the net, as this can damage fragile wings. As soon as the insect is in the net, fold it with a quick flick of the wrist, trapping the insect inside. You can now maneuver your subject by lifting up the end of the net bag and allowing the insect to fly or crawl up toward the light.

Nets may be great for catching your subject, but they are surprisingly difficult to see details through. For this you need a specialist bit of equipment known as a pillbox, which normally comes as a set of varying sizes that sit inside each other like Russian dolls. A pillbox is simply a cardboard pot with a clear bottom, and is fantastically useful for all insects, as it is dark, offers a perch for the insect to grip, and, most important of all, being cardboard, breathes, so condensation doesn't build up and the insect doesn't get wet and stick to the sides. If you cannot source purpose-made pillboxes, fashion your own from the cardboard tube that comes in the center of toilet or kitchen-paper rolls.

To transfer a butterfly or moth from your net, simply cup the pillbox over the insect, wait for it to crawl toward the light, and slide the lid on. (Another advantage of this design is that it greatly reduces the risk of inadvertently trapping wings and legs, because the insect instinctively heads toward the other end of the box.) Use a small flashlight to help you pick out tiny details, and, as always, as soon as you have finished, release it in the same area that you caught it.

Smaller kit
at the sharp end

Tweezers or forceps are useful for manipulating something you don't actually want to touch, like a stinging nettle, or aren't afraid of damaging, like a snail or beetle. Don't use them on small or delicate animals, though – go for cocktail sticks or large sewing needles, which give you more control over the pressure you are exerting.

With those frustrating creatures that curl up their legs the moment you look at them, try picking them up in a tablespoon or combine this with a small camel hair paintbrush and use them like a dustpan and brush to dislodge your subjects from a plant or scoop them up off the ground. If you don't want to touch slugs, snails, and the like, using two spoons to pick them up gets round the problem.

If you become fascinated by insects and creepy-crawlies generally, you will often find yourself poking and prodding in dark places, and so it can be handy to have something to illuminate the subject. I always carry a pocket flashlight, and the other device I find useful for bouncing light about is a pocket-size, travel-type shaving mirror. These are great for looking under ledges and rocks. For nocturnal hunting, use a head lamp, keeping both hands free for manipulating any small creatures you may come across.

Pots: you can't have too many

Whatever your passion as a naturalist may be, whether you are collecting seeds, droppings, shells – in fact anything living or dead that needs a bit of protection in your field bag or back at base – you will need pots, and you will soon be recognizing the potential of an eclectic range of containers. From ice-cream tubs to the tiny plastic boxes that peppermints come in, you'll find a use for them.

Obviously, if your subject is dead, you can keep it in pretty well anything, but with living creatures, don't forget light and ventilation. Punch a few holes in the lid of a margarine pot, and your spider will be perfectly happy; use an elastic band to hold a piece of netting in place over a take-out container, and caterpillars will crawl around to their heart's content. Use your imagination and think how much your recycling efforts are helping the planet!

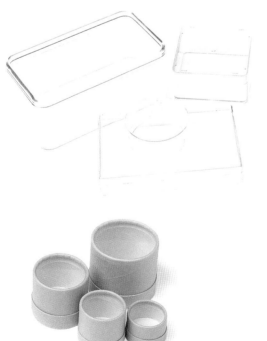

Try to collect an assortment of cardboard and plastic pots of different shapes and sizes.

Feathered and flighty
birds

Birds present the amateur naturalist with some of his or her greatest challenges, for the simple reason that they cannot differentiate between the well-meaning naturalist and the life-threatening predator. So their first instinct is to put as much space as possible between us and them. The same is true of mammals, of course, but birds have the extra disadvantage from the naturalist's point of view of being blessed with wings, making them flighty masters of three dimensions.

Having said that, birds do tend to be visible. Step off a plane into a new and exciting country and the first living creatures you see when leaving the airport are birds. But catching brief glimpses and getting long, protracted views of them doing what birds do when they are not flying around airports are two totally different ball games! Another important and user-friendly aspect of birds is that many of them vocalize as part of their everyday pattern of behavior. Generally speaking they are much noisier than mammals, although this behavior can be seasonal and related to breeding or to environmental conditions.

Above: Swallows
(*Hirundo rustica*) flocking
Right: Detail of a jay's
wing (*Garrulus glandarius*)

'Merely glorified reptiles'

That's what the great Victorian biologist Thomas Huxley called birds, and, though to the naturalist they present many of the same challenges as do mammals, it may come as a surprise to learn that birds are closely related to reptiles. Some scientists think the two groups have so much in common that they put them in the same class, the Sauropsida.

Of all the terrestrial vertebrates, birds are the most numerous, with something like 9,000 species – there are about twice the numbers of feathered creatures as there are furred! In recent years birdwatching has reached the masses and is huge business in Europe and America, with countless societies dedicated to watching and studying them (in the U.K., the Royal Society for the Protection of Birds has over a million members, while in the U.S., the Audubon Society has numerous centers in every state, where it is estimated there may be as many as 70 million birdwatchers). There are holiday companies that specialise in birdwatching and trade fairs dedicated to all those with an ornithological leaning. The birdwatcher's image has changed, too, and it is a great pleasure now to see people from all walks of life watching birds.

So why are birds so popular? To claim that they are easy to get to know is inaccurate – they can be some of the most frustrating creatures on the planet to study. But as a group they are active and conspicuous, which makes them appealingly accessible. In almost any city in the world you can look out of your window and see a bird. Many are fabulous to look at and have a deep aesthetic appeal; they can also be capable of extraordinary feats of migration and some fascinatingly diverse habits and survival strategies.

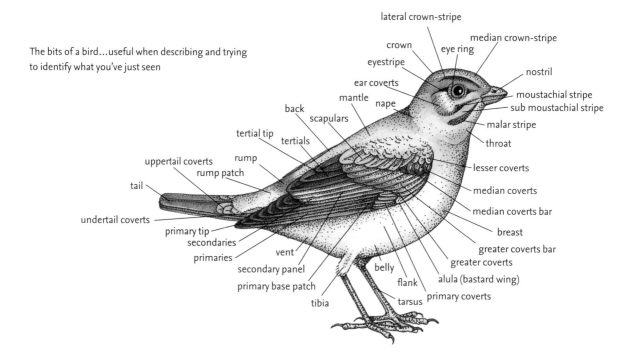

The bits of a bird…useful when describing and trying to identify what you've just seen

Feathers
hundreds of uses for dead keratin

Feathers are the most obvious thing that separates the birds from all other living things. These versatile, disposable, flexible, insulating, lightweight, easily maintained, interlocking, "scale-like" structures are unique to the birds.

They are also the secret to their success, as bats are the only other masters of true flight, and feathers really do have the edge over the patagium (that flexible thin skin that is the wing of a bat). For a start, if feathers are damaged they can be regrown, which the patagium cannot, and feathers mean that birds don't have to have long, thin, fragile bones, and so their wings are much more robust than a bat's. Feathers make great insulation, which is why birds can maintain their body temperature more efficiently than any mammal – and why we make duvets out of them. A bat's wings, on the other hand, act like giant radiators, which limits where they can live and when they can be active. The fact that a bird's wings (unlike the front limbs of a mammal) are independent of its legs also means that all the other diverse uses to which it puts its feet, such as grasping, preening, and manipulating, have been honed to perfection.

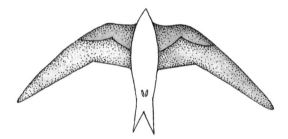

A **swift** has slender, swept-back wings designed for high-speed flight. They are long and narrow to minimize turbulence.

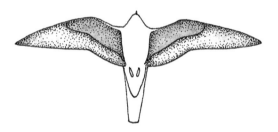

The wings of a **falcon**, like those of a swift, are pointed to allow them to soar well.

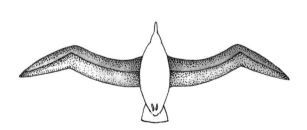

An **albatross** has long, thin wings for great lift and gliding with low effort and maximum efficiency.

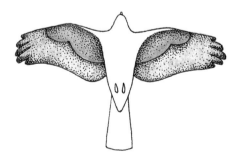

The round wings and long tail of a **hawk**, are ideal for moveability and soaring, allowing it to glide effortlessly while on the lookout for food.

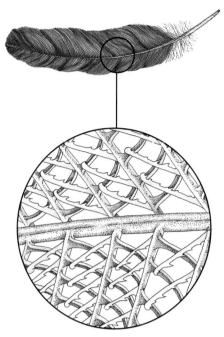

The apparently perfect flat surface of a feather is made up of a complex series of interlocking "branches." The barbs are attached to the central shaft and are locked together by the tiny side branches called barbules.

As a boy I was obsessed with feathers. Even today, while I do not go to quite the same lengths to obtain them (I once suspended my unfortunate younger brother by his legs into the ostrich pen at a local zoo to procure a fine fluffy specimen for me), I still cannot help but bend down and pick them up whenever I see them. Not only are they the most perfectly beautiful example of form and function in the natural world, but many also come in fabulous colors, and for the expert naturalist, every feather tells a tale.

Feathers are made of a flexible protein called keratin, the same stuff as human hair and nails. The reason they are so light for the area they cover is that the shafts are hollow. All the other parts are made up of tiny interlocking strips called barbs, "zipped" together by little hooks called barbules. If you run your finger backward along a flight feather, you mess it up, because you have "unzipped" the barbules. This happens to a lesser extent during everyday wear and tear. If you smooth your finger back up the feather you cause the barbules to "zip up" again, which is exactly what a bird is doing when it preens itself. Despite their proverbial lightness, feathers make up nearly a quarter of a bird's total weight. They can actually be heavier than its skeleton!

Cross section of a wing. The bones are similar to those of the human arm, but the hand and wrist areas are much simplified.

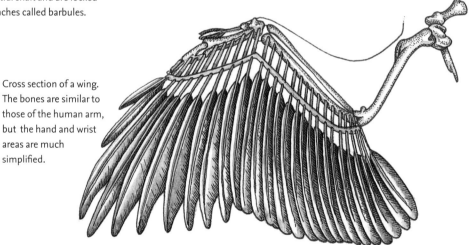

To a naturalist the feather is much more than a bit of windblown fluff; it can tell an awful lot about the previous owner. Different feathers on a bird's body grow from distinct places, or tracts, known as pterylae. When fully developed these feathers take on their own distinctive shape and appearance, and with a little practice, you can identify these. The next level of expertise is to be able to identify the difference not only between species but also between sexes, ages, and molts. I have a friend who works on prey selection of certain species of

Soft downy feathers trap a layer of air and act as insulation. They are used in duvets and down jackets because they are excellent at providing warmth.

This is a primary feather for the left-hand wing.

The plumage of the starling changes color throughout the year.

raptor such as the peregrine falcon (*Falco peregrinus*), and because these birds are messy eaters, if you can retrieve the feathers and meal remains, you can construct a fairly good idea of the bird's menu. Sometimes these dinner remains throw up some real surprises, like new records for species of bird in the area.

Growing feathers

The growth and renewal of feathers, known as a molt, is controlled by hormones and is a fairly energy-expensive operation, requiring a lot of effort and a reduction in efficiency, and so molting periods are synchronized with other major events in the bird's annual life cycle, such as breeding and migration. An example of this occurs on the predator-free mudflats of the Severn estuary, where in the late summer, after breeding, shelducks (*Tadorna tadorna*) congregate to molt. This mass molting is so spectacular that the first time I witnessed it, I thought I was looking at an unseasonable fall of snow – there were literally millions of feathers blowing around in drifts on the muddy shore. Shelducks and other waterfowl become very vulnerable at this stage, as their powers of flight are often totally compromised, and so some enter "eclipse" plumage, becoming very dowdy in appearance to avoid unwanted attention from predatory eyes.

Most birds molt completely two or three times every year for a variety of reasons other than simply to renew the feathers. Some molt into gaudier plumage prior to breeding to display to potential mates. But to continue this beyond the breeding season would only advertise yourself to predators, and so a second molt restores the bird's previous low profile. In other species, feather wear has evolved to occur at a certain pace. The European house sparrow (*Passer domesticus*), starling (*Sturnus vulgaris*) and chaffinch (*Fringilla coelebs*), for instance, all seem to change color and brightness as winter turns into spring. In reality they do not molt at all – the feather fringes simply wear off and create the illusion of a brighter bird.

Tracking birds

Despite spending a lot of their time above the ground, birds leave a surprising amount of evidence on the ground in the form of nests, feathers, and egg fragments. And when they do finally come to earth, they leave tracks. It is a little harder than with mammals to identify individual species by these alone, but once again, combine the physical clues in the footprints and field signs with other information such as the distribution and knowledge of an animal's habitat use, and you can start making good guesses.

ground bird

perching bird

woodpecker

To help you narrow down your choices and obtain a positive identification, bird tracks can be divided into three main categories. None of these is linked to phylogenetic relationships; the tracks just coincidentally show a number of shared features.

Ground birds, waterfowl, waders, and shorebirds include game birds such as grouse and pheasants, waders such as sandpipers, cranes, gulls, and waterfowl such as ducks and geese. All these birds have three toes pointing forward and one short one pointing backward. The pattern of the toes tends to be symmetrical. With ducks, geese, and gulls, the rearward pointing toe doesn't always register, while with game birds, if it registers, it is as a nail hole. Webbing between the toes of gulls, ducks, and geese will show on a soft substrate such as mud and can give you a big clue to the treader's identity, but it doesn't always show up. So always check the shape of the two side toes – if they curve inward, the track belongs to a web-footed bird.

Perching birds, herons, and ibis make up a huge category that includes pretty much every bird capable of gripping a branch – songbirds, birds of prey (excluding owls), pigeons, and crows among them. This category encompasses many sizes and lifestyles, and as a result there is large variation in size and a degree of asymmetry between the forward-pointing toes. But the big distinction is that the rear-pointing toe is often nearly as long, if not as long, as the toes pointing forward. Because of their raptorial purpose, a hawk's toes need to be sturdy and well constructed, which is reflected in its footprints.

Woodpeckers, cuckoos, roadrunners, and owls often have two toes pointing backward or certainly not forward, giving a rough X or K shape.

You can also glean a limited amount of information about the bird's gait from its footprints. Stride length can give you an idea of leg length, and a walking bird will leave an alternating pattern whereas a hopping bird leaves pairs of tracks next to each other. Shelduck footprints resemble those of any similar-size waterfowl, but because this bird has a characteristic method of feeding, with a repetitive sideways sweeping of the bill, it leaves a trail of horseshoe-shaped beak tracks as it walks. Dunlin (*Calidris alpina*) work their way across the mud, randomly probing with their bills and leaving a trail of single holes like stitch marks. Snipe (*Gallinago gallinago*), on the other hand, probe with their bills held open, leaving paired "double stitch marks."

Who had the eggs for breakfast?

This egg has hatched naturally – note how the membrane of the egg just protrudes outside the shell.

Eggshells often turn up on lawns, or you may stumble upon them out in the field, especially in the spring. The big question is, did it hatch naturally or was it predated? When a chick hatches naturally, it chips away at the shell using its "egg tooth" and usually makes a neat job near the blunt end. The papery membrane within the egg is preserved and its edge protrudes outside the shell, often curling inward when it dries. The inside of the shell will also be clean. The presence of eggshell doesn't mean there is a nest nearby: Once the chicks have hatched, the adult often dumps the shells far away so as not to attract predators. A complete egg, particularly if it is pale blue, can be explained by the behavior of starlings: one will often nip into another starling's nest, lay an egg of her own, and remove one of the original clutch.

A predated egg, on the other hand, is clearly a predated egg. Whether the egg thief is a bird or a mammal, the job is usually messy; the shell may be split into more than two pieces or simply have a small hole in it; there may also be remains of yolk, egg white, or blood (if the embryo was well developed). If the predator was a mammal, the shell may bear witness to this by showing the punctures made by canine teeth. The distance between the marks can also hint at the identity of the predator. The best clue, though, is that the membrane in a predated egg rarely projects beyond the edge of the shell.

The shells of ground-nesting birds such as ducks, gulls, and game birds often remain in the nest after hatching. Their remains may be found crushed in the nest or abandoned as the chicks are frog-marched out of the area by the parent birds. A nest like this is worth closer inspection, as it may have been raided (whole clutches can be consumed by predators), and you can use your detecting skills to deduce what has happened.

Note the split shells of these predated eggs.

Time to bring up pellets!

We'll talk a lot more about excrement in the Mammals chapter (see p. 90), and some of that information applies to birds too. But birds of prey do it differently. They excrete only liquid waste from their vent; their solid matter comes back up the way it came in.

Goshawk (*Accipter gentilis*) feeding. Its food remains may even include feathers, giving good clues to the identity of its prey.

Pellets of a great horned owl (*Bubo virginianus*). This bird can grow to an impressive 85 cm (2 ft 10 in) and feeds on animals as large as rabbits or skunks. With practice and a feel for the sorts of places pellets are deposited, you can begin to identify what coughed it up. Barn owls produce more rounded, smoother pellets than the other owls, often encased in a black/gray crust. Tawny owls (*Strix aluco*) have a lumpier but more elongated pellet. Those of the small, primarily insectivorous owls such as the little owl (*Athene noctua*) produce pellets that reflect their diet, often packed with the hard wing cases and legs of beetles and the like.

The nondigestible portions of a bird's diet that never make it through the system are regurgitated back up the gullet in the form of a pellet, or cast. Owls are famous pellet-producing birds, but all raptors, members of the heron (Ardeidae), crow (Corvidae), and gull (Laridae) families at some time or another eject these nuggets of indigestible stuff. In the absence of any other evidence, it can be hard to tell which species produced which pellet. But there are a few guidelines that can help you sort this out, starting with the most frequently encountered pellets, those of owls and hawks.

Hawks have much stronger digestive processes than owls and a different way of feeding – they generally tear and pull the flesh from the bone. This means their casts are of a finer texture. All but the biggest bone fragments are dissolved, and in most cases, just the fur and feather fibers make up the bulk.

An owl's pellets tend to be much coarser and fibrous, as most of their diet consists of smaller prey items that are entirely consumed and sometimes even swallowed whole. Therefore the pellets tend to be more revealing about its diet, and pellet analysis is not only a major part of owl dietary study in its own right, but also a very important way of monitoring the populations of small mammals in an area. These in turn can be sensitive indicators of environmental variations such as land-use change or the arrival of an introduced species.

Finding pellets

The best way to discover these revealing deposits, especially in the case of hawks and owls, is to locate roosts. Owls tend to return to the same places to roost in disused farm buildings, outhouses, tree cavities and even large parkland trees. They may also make themselves more prominent by being "whitewashed" by the birds' liquid waste. Hawks also have favorite roost sites, be they fence posts or old trees, and these are your best bet, though the pellets are harder to find, as they are produced and "lost" as the bird goes about its wide-ranging daily business.

With other pellet-producing birds, look around nest sites or under rookeries and heronries. Gull pellets are a common find anywhere on the coast, particularly among tussocky hummocks on cliff tops, but they can turn up pretty much anywhere a gull has stopped. Being scavengers, the contents of gull pellets tend to be very varied and interesting – you can find anything from foil and string to more natural and expected dietary items such as fish bones.

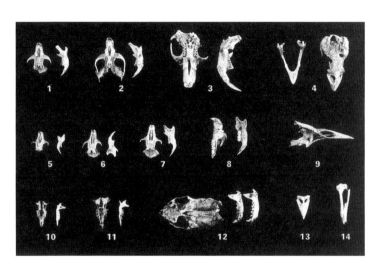

Skull fragments found in the pellet of the long-eared owl (*Asio otus*):

1. Bank vole	8. Rat
2. Field vole	9. Starling
3. Water vole	10. Common shrew
4. House sparrow	11. Water shrew
5. Harvest mouse	12. Weasel
6. House mouse	13. Chaffinch
7. Wood mouse	14. Blackbird

You are most likely to find those of voles, recognised by the long cheek teeth with a zigzag pattern to their grinding crowns; shrews, with their small, pointed, orange-tipped teeth; and mice, with big incisors and more individual and rounded cheek teeth. Lower jaws are similarly distinctive.

Pellet analysis

Pull apart an owl pellet, and you will find all manner of bones, not just the big and bulky ones, but also complete skulls of small mammals, small birds, even frogs, and lizards. There are two ways to do this, the wet and the dry. Before embarking on either, record the appearance and weight of your pellet.

The wet method: carefully break the pellet into chunks and soak in warm soapy water for a few hours. Tease them out and gently stir or agitate the solution. The heavy stuff such as bones and teeth will sink to the bottom, allowing you to decant and tip away the lighter debris such as fur and feathers. Use a sieve in case you overpour and lose some of the bones, which can be picked up with forceps and returned to the pot. Repeat this process several times until only the bones remain. Transfer them to a shallow dish and sort through them with cocktail sticks or dissecting needles. Use a fine paintbrush to remove any remaining traces of softer tissue.

I prefer **the dry method** because the fur and feathers can also give you subtle clues to what has been going down with the owl! Using a pointed implement to tease the pellet contents apart, sort them into piles of recognizable pieces – fur in one place, lower jawbones in another, skulls in another, etc. Try to identify and match up the skulls and teeth as you go.

Once you have extracted the bones from the pellet, you can, if you like, bleach them (see p. 100). Do not leave bones this size in the bleaching solution for long, as they will become even more fragile and the teeth have a tendency to fall out. Display and store your collection of fiddly fragments by gluing them to a piece of black cardboard, and then add the written notes you took before you started.

Birdwatching

Do not mistake simply looking at and identifying birds as birdwatching; for me it means much more – observing their behavior and learning about their lives and how they interact and work to survive. For example, you might identify eight species among a bunch of waders tottering around on estuary mud, but the true birdwatcher will see how they are spaced out so as not to interfere with each other's easily disturbed prey items; notice that the plovers are involved in a feeding sequence – look, dash, look, peck – while a dunlin randomly stitches its way across the mud. You might even notice three different feeding strategies employed by one species of oystercatcher!

That is the detail, the fascination of birdwatching. The identity thing, though important, becomes second nature, especially on your home patch. On paper, trying to describe a pigeon and a peregrine falcon flying is very much the same, but as soon as you gain experience you will almost instinctively pick up on the GISS of a bird. Though this is often written as "jizz," it is really an acronym for General Impression Size and Shape and refers to the quick summary, or "feel," that allows you to identify a species at a glance.

Birding by ear: the art of hearing

Most birds produce a rich range of sounds. Mostly uttered by the bird's syrinx (voice box), these are not just loud, proud territorial claims made mainly by males during the breeding season; the repertoire also includes a complicated array of more subtle avian small talk that is used all year round simply to communicate. There are alarm calls, songs, subsongs, whispered songs, begging calls, and contact calls to take into consideration. Some birds also produce sounds other than calls: The "drumming" display of snipe over a sodden grassland, the irritated "clack" of an owl's bill, or the percussive drumroll of a woodpecker are good examples.

A noise can be thought of as an audio fingerprint to a species, and it is often easier to make a positive identification of a bird by its call than by its appearance. Take, for instance, the marsh tit (*Parus palustris*) and the closely related willow tit (*Parus montanus*) – two birds that, even when you have one in each of your hands, still confound many of us! But listen to them call, and you will be in no doubt – if it's sneezy and wheezy, it's a marsh tit; if it's more aggressive and scolding, it's a willow.

A rich, liquid warbling from the bushes could be any bird to the untrained ear. But combine the sight and sound, in this case, of a robin (*Erithacus rubecula*), and you will soon be noticing the difference not only between species but between seasons!

When I started going out on dawn-chorus walks, I was invariably surrounded by people who really knew their stuff. At first I was inspired by the ability of these superior beings to distinguish the subsong of a blackcap (*Sylvia atricapilla*) from all the other subsongs of a bunch of newly arrived warblers, but soon it became daunting. I retreated into my ignorance and stopped asking questions before slinking off to cry into the pages of my field guide.

It took me years to recover, but here is how I did it. I finally realized that these knowledgeable people were not in possession of a divine gift but had actually learned their skill over time. And that is the key: *It takes time.* Seeing with your ears is a two-part process. First you have to hear the bird, then you have to make the connection between the noise and the vision. You need to get to the stage where the sound of a song or call instantly takes you back to the moment you first saw it being created. It is a matter of basic association in the same way as a certain piece of music can act as a shortcut to memories of your first kiss or your first pair of binoculars (is he joking, you have to ask yourself). Collecting these experiences really does boil down to time taken in the field – the more you look, the better you get. Having said that, there are a few "tricks" that can help you get there faster.

1. **Make life easier for yourself:** start by working with a few familiar species in your neighborhood. Get to know their repertoire and move on to other species as you become familiar with those that create the local "audio wallpaper." In temperate climes, the best time to do this is at the beginning of the year before all the migrants arrive and confuse things. Teach yourself to listen and hear each voice, then, using all the skills of stealth and patience so key to a naturalist's activities, persist in trying to see and identify the bird making the sound. To home in on different calls and the direction they are coming from, try cupping your hands behind your ears and moving your head about.

2. **Sound associations:** many bird calls are very distinctive, but to help you remember them, there are various phonetic renderings that can be applied. In Europe the song of the yellowhammer (*Emberiza citrinella*) can be heard, with a little poetic license, as "a little bit of bread and no cheese," the quail *Coturnix coturnixas* "wet my lips." With others just the cadence or the sounds can be likened to familiar things: Bobolinks (*Dolichonyx oryzivorus*) have been described as R2D2 shorting out; the common song of the European chaffinch allegedly has the pace of the footsteps of a fast bowler winding up to bowl; and the wood warbler (*Phylloscopus sibilatrix*) sounds like a coin spinning.

3. **Expand on the above:** mnemonic phrases – those little descriptions you often see in field guides that write the sounds of bird songs and calls as collections of letters – can help once you are at a certain stage of expertise. It is also a neat little trick to draw these sounds! That may seem odd, but when I think of a sound, I often make a mental picture of it. Try drawing things like a wavy line for a rising and falling song, a broken line for short, staccato sounds, or an upward curve for a short call that starts low and ends high. This is a technique and a language that will be distinct to you.

4. **Keep testing yourself:** nobody knows everything; even an experienced birder on his or her own patch will sometimes hear unfamiliar sounds. Never become complacent. Hear a bird, identify it in your head, then go and see if you can catch sight of it and find out if you guessed right. No matter how experienced you are, this is a good way of staying sharp. I often have to relearn the songs of all the migrants that, in the U.K., sing only for a month or so every springtime.

5. **Use sound references:** in the same way as you may use a reference book on your return from the field to help interpret your observation, you can do the same with bird songs and calls. There are a large number of CDs and DVDs that act as audio field guides, helping you to reach positive identifications or remove any niggling doubts about the sounds you have heard.

Male blackbirds (*Turdus merula*) can be very territorially aggressive and will raise a rattling alarm call to chase off other males. their song is distinctive and tuneful with clear phrases.

Willow warbler (*Phylloscopus tronchilus*). In the spring males often sing from a prominent perch. The song is a series of notes down the scale that can sound quite plaintive.

Mapping territories

The breeding season, particularly the spring for temperate species, is a time for birds to do battle – not with beak and claw but with their voices. Common garden birds are setting up their territories and defending them against their neighbors by shouting all about it.

Now is the perfect time for you to map the territories of the birds in your patch. Simply get up early and look for males singing – they usually choose high perches in the center of their kingdoms, overlooking as much of their territories as possible. Jot the positions on a map (using different colors for different birds), watch where they fly and try to shadow them, but do not worry if you lose track – you can pick up where you left off the next day. If you see two male birds close to each other, you can assume that each is on the boundary of his territory. Over a few weeks you will start to notice the invisible lines that are the territorial boundaries within which most birds move. Soon you will not only have a unique record of the movements of the birds in your neighborhood, you will also become a top bird spotter and learn a lot about bird song. If you supply a variety of nesting materials such as bunches of animal hair, wool string, fluff, and even a shallow dish of mud, it won't be long before the locals start visiting; by watching which way they fly off with their beaks full, you can often work out the locations of their nests, too.

Another famous territory exercise is one that should be tried only occasionally. If you repeat it, you will cause the birds a lot of disruption, stress, and wasted energy. But it works particularly well with the European robin and is worth doing once to observe the ferocity of these seemingly harmless little songsters. Just as a male stickleback responds to the stimulus of a red model fish (see p. 156), so the male robin will attack a model robin (it doesn't even have to look realistic, just have a red breast) with a fury and boldness that will surprise all who witness it!

Sound recording: catching a song

This technique is not restricted to birds, and much of the following advice can be used to record pretty much any animal vocalization. As so often, the better the equipment, the more expensive it will be, but to start with cheapish recording gear is fine.

Recording bird song with a microphone and headphones

Microphones: the biggest obstacle for anyone trying to record wildlife sound (especially bird song) is distance; just by halving the distance between you and your subject increases the power of the recording by a factor of four. This problem can be overcome in many cunning ways, such as leaving microphones next to singing posts. But the easiest way around it is a decent microphone. As with binoculars, it pays to go for quality, since cheap mikes do not usually have the necessary sensitivity. To "catch" a song and leave out the other enemy of the sound recordist, background noise, you really need directional microphones or a dish-shaped device called a parabolic reflector, or parabola. Parabolas come in a variety of sizes – the larger the dish, the more the sound is amplified. But it is worth noting that low-frequency sounds such as those uttered by owls and pigeons do not record well if the diameter of the dish is less than the wavelength of the sound – the recording may sound a bit weak and watery as a result.

Recorders: the requirements here are simple. Recorders need to be portable – that reads as lightweight – strong, robust, and reliable. Other factors governing your choice depend on your purpose, budget, and the environment you are working in.

Mini disc recorders are ideal for capturing bird song.

Cassette recorders are cheap, but who uses cassettes any more? "Reel to reel" is the traditional choice of the professional, but they are heavy and fragile, with lots of moving parts to damage. DAT (digital audio tape) recorders are great but hate moisture.

For the amateur, I recommend MDs (mini discs), as the recorders are very small and the discs practically indestructible. The only problem is that the sound that is recorded is "compressed." This is supposed to be undetectable to the human ear, but audio purists are not convinced, and the matter continues to be one of hot debate. The last of the many ways to "skin the audio cat" is recording onto solid-state formats such as disk drives and memory cards. The limiting factors are the amount of memory these recordings take up, the small amounts of memory available at a time, and the high price of the cards.

But memory is getting cheaper, and so very soon, the maintenance-free and totally robust solid-state technology will probably be what every field naturalist will use.

Evening the odds: attracting birds to you

It's hard being a human when all you want to do is get close to birds and all they want to do is "vote with their wings" at the slightest perception of a threat. Fortunately there are ways of tricking them into showing their beaks. Become a bird impressionist and you can sometimes "call them in" so that you can have a closer look.

The most universal technique, which works well with lots of small passerine birds throughout the world, is a stylized form of alarm call known as "pishing," produced by blowing air sharply over your tongue while it is squashed between the roof of your mouth and your lower teeth. The noise you are aiming for is a kind of "pursheeee" – a bit like the noise my mum used to make to scare the cats away from her herbaceous border. It works best in a sequence of three, repeated at intervals. The birds hear you sounding the alarm and come to see what predator they have missed – a piece of behavior you may have seen when small birds "mob" magpies, crows, owls, and raptors. The sequence can then be topped off by the "death call," a high-pitched squeak created by drawing air through tightly pressed lips, while making a kissing sound against the back of your hands or the gap between forefinger and thumb. Do this correctly and the birds will get really agitated, thinking that one of their number has succumbed and gone to the big bird house in the sky. The cumulative effect can be spectacular, as your performance may spark off the alarm calls of the most gullible birds, which, being real, agitate and attract species that are less easily fooled by a squeaking ornithologist.

"Calling in" works equally well for predators such as foxes, stoats, and barn owls.

Make an owl call by blowing between your thumbs.

Put your thumbs together and blow

You may think that, being nocturnal, well-camouflaged, woodland birds, owls would be pretty well impossible to see. But Europe's tawny owl is fairly "birder friendly" as owls go. It is an adaptable bird and, although principally a creature of woodland, it is tolerant of human disturbance and the only owl to have populations in our cities – in fact, some of my best owling moments have taken place in a parking lot in Bristol, watching a tawny hunt young rats foraging around a trash can from the vantage point of a No Parking sign.

Calling them in works best in the autumn and winter. For a start, the leaves are falling, allowing better views. But also at this time of year there is a lot of shouting in the owl world after dark – the young have been ousted from the territories in which they were raised, and they and other birds are competing for territories that must not only supply food through the coming winter but also have suitable resources such as roosts and nest holes for the late-winter breeding season.

Blowing between your thumbs into an airtight cavity produced by your cupped hands generates a tawny-owl impression that, though not a patch on the real thing, is often enough to start the blood of a resident male boiling. Do this near where you hear owls calling, and with the use of a flashlight, you are almost guaranteed to see an owl. At close quarters you will also appreciate that cliché sound of the night, not as the well-known and oversimplified "hoo-hoo-hooo" but as a throaty affair with wavers and croaks. Play fair, though – once you have set eyes on your bird, stop the impressions and let the owl go back to its business undisturbed. This technique can be

Barn owl (*Tyto alba*). Don't be deceived by that beautiful face and the duvet-soft feathers – this is a serious predator with beak and talons designed to kill.

modified to imitate the hoots of other owl species native to the area.

When pishing fails, try chipping – a short, sharp, kissing noise between tight lips. This is sometimes enough to make the birds appear, if briefly, out in the open, though some species, notably sparrows and the like, do not respond well to it. When birds are flying overhead and you have no time to reach for your binoculars, try a short "pew-pew" or a single loud "pish"; these calls are sometimes enough to cause the flyer to plummet out of the sky to avoid the imaginary predator that you have just warned it of.

Probably the most bizarre method of calling a bird in is that used to attract the European nightjar (*Caprimulgus europaeus*) in spring when the birds have just arrived back on their heathland breeding grounds and are setting up territories. If you approach a site at dusk, just as the birds are getting up for the night, and wave white handkerchiefs in the air while clapping your hands together like a Morris dancer, you may well lure in a testosterone-laden male bird, also flashing his white wing patches and clapping them together in a bid to challenge you.

This last trick can be much improved (and I have had a nightjar think about perching on my head while I was doing this) by playing a recording of its own call back through speakers. This way you do not even have to attempt to impersonate the bird, and nearly every time I have tried this I have had success. Not just with nightjars, either – many other species are attracted to their own voices.

All the above tricks are just that, and you should use them with great respect for the birds and awareness of their needs. The golden rule is, once you have had a look, quit calling them. They are, after all, responding in an agitated manner to a perceived threat, whether territorial or predatory, and being stressed uses energy that birds do not always have to spare. So never call them during their breeding seasons or when the conditions are cold, especially first thing in the morning, as many small birds are on very tight energy budgets. These techniques can be a bit like "crying wolf," too – the birds eventually get bored with all the commotion, and that is when a predatory hawk, also attracted to the noises, is most likely to strike.

Nightjars generally use their far-carrying froglike call only in the mating season. Males also clap their wings together as part of the courtship ritual or to warn off rival males. But note that nightjars are a schedule one species and as such are protected by the law, so disturbing one at the nest is a serious offense.

The way to a bird's confidence is through its stomach

When you feed birds in the park or put up a nest box for them in your backyard, you are providing a necessary resource and locating it so as to maximize your involvement with it. Improving bird habitats is a very good way of shortening the distance between you, the naturalist, and them, the wild creatures, and there are almost as many ways to do this as there are birds. There are many books and websites dedicated to this vast subject, so once again what I will do here is point you in the right direction and suggest a few of the cheaper and more eco-friendly ways of achieving the desired results.

Feeding first: There is a battery of different feeders available to dispense seeds, nuts, kitchen scraps, suet-based recipes, and water to your birds; they vary in design from a piece of board to a top-of-the-range, squirrel-proof affair that comes as part of a huge and burgeoning market in custom-built, designer bird feeders.

Tins of the kind coffee and baby food come in can be turned into seed feeders by drilling three holes in the sides close to the bottom, then one through the center of the base. Align this with a hole in a plastic saucer or drip tray, then either screw the whole thing onto a post or suspend it and fill it with seed.

The cheapest nut feeder is no more than an old net orange bag of the type supermarket fruit comes in. These are surprisingly effective and the bright color seems to attract birds that do not come to other feeders. Don't ask me why, but I rarely get siskins anywhere else, and I have been told that it is a color choice!

Right: The bullfinch (*Pyrrhula pyrrhula*) feeds on various kinds of seeds. It may nest in trees of larger gardens, and so if you are lucky enough to have a resident pair, it is easy to attract them to a feeder.

Below: Blue tits (*Parus caeruleus*) are the most common visitors to nut feeders in most parts of Britain.

Step **1**

Making a seed feeder

You can make your own seed feeder from those horrible plastic milk bottles that seem to have taken over the supermarket shelves recently. I recommend the 1 litre (2 pints) or larger sizes, unless you do not mind refilling them twice a day.

You will need:
- a large plastic bottle
- a knife strong enough to cut through it
- a pen
- twigs or any straight bits of wood, and string or wire to attach them to branches

1 Draw a line on the bottle 1.5 cm (½ in) from the bottom on the side opposite the handle, parallel to the base, and cut carefully along it. At each end of the incision, cut up about 3 cm (1 in).

2 Fold the flap you have just created back into the bottle and, hey presto, the bottom of the bottle becomes a feeding tray.

3 Make a couple of perches from the wood and stick them into holes below the feeding tray.

4 fill from the top with seeds and hang in the garden.

Step **2**

Step **3**

Bird cake or pudding, made from warmed suet mixed with any variety of seeds, fruits, nuts, or insects and left to set, can be served up in many ways. Put it in a tin wedged in place between three blocks screwed to your bird table, hang it in pots, cartons, or half coconuts, or jam it into large holes drilled in logs – a favorite for woodpeckers.

Mealworms

These are the wriggly larvae of beetles and can be bought in many pet shops, especially those that deal with reptiles and amphibians. There are many mail-order stockists, too, and so a fresh tub will turn up every Wednesday if you so desire. Mealworms are also easy to raise in the airing cupboard – keep them in a well-ventilated box with a tight-fitting lid and feed them on oatmeal, bread, cookies, and the like.

When buying mealworms, do not be tempted by cheaper imitations – to the uninitiated, there may not be much difference between maggots and mealworms, but remember that maggots are commercially grown for fishing and may contain chemicals; also they have been brought up on dead-animal material and may contain contaminants that are bad for your birds. Mealworms, being vegetarian, are much more like the caterpillars and grubs that birds feed on in the wild.

A handful of wriggling mealworms may not seem very appetizing to you, but robins find then irresistible. Start by putting a small margarine tub with a few mealworms in it on your lawn to get your local robin interested. As the days go by, stand out in the garden while it is feeding, inching closer every day. Different robins have different tolerance levels. So there are no rules about how long getting to within arm's length will take. Just be patient. Keeping low or even lying down may help. Now comes the hard bit – making contact. Offer the mealworm in the same tub, but hold the tub in your outstretched hand. If your robin is at the right stage of conditioning, it should feed fairly happily. Let him or her settle in to this pattern for a few days, then when he or she seems relaxed, remove the tub and place the worms in your palm. And you should have a hand-tame robin!

If at any stage you fail, go back a step and keep trying – it is worth it both for the robin, who gets vital food of the right kind, and for you, who will get the rare thrill of contact with a wild bird.

Feeding mealworms to birds can be tricky, as they have a tendency to crawl off, something a peanut cannot do. This can be overcome by serving them up in slippery-sided containers. Watch for rain, though; drill a drainage hole in the bottom to stop your worms drowning – if they are dead, they stop wriggling and soon go moldy.

Points to remember about feeding

Be patient. If you have just started feeding the birds in your garden, it may take them a while to learn about your service and add you to their daily rounds.

☀ Keep areas under feeders clean. If they are positioned over hard standing, sweep and disinfect it regularly; wash and scrub down your feeding devices as well. Feeding stations, with their high numbers of visitors, are perfect places for disease transfer. Plus the tidier your feeders are, the less likely you are to attract unwanted guests such as rats. (Though if mammals are your thing, this may be a bonus!)

Chaffinch (*Fringilla coelebs*)

☀ Use good-quality foods, ideally from a purveyor of seeds and the like aimed at garden birds. Many of the selections you see in the bargain basement have a high concentration of wheat (not a problem if you want to feed pigeons, pheasants and chickens, but not attractive for smaller birds). Peanuts that have been badly stored may contain a fungus called aflotoxin that is lethal to small birds. So buy wisely.

☀ Choose a variety of foods. Not all birds like eating the same things: Hummingbirds have specialist requirements and need a sugary liquid; finches go for seeds such as niger and sunflower; tits are crazy about nuts; thrushes like fruit; and woodpeckers love fatty, suet-based stuff. Provide water nearby, so that the birds can drink and wash between meals. This is especially important in the winter if temperatures fall below freezing. Keep the ice away by placing hand warmers or candles below a metal dish of water, regularly pouring in hot water from the kettle, floating a ball in the water or splashing the cash on a heated bird bath (yes, they really do exist).

American goldfinch (*Spinus tristis*) feeding on thistle seeds

☀ Put your feeders in an open location but with cover nearby. This means that next door's cat cannot sneak up unawares, but the birds will feel secure knowing there is natural cover into which to dive if a predator such as a hawk shows up. Feed in various locations. Some birds are bold, others shy, so by all means provide food close to the house, but don't forget the nervous ones – put a little at the end of the garden, too. Also bear in mind that different birds feed in different ways; some rarely get onto the bird table but prefer to stay on the ground; others like flat surfaces; some like to hang.

Bird cake or pudding: This animal fat-based food made from warmed suet mixed with any variety of seeds, fruits, nuts, or insects and left to set can be served up in many ways. You can provide it in a tin that is simply wedged in place between three blocks screwed to your birdtable, it can be hung in pots and cartons as well as half coconuts, or jammed into large holes drilled in logs – a favorite for woodpeckers.

❋ There is a myth that you must stop feeding the birds in the summer/breeding months. This is just not true, as birds are more pressed than ever to meet the demands of their nestlings. What you should do, however, is avoid large food items such as peanuts or bread crusts that can be removed whole, as these, when fed to nestlings, may cause them to choke and die. In summer keep the food small and soft.

❋ Many people worry that the birds in their garden may become so dependent on their feeding that, when they go away, the birds will starve. Well, don't feel you have to cancel your holidays. It is thought that many garden birds treat feeding stations as they do patchy food resources in the wild: As soon as food dries up, they move on to somewhere else in the neighborhood.

❋ Don't be afraid to experiment and have fun while providing for your birds. Rather than putting nuts in feeders and crumbs on the lawn, attract a few more finches by collecting teasel seedheads and sprinkling tiny black niger seeds into the natural seed chambers. This makes the seedheads recyclable, whereas in the wild they would be used only once. Try melting fats into some of the seedheads – blue tits love it. Alternatively, drill holes in a log, fill them with suet and you have the perfect woodpecker feeder.

A variation on the theme

As well as putting food out for the birds during the winter, how about putting nesting materials out in the spring? When out walking, collect tufts of sheep's wool caught on barbed-wire fences, horse's hair, feathers, dry grass, and hay. Add long hairs from the hairbrush and the fluff from the Hoover bag, bundle it up, hang it around the garden or on the birdtable and see who comes and takes what for their nests.

Living in a box
nesting sites for birds

The bird box has been a feature of many gardens for some time, but with the continual squeeze on wild bird nesting places in many parts of the world, due to urban development and drastic changes in land management and farming practice, the back garden is becoming an important sanctuary.

Lack of suitable nest sites holds many bird populations back, and providing them is one way that the amateur naturalist can plow back a little. This is a two-way relationship – you give them nest boxes; in return you get a focus for your studies – and with a bit of techno-wizardry, you can elevate the humble tit box to new heights.

Having birds use a box in your garden allows you to become familiar with intimate goings on that would usually be hidden in the tangles of the wild. One rather frosty evening, I watched a wren enter an old nest box hanging on my garden wall. I was surprised, as up till then no bird had ever condescended to use my home-made box in the breeding season, but I watched with interest, thinking he might be hunting for spiders. Fifteen minutes later, without having noticed him

Great tit *(Parus major)* – a bold bird, likely to be an early colonizer of your nest box. A nest box camera (see p. 67) gives you a privileged look at your tenants' family life.

leave, I saw him go in again. After the fifth sighting, I got suspicious and stayed with my eyes glued to the box hole. It soon became apparent that, unless my box had sprung a leak, there were many birds sheltering there; by the time dusk had fallen I had counted 23 wrens.

Since then I have done a bit of homework and discovered that the record is 60 wrens in a standard blue-tit box – the ornithological equivalent of cramming students into a phone booth, I guess. The explanation is that the birds are effectively creating one superwren, huddling together and reducing the surface area through which they lose body heat.

Come the beginning of spring, as the birds begin to start calling and warming up for breeding, you will see them beginning to inspect cavities and eventually taking up residence. The real action starts when the eggs inside hatch and the parents' comings and goings increase in response to the demand for food. Just counting these visits and noting the sort of prey they bring in is the key to a much greater understanding of even our most common birds.

Nest boxes are not all boxlike – they can be anything from the classic cavity box with a hole to the very latest in woodcrete architecture (a secret combination of wood and concrete that is supposed to have insulating properties and allow the cavity to breathe). They can be a floating raft for moorhens or a floating beach for terns, a construction the size of a tea chest for owls, a drainpipe for tits, or a little woven reed or rope ball for bearded tits (*Parnuris biamicus*); and these are just those *intended* for nesting. Birds can also be surprisingly good at improvising – every year I hear of a selection of bizarre nest sites that has included overcoat pockets, car exhaust pipes, crash helmets, and even a human skull.

The following are a few ideas to be getting on with, but as usual be creative, check out some of the books recommended at the back of this one, and you are sure to come up with a desirable residence for the birds in your garden.

A great tit checks out "woodcrete," the latest in nest box materials.

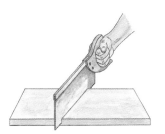

Step **1**

Step **2**

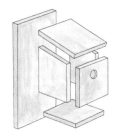

Step **3**

Step **4**

Step **5**

Making your own bird box

This is the most common form, attractive to a whole host of small birds. A hole with a maximum diameter of 3 cm (1 ⅛ in) is good for most tits, tree sparrows, and nuthatches.

You will need:
- a plank of wood about 15 cm (6 in) wide, 122.5 cm (50 in) long, and 18 mm (¾ in) deep, treated with wood preservative
- another piece of treated wood, 40 cm (16 in) x 10 cm (4 in), for a batten
- a saw and drill
- nails, screws, or glue
- a brass hinge

1 Working on a solid surface such as a workbench, saw a 45 cm (18 in) length of wood off the plank. Cut this again on the diagonal so that you have two identical pieces, each with one long side measuring 25 cm (10 in) and the other 20 cm (8 in). These will make the sides of your box.

2 Drill a hole near the top of the piece that will be the front. (Its size will depend on the size of the bird you want to attract – see p. 66.)

3 Cut the remaining length of plank into four pieces, measuring: 25 cm (10 in) long for the back; 20 cm (8 in) for the front; 21.5 cm (8 ½ in) for the top; and 11 cm (4 ½ in) for the floor.

4 Screw, nail, or glue the back to the batten, which should stick out a bit at both top and bottom. Then fix the rest of the box together with the longer ends of each side toward the back. Leave the roof till last and fix it on with the hinge. Don't worry about making all the joins perfect – any gaps will be useful for drainage and ventilation (in fact, if you are a master carpenter, you should drill a few holes to supply these needs).

5 Nail through the top and bottom of the batten to fix your box to a tree or wall, high enough to be safe from cats and other predators. See p. 66 for advice on positioning.

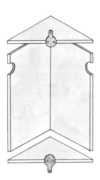

Treecreeper box

Location is the single most important factor in the success of your nest box. Make sure it is high enough off the ground to be safe from predators and facing away from the prevailing wind.

Specialized bird boxes for fussier birds

If you want to attract robins, wagtails, and spotted flycatchers, make an open-fronted box using the dimensions given on p. 165, but with the front piece only about 7½ cm (3 in) high. Nail it to a tree or wall in a sheltered spot and partially cover it with climbing plants. Adding a handful of straw or similar material will make it even more attractive. An open-fronted box about twice this size may lure kestrels, sparrowhawks, or little owls.

Treecreepers will visit a box that mimics their preferred natural nesting sites – a crevice in a tree or under a piece of loose bark. Cut two rectangular pieces of wood about 165 mm (6½ in) by 305 mm (12 in) and two triangular pieces with two sides measuring 165 mm (6½ in) and the other 235 mm (9¼ in). Cut a semicircular notch about 2.5 cm (1 in) in diameter out of one long side of each of the rectangles, about 50 mm (2 in) from the end. Nail the two rectangles together at an angle as shown, with the notches on the outside and near the top, then add the triangular pieces to make a roof and a base. Use mirror plates at top and bottom to fix it all to a tree, which forms the back of the box, and glue a few strips of bark to the outside so that it blends in with its background.

If a swift can't find a suitable roof to nest in – quite likely if your area consists of predominantly new houses – it will appreciate a special bird box. Make a conventional box as described above, but reinforce the entrance by screwing on a metal plate with a circular hole, making sure you file down any rough edges. This prevents other, larger birds extending the entrance.

Fix the box at least 6 m (20 ft) off the ground, preferably at roof level, under the eaves, and be patient – it may take the swifts a few years to move in.

'Location, location, location': positioning the box

You can have the most fabulous, comfortable, centrally heated "des res" with mealworms on tap, but if it is sited incorrectly, it will house nothing but the beetles you placed in there in the first place. The positioning of your bird boxes is critical; different species have different requirements such as height and relative positioning to other garden features. Robins and spotted flycatchers (*Muscicapa striata*) seem to prefer more open boxes than tits, and sparrows like theirs next to thick bushes; they also choose their nest sites early in the season, and so in the Northern Hemisphere put your box up by Christmas if you want to attract sparrows.

The two most important things to take into consideration are shelter from inclement weather, not just rain and wind, but extremes of temperature, too; and safety from predators such as cats. These needs then have to be balanced with your own – how viewable you wish the boxes to be and how easy they are to clean and service (by this I mean an annual scraping out of debris and any necessary external repairs). The time to do any maintenance is during the winter months; this is also the season to reposition the boxes if for some reason you didn't get it right the first time.

Watch the birdie: nest box cameras

Thanks to technology continuing to make everything smaller and cheaper, it is now possible to buy reasonably priced kits that allow you to view the most secret lives of birds in your nest boxes. A kit consists of a very small infrared camera with a length of lead that simply plugs into the back of your computer, video, or TV. So when there is nothing on TV except reruns of *Friends*, you can flick over to see what the tits are doing.

The cameras are intended to be fixed into the roof of the nest box and with some of them you don't even have to do this yourself – the kit comes with its own box. All you have to do is nail it up and plug in, and the birds will do the rest. The lenses are fixed, but because the field of view is so wide, the entire contents of the nest box will be in focus. With the camera high up in the box, the lens remains fairly clean and splatter-free, though when the nestlings start getting cabin fever and realize what their wings are for, the dust does begin to fly. Any muck that gets on the lens can be quickly polished off while mum and dad are away. When your nestlings have moved off, keep watching, because the parents may try for a second family or another pair may move in. If it all goes quiet, you can simply reposition the camera, perhaps in a hedgehog box or on the mammal table.

Once you start "bugging" your box like this, there is no limit to the possibilities – color pictures, night vision, microphones, light sensors that allow internal lights to come on and go off. And why limit yourself to the inside of a box? Why not try some of the waterproof units that will allow you CCTV coverage of pretty much every inch of your estate?

With all these hungry mouths to feed, the parent birds – here, great tits – will welcome any contribution from you – they will eat seeds, suet, beech nuts, and insects.

Hides and blinds
you're 'outa sight'

There is a lot to be said for simply sitting still without moving a muscle, and although this may sound like a great excuse for sloth, there is a point to it. Watching and waiting for something to happen is one of the best things a naturalist can do in the field, and this applies just as much to other wildlife as it does to birds. Obviously you can increase your chances of seeing something interesting by knowing some of the habits of the creature you are trying to watch, but simply doing nothing in the right place at the right time is a technique that has never failed to amaze me. I've had badgers run into my legs and knock them from under me, I've nearly been stepped on by a giraffe, I've had a grizzly bear eat a fish so close I got an eyeful of milt, and I've had a sparrowhawk pluck a thrush before my very eyes.

Keep your distance and be as quiet as possible.

The technique is universal, and I remember once having a chat with a naturalist about someone who had named the art of sitting still. The problem is that I cannot remember who it was. Recent conversations seem to suggest a Canadian called Ernest Thompson Seton, though a correspondent of mine who is a member of the Seton Trust has never heard of it but agrees that if it isn't called the Seton technique it should be. So you may well have heard it here first: "The Seton technique, simply sit and wait!"

Sitting and waiting works even better if you cannot be seen by your quarry. There are purpose-built bird hides, or blinds, on many nature reserves now; they can be anything from a draughty shed to a centrally heated, double-glazed monstrosity complete with coffee machine. But the object is the same – they allow you to be human without disturbing the animals you have come to watch. For me the best thing about them is the social scene within: Hides are simply the best place to meet other "birders," from full-blown bird nuts to casual Sunday-afternoon binocular claspers. The hide becomes one big "superbirder" with as many pairs of eyes as there are people gathered inside, and the more eyes there are looking, the less chance a bird has of sneaking past without being seen.

Remember hide etiquette, though – keep the noise down and do not, whatever you do, stick your hands out of the slots to point at something. I've seen it happen, and the person who scares off a huge flock of mixed waterfowl by doing this will wish he or she had wings, too! One other thing – when you leave, shut the viewing "slots" behind you and don't let the door slam.

At the other end of the hide or blind scale are the ones a versatile naturalist will want to build and position himself. There were once a couple of nature photographers, the Kearton brothers, who used to get close to animals in many remarkable and bizarre ways, such as making model cows and sheep to hide themselves and their cameras in. Although there is no limit to how inventive you can be in order to achieve your goal, simpler options are available, and what you opt for depends on your needs.

Probably the most basic form of hide and one you can carry around with you is a bit of military camouflage scrim. Scrim is that netting with various bits and pieces stuck to it, used to break up your outline. Its big advantage is that it is lightweight and you can carry it in your pack. If you stumble across a situation where you need to vanish, simply throw it over yourself or fashion a basic support from the available vegetation and you have a hide. The disadvantages are that it is flimsy, will blow around, and doesn't protect you from the elements.

You can achieve similar results with natural materials such as bent branches, string, and leafy vegetation or, if you want something more robust and permanent, incorporate waterproof canvas and scrim, add a chair and a flask of hot coffee, and you have a setup that should allow you to outlast even the most patience-testing bird.

The other option is the "throw money at it" one. There are hides on the market that are practically camouflaged tents and come in a huge range of designs to suit an equally diverse range of budgets.

The art of not being seen

It's lucky for the naturalist that birds cannot count – even smart birds like ravens (*Corvus corax*) have trouble with mental arithmetic. If you are planning to spend some time in a hide which has an unprotected approach that means you will be seen by your quarry, rope a friend in to walk you to the door. If you both go in, wait for a minute or two, and then your friend goes back, the animals will perceive the threat as having left. You can now relax and get down to watching the animals as they go about their business.

Do your research before building or locating your hide. Get to know the area and how the animals are using it. I once spent a long time creating what I thought was a hide masterpiece, perfectly positioned close to the holt of a giant otter (*Pteronura brasiliensis*). After waiting for several hours, I became aware of a rumbling noise that appeared to come from below my feet. It wasn't until a strong smell of fish started permeating the hide that I looked out to find that the "back" door to this otter's holt (actually its front door, as it turned out) opened behind my hide. The rumbling was the otters passing backward and forward beneath my feet and the smell of fish came from what they were having for dinner while I was pointing in the other direction!

Make a note of the prevailing wind direction of your site and try to pitch your position downwind. This is not as important with birds as it is with mammals, but is still worth taking into account: You may have come for the oystercatchers, but if an otter was to turn up, you would kick yourself if it sussed you out and ran away.

Prepare yourself for your period of isolation. Take food and a drink of a suitable temperature. Hides can get surprisingly hot or cold, and a drink will help alleviate discomfort. Once inside your hide, do not be lured into a false sense of security. You may be hidden, but any noise you make will pass through the flimsy material of the hide. Avoid rustling clothes, potato chip packets, and food wrappers. Opt for a quiet sandwich instead. When it's time to go home, always leave as quietly as you arrived.

Try to keep quiet and well camouflaged.

Birds of a feather

Many bird species find advantage in flocking together for the winter. This whole mass-roosting thing is a bit of an enigma. The first obvious theory is communal thermal regulation – combining lots of little bodies to form one large one with a relatively smaller surface area. This would make sense for a lot of small birds, but if you look at roosts of pied wagtails (*Motacilla alba*) and starlings you will see that the birds are not huddled but very spaced out, and so the theory doesn't seem to work there. Those desperate to conserve warmth, such as wrens and several members of the tit family, will jam themselves into old nest boxes and crevices, as I described earlier.

So what is going on with the big roosts of birds that aggregate for the night only? An obvious advantage is safety in numbers – lots of birds milling around makes for confusing hunting, and if you watch a flock of dunlin seethe, shimmer, and condense at the attack of a peregrine, you can understand how this works. This would apply equally to the activities of sparrowhawks (*Accipiter nisus*) and tawny owls, which are regularly seen having a pop at big roosts. Added to the confusion is the fact that, with so many birds to eat, all the predators in a small area are sated quickly, and each individual in a flock stands less chance of being nobbled.

Another theory is that a lot of the bird equivalent of gossiping occurs at a roost, each bird communicating with others if they have split up during the day to feed, as starlings do. Those returning to the roost with a full crop somehow by appearance or sound pass on the message that they have fed well and that any less successful birds may benefit from joining up with them the next day.

A "chorus line" performance observed on safari in East Africa – little bee-eaters (*Merops pusillis*) roosting

Sticks and homes
retro birding

For much of the year woodlands, copses, and hedgerows act as living leafy shrouds, obscuring the details of private lives. During the bare winter months, however, things become more transparent. Back-lit against a watery gray sky, the trees not only reveal their own profiles but also betray many of the summer's secrets.

Song thrushes make neat, circular nests lined with mud.

Birds' nests are among the things that are revealed. It's taboo to go looking for these in spring and high summer when they are fulfilling their function, but now that they lie vacant – of birds, at least – the amateur naturalist can revel in them.

Dense bundles of twigs and vegetation give away where birds' nests were built, and so if you failed to discover where that long-tailed tit (*Aegithalos caudatus*) was heading with all those strands of horsehair and moss back in the summer, now is your chance. If this sounds like a waste of time, bear in mind that some birds return to the same areas year after year or at least select the same habitat or height, and so finding and identifying nests and their positions now can stand you in good stead next year.

At first and to the inexperienced eye, one nest may look very much like the next, just a tangle of sticks, straw, and a bit of mud. But with a little practice, a touch of guesswork, and the usual healthy helping of dogged persistence, you can soon start linking them to their avian originators.

Distinctive constructions such as the large, loose-domed stick nests of magpies, the tree-top communities of platforms constructed by rooks, or the solitary efforts of carrion crows are relatively easy even from a distance. Slightly more taxing are the similar-size nests of various garden birds such as blackbirds (*Turdus merula*) and song thrushes (*Turdus philomelos*), but these can be separated on constructional merits. Song thrushes are unique among British birds in having a hard lining of mud to their nests, while blackbirds use mud in the construction but actually line the nest with fine grasses. The masterpieces of wrens look like moss footballs, each with a hole punched in its side, built close to stumps and in dense vegetation.

After some searching you will discover the small cup-shaped nests of finches – often made of finer materials than the thrushes' – grass, hair, wool, and moss. Greenfinches (*Carduelis chloris*) and chaffinches are less fussy than their relatives about location; their nests are the ones you are most likely to find in a garden hedge – the chaffinch's is a rather neater cup-shape than the greenfinch's. For the other finches, you need to look a little higher, either in the forks of trees close to the trunk or toward the ends of branches.

While nest-watching, look out for stashes of seeds and fruits, as hedgerow nests are often used by squatters such as voles and wood mice. And, just as we have a microcosm of life in our own households, so do birds. Take a disused nest home, break it open on a sheet of white paper, and watch as pseudoscorpions, spiders, and mites come tottering out.

For the observant master class of nest-spotters, look for the bored-out nest holes created by woodpeckers. Green (*Picus viridis*) and great spotted woodpeckers (*Dendrocopos major*) have a nest entrance of around 7–8 cm (2 ¾–3 in) in diameter, while the lesser spotted (*Dendrocopos minor*) has a tiny doorway of about 4 cm (1 ½ in). But there is more to this than the size of the holes. Green woodpeckers prefer to knock holes in healthy-looking trees with rotten hearts, great spotted tend to use trees that are obviously on the way out, and lesser spotted nest holes are often higher and on the underside of a sloping branch.

It's not just birds' architectural activities that you are likely to come across while scanning the lofty levels of a woodland. You may well notice the summer drey of a gray squirrel, but the chances are that you wouldn't know that was what it was, as they resemble a hollowed-out crow's nest built high and out on the branches. Larger and much more distinctive is the dense winter drey, also used as a nursery. This is often constructed with leafy twigs, lined with mosses and grass and built close to the trunk where it is less prone to the buffeting of gales.

Catch the creeper

Another ornithological extra worth looking for requires first identifying a tree. Old parks and churchyards are the best places in the U.K. to find mature wellingtonia trees. These unmistakable giant conifers native to California have a soft, deep, and fibrous bark. Check this over in daylight, and the chances are you will find small oval depressions in the bark, made more obvious by a trickle of white bird droppings below each one. Return on a cold night, and you will find these plugged with the tiny tawny-streaked bodies of treecreepers (*Certhia familiaris*). The birds hollow out these customized and insulated snugs, and a single tree can attract birds from all over the neighborhood seeking sanctuary from the cold; as many as 25 can be seen on one large tree.

The green woodpecker is not an agile climber, though it nests in trees and is often seen on the ground feeding on ants, its principal food.

Treecreepers have inobtrusive plumage but a distinctive habit of "creeping" up tree trunks.

The sticky-out bits
watching migrants

From little brown jobs (LBJs) to large white ones, unexpected animals can throw the ornithological world into turmoil at certain seasons. Headlands can be as busy as a bank holiday weekend at Heathrow Airport when the autumn migration is in full swing, what with winter visitors flying in, summer breeders checking out, a few species in transit landing for a refuel and fuselage check, and individuals who alight lost, way off their intended course.

Swallows (*Hirundo rustica*) and house martins (*Delichon urbica*) belong to the same family and in summer are often seen gathering together on telegraph wires.

Despite the many clues – swallows gathering on wires, the disappearance of that spotted flycatcher that was always in the garden, the emptiness echoing in the shrubs, the lack of calls from willow warblers, whitethroats (*Sylvia communis*), and chiffchaffs (*Phylloscopus collybita*) – the autumn migration is not as obvious as its spring equivalent. In spring the birds are driven by a lustful urgency to set up territories and get a head start on the breeding season; by autumn the pressure is off and the outflux is a gradual one. This apathy is obvious in many streets; while some nests of house martins (*Delichon urbica*) lie abandoned, their owners already on their way, others still have their entrances stuffed full of the pied "yippering" heads of the last generation of the year.

Millions of birds that have visited for the summer breeding season and their offspring are southbound again. Many that have boarded farther north, in places such as Iceland, Greenland, and Scandinavia, either join us for the winter or use our temperate zones like convenient avian highway services before continuing south to the Mediterranean and Africa.

The knack of beholding the migration spectacle is simply being in the right place at the right time. And the right place is one of the many "sticky-out" bits: Headlands, bills, mulls, and peninsulas become the focal points for birds that are passing through, funneling those moving over land to the shortest over-sea jumps and providing good vantage points from which to spy seabirds passing offshore.

If you don't live near moorland and fancy seeing a ring ouzel, or want to learn your warblers all in one day, are turned on by rarities such as a red-breasted flycatcher (*Ficedula parva*), or simply wish to witness the spectacle of swallows doing what they are famous for, the time to act is now. Choose your day carefully and according to the weather. For best results, think like a bird that has to conserve its resources; early mornings on days with an inshore wind are best, as any birds wanting to leave land are likely to "bunch up," waiting for more favorable weather. These conditions also help birds traveling the opposite way and heading for landfall.

Do not be put off by the thought of being surrounded by thousands of unidentifiable LBJs. The beauty of the autumn migration is that, with a bit of luck, you will get plenty of easy "spots." A good wind may carry with it the first "fall" of redwings (*Turdus iliacus*) and fieldfares (*T. pilaris*) on the same day that scores of pied (*Ficedula hypoleuca*) and spotted flycatchers, whitethroats, garden warblers (*Sylvia borin*), wheatears (*Oenanthe oenanthe*), and whinchats (*Saxicola rubetra*) are lining up to check out. In the West it is not unknown for a few treats to turn up – such as bluethroats (*Luscinia svecica*), wrynecks (*Jynx torquilla*), or the ungainly bulk of an incoming woodcock (*Scolopax rusticola*) or two.

Big game
mammals

Mammals are the top of the range as far as the amateur naturalist is concerned, simply the best that Mother Nature and millions of years of evolution have come up with. Like us, they are "warm blooded" and have highly developed central nervous systems. Many are also blessed with supersenses hundreds if not thousands of times more sensitive than ours – very handy for their everyday survival, but a total pain in the neck for those wishing to study them.

Part of the problem is that the majority of wild terrestrial mammals are small, highly strung, and twitchy, and, like it or not, they see us humans as predators – which is why almost any encounter with one provokes the same reaction – immediate flight. So the naturalist has to find other ways of approaching them and of finding out about their lives.

Above: Badger (*Meles meles*) hair caught in barbed wire
Right: Red deer (*Cervus elaphus*) roaring

Attracting your subjects

It is hardly surprising that so many small mammals are of a nervous disposition. They have the misfortune of being a critical link in a lot of food chains and there is a good chance that pretty much every other animal around that is armed with sharp teeth and claws is going to want a piece of their hide. Many of them have very fast metabolisms, which means they have to spend a lot of their time eating. So if you want to lure them into your garden, you have to provide food and you have to make them feel safe.

The mammal table

European red fox
(*Vulpes vulpes*)

The principle of a mammal table is exactly the same as that of a bird table. You put food out and hope to lure some of the shyer furry residents of your backyard within intimate viewing range. It is also perfect for the lazier armchair naturalist who happens to own a set of glass patio doors.

I have seen all sorts of variations on the theme of a mammal table – foxes, badgers, deer, opossums, moose, pine martens, brown bears, and hyenas are all very much up for an easy meal – but here I am going to concentrate on the ubiquitous, but still rather exciting, small mammal fauna.

To set up a successful feeding station, you need to combine the animals' needs with your own wishes. You will want to view with a degree of comfort, and so situate your table near a window. The lower the table, the better, as most small mammals, even those that are good at climbing, will come down to ground level to feed, but not all those at ground level have a head for heights. For the table itself, a piece of smooth wood such as an old tray or a spare plank is ideal.

Providing a certain amount of shelter is important. Covering the platform with chicken wire enables you to see the animals while at the same time dissuading predators from having a go. Try covered approaches leading from suitable habitats nearby:
I have used offcuts from roof gutters and old downpipes with much success. Or you could make the whole table an enclosed box, with one open side facing your glass, for good and secure viewing.

Remember also that these animals are very sensitive to noise and disturbance, and so keep this down and put red filters over your flashlight or any other lights (most nocturnal creatures are less sensitive to light in the red end of the spectrum). Bait the table with a variety of food such as grain, cheese, cat food, mealworms, and fruit.

Somewhere to call home

The small and medium-size visitors to your table will be more numerous if you encourage them to take up residence near your home. This not only makes it a lot easier for you to monitor their comings and goings, but it is also a way of "putting a little back," as many natural den sites and habitats in and around human habitation have been lost or damaged by our activities.

Dawn and dusk are the best times to see mammal activity. These are the times when the day and night shifts change over and most mammals are active, either heading out or heading home. This wood mouse (*Apodemus saylvaticus*), or long-tailed field mouse, is feeding among leaf litter under the cover of darkness.

This need not involve great cost, heavy construction, or sore thumbs. Simply modifying parts of your home or outhouses can make a difference. You could create a bat box or simply leave access points in your own eaves and allow the local bats to occupy existing cavities; the amount of effort you put into this is entirely up to you.

Tips for the mammal-watcher

Bearing in mind the natural nervousness of most small mammals (and quite a lot of large ones, come to that) when faced with a member of the human race, there are a few commonsense rules you should bear in mind when attempting to watch them.

There is an inverse ratio between the number and length of sightings made and the number of people in your party. The fewer observers, the more you will observe.

Keep the wind in your face and be aware of natural cover, whether it is vegetation or a bend in the track. Position yourself in such a way as to minimize the likelihood of a surprise encounter. Always expect an animal to appear, act accordingly, and be rewarded.

If hides are available, make use of them, remembering to consider the needs of other mammal-watchers too. Alternatively, build your own (see p. 68).

If spotted, try to look as unhuman as you can. Get down low and move slowly and inconsistently: Take a few steps, wait, take a single step, wait, then continue. You are less likely to be thought of as a potential predator if you don't behave like one.

Reading the signs
the 'art of seeing'

Encouraging wildlife into your garden is only the first step toward learning more about it. The keen naturalist is also going to want to get out there and study the signs the animals leave as they get on with their lives.

Measuring black rhino (*Diceros bicornis*) tracks in Namibia. The local people are so expert at following rhino trails that just a tiny pebble kicked out of the way can tell them in which direction it went and at what speed.

Why track animals? Funnily enough, the answer isn't necessarily to find the animal that made the tracks. Learning how to track is like learning to read all over again. And just as with reading, the aim is not to get to the end of the story as fast as you can but to "experience" the words.

Tracking an animal is not just a way of getting close to its physical presence but a way of finding out what makes it do what it does. When you begin to understand an animal's ways, you are better able to predict where it is going to be, which leads to a higher chance of actually seeing it, because by using your knowledge you can position yourself accordingly. Any fool can stop and look, but not everyone can stop and look in the right place.

So first you have to learn to recognize "field signs." Look close enough and you will find every square foot of a habitat has something to tell you about the creatures that live in it or move through it. Some of the signs are very subtle and tell you things in an easily missed "whisper" – a single hair on a fence post, say. Others are more obvious: Uprooted trees with branches twisted off scream "Elephants were here!"

Interpreting field signs is vital when working with timid and secretive creatures, as it is often the only way we can piece together their private lives without trapping them. I know somebody who did a doctorate on the behavior of otters in an English river and during the three years of the study never set eyes on the elusive beasts themselves.

So the nature detective spends a lot of time looking at the ground.

It never fails to amaze me to see, early in the morning, the trails left by nocturnal creatures. Most are made by domestic animals, but look closely and you will soon start noticing other trails. A lot depends on the substrate where you are looking: To find good tracks you need the soft stuff. Mud and sand have the advantage of being available in most habitats in most seasons.

Let's start with a couple of definitions. It may seem a bit boring, but if you are working with others or trying to interpret someone else's notes, it makes sense to ensure that you are all talking about the same thing.

So, a **track** is specifically the impression made by the feet (or any part of the body involved in locomotion). A **trail** is the overall impression made by an animal's passing by. It can indicate size, gait, and the speed at which the creature was traveling. The term trail also refers to marks made by other parts of the animal's body, such as tail drag, and its physical effects on the surrounding environment, such as stripped bark or trampled vegetation.

Tracks

The track, or footprint, of an animal is a good starting point for practicing your detecting skills. Roughly speaking tracks can be separated into four categories:
birds;
hoofed mammals such as deer, sheep, and horses;
animals with "pads and toes," which can be anything from a bear to a mouse;
everything else, from reptiles to insects – after all, even the lowliest worm can leave a track if the conditions are right.

So, for the purposes of tracking, mammals fall into two main categories: those whose limbs terminate in hooves, or cleaves, and those that have paws, with pads and toes.

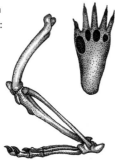

Skeletal leg and foot of a squirrel and its footprint: a typical plantigrade print

When mammals evolved 200 million years ago, they started off with a basic, archetypal foot plan that can be likened to the human hand, with five digits. The digits are conventionally numbered one to five, with number one, the inner toe, always being the shortest, analogous to the human thumb. This is relevant to the tracking naturalist because the world is still walked upon by animals with primitive foot layouts – flat-footed, or **plantigrade** creatures include insectivores such as hedgehogs and shrews; bears; mustelids (the group to which weasels, badgers, skunks, and otters belong); and primates.

This may sound like an unnecessary amount of detail, but it is just the sort of thing you need to know if you are to interpret field signs to the full. If you find a track showing five toes, you can start making guesses about what sort of creature made it, and if you can identify the inner toe, you can tell from its position whether the track is that of a right or a left foot.

Skeletal leg and foot of a dog and its footprint: a typical digitigrade print

Now, the problem with being flat-footed is that you have a lot of resistance – every time the foot goes down it acts as a brake, wasting valuable energy. So mammals that needed to travel fast had to adapt. Over time, the weight of the body moved forward, the legs became longer, and mammals started to run on their toes. One of the accompanying changes was that the number of toes was reduced, and the toe to go was our friend digit number one. Look at the footprint of a dog or cat, and you will see it registers only four toes on each foot. In such **digitigrade** animals, the remaining four toes became larger, and if there is a short toe, it is now the outer one, digit five.

Skeletal leg and foot of a deer and its footprint: a typical unguligrade print

This process continued with the further reduction of toes in **unguligrade** animals. Deer and sheep produce footprints that register two toes per foot; these cleaves, or slots, correspond to two hooves representing digits three and four. The most extreme toe reduction is found in the equines, or horses. A horse stands on the tip of digit three; all the other toes have disappeared.

Plantigrade footprint of a badger

The pads of a mammal's feet can also help with identification. Next time you are curled up on the sofa with the household cat or dog, check out its feet. The undersides have tough leathery pads that act as springy cushions and are reinforced with protective ligaments. Below the tip of each toe is a corresponding toe pad, then behind these there can be various arrangements of other pads. In some species these blend together to form the central or hind pad (also called the palm or heel pad). The footprint of a human or a badger shows this well.

In some animals, the pads on the feet provide individual signposts.

If I'm going somewhere where I'm likely to pick up track, I usually take enough equipment with me to make casts of four or five dog-size prints – this is a reasonable amount to carry on a day trip. But if there is a chance you will find *big* prints, you need *big* quantities as well as *big* vessels to mix or melt in. The example that springs to mind is my quest for polar bear prints in the Canadian tundra. These huge predators leave deep, dinner platter-size pugmarks, and I thought a print of one of them would be the ultimate addition to the collection.

It was this vision that drove me to the madness and inconvenience of lugging a 15 kg (33 lb) sack of plaster and bucket with me wherever I went. We were traveling everywhere by helicopter, and the sack kept springing leaks and puffing forth the fine white powder, enough to test the patience of any pilot, especially one who clearly took a lot of pride in the interior of his helicopter. On top of this we were working as part of a film crew, and my bulky bag was simply getting in the way. When I was carrying it in my backpack it nearly killed me. It all seemed as if it was going to be worth it when, much sweating, puffing, and panting later, I found my dream footprint beautifully registered in some frozen mud. But I was in the subarctic in early winter, and I had forgotten one rather obvious fact – that all the available water was frozen solid and I had nothing to mix my plaster with.

As so often, a bit of planning and research would have gone a long way to avoid much discomfort and suffering.

Trail patterns

Now let's look beyond individual tracks and consider the overall impression. Even if you are having trouble reading the tracks, it doesn't mean you can't identify the animal.

The footprints of many wild canines are very similar to those of domestic dogs; but look up from the tracks, look at the *way* the animal has moved and you can learn to read its trail. This is the master class of tracking, the difference between being an Inspector Clouseau and a Sherlock Holmes.

Mammals' gaits are all variations on four themes: walking, trotting, running, and bounding or hopping. Not every mammal uses all four – rabbits and squirrels, for example, never walk; even when moving slowly they hop. In the field, look out for any distinctions between fore- and hindfeet; many animals have them.

Walking shows as a pattern of alternating footfalls. The left hind foot moves first, then the left forefoot, then the right hind, then the right fore, before the process repeats. The spacing between the footfalls depends on the speed the animal is moving and also the type of animal. At one extreme the front and rear tracks superimpose totally, known as perfect registration (seen in some deer); sometimes the registration is imperfect and the hind foot and forefoot overlap partially, as with a walking badger. So the trail pattern appears as two parallel lines of tracks.

With **running** there are no alternating movements. When an animal takes off with a burst of speed, both front legs leave the ground, then both hind legs, and for a moment in the stride all feet will be off the ground – the animal is literally flying along. The feet land not simultaneously but offset from each other. The rear legs are used for push off and their impressions are left well in advance of those of the forefeet. When an animal runs, the front and rear track never register and often there is fine evidence of the toes splaying.

Trotting is a very energy-efficient way for an animal to move. Alternate feet leave the ground at the same time, e.g., right forefoot and left hind foot. As the speed increases, so does the length of the stride, while the width of the trail decreases.

A **bounding** animal is also airborne at some point in its stride. It pushes off with its hind limbs and lands on its fore, then takes off again on its front feet before the rear legs have had a chance to land. The tracks show the hind feet in front of the fore.

The perfect print
making a good impression

If you want a permanent record of an animal's footprint, making a plaster cast is fun. It's also easier and more accurate than drawing and is the best way to compare and contrast different tracks. On top of that, at the end of the day you have a trophy, which counts for a lot when working with mammals – usually all you have is the experience and a story to tell.

Do not necessarily restrict yourself to individual or perfect footprints; different gaits and substrates leave different degrees of registration. The track left by a running animal is very different from that made by the same animal standing still; the same applies to hard or soft ground. Take a variety of casts to illustrate these differences. With small creatures, try casting a number of tracks together, to record the gait.

You will need:
- plaster of paris/wax beads or chips
- a bottle of water (if using plaster)
- a piece of card
- a paperclip
- a container for mixing the plaster (I usually use a couple of plastic bottles with the tops cut off) or a tin and a small stove for melting the wax
- a soft brush and a mixing stick
- an old knife that you don't mind digging with
- newspaper or other packing material to protect the cast when complete

1 Once you have found a clear footprint that you wish to keep or identify back at base, make a mold around it. If the print is the right size, you can trim a ring from a plastic bottle; otherwise fold a strip of card round the print and hold it in place with a paperclip. Or, if the substrate is something suitable such as sand or mud, heap this up around the print. Whatever method you use, make the mold deep enough to contain at least 2.5 cm (1 in) of plaster – any less and the resulting cast may be brittle.

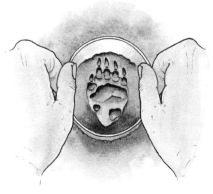

Step **1**

2 Mix the plaster of paris quickly with enough water to make a treacly consistency, stir to remove any lumps, and pour it evenly into the mold. Tap the mold gently a few times to release any air bubbles and wait for 10–15 minutes for the plaster to harden. The time this takes varies according to the consistency of the mix, the depth of the mold and the temperature. If you are using wax, the same principles apply, but you need to melt it in a tin on the stove first.

3 When the cast is hard, lift it up and gently pick and brush off any dirt sticking to the print. You should now have a beautiful positive impression of the footprint. It will take a few hours for the plaster to set as hard as it is going to, and so wrap it up to protect it on the way home.

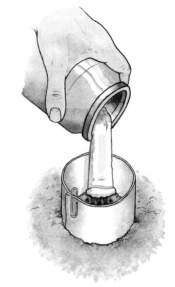

Step **2**

✳ Plaster cast tips

You can't take plaster or wax casts in the snow: The plaster or wax warms it enough to turn all but the hardest, iciest print into slush before it has had a chance to set. In these conditions, photography is the answer. Just pay attention to the light source – the lower and further away it is from the vertical, the better it is at picking up the details of the impressions left in the snow.

Step **3**

If you add too much water and the plaster is runny, mix in some salt to speed up the hardening process.

Mix a little soap into the water and plaster to make the resulting cast less brittle.

You can ink or paint the print to help it to show up. Alternatively, if you paint the surface with several layers of PVA glue or petroleum jelly and then press the cast into modeling clay, you can make a reverse negative cast of the positive you created in the field – you follow the same procedure, but the PVA or Vaseline keeps the new plaster from sticking to the old. Leave for a day to harden and then trim the edges of the cast with a knife until you see the line separating the two. Repeat all the way around and then gently lever the two apart with a knife blade.

Wonderfully clear jaguar (*Panthera onca*) tracks in soft wet mud on a river bank in Brazil. Prints are the only sign you are likely to get that this elusive nocturnal predator has been in the area.

Tracking beds

Away from the wet and soft stuff, the budding mammal detective has his or her work cut out. Tracking becomes a much more subtle art.

If you don't aspire to the sort of skills used by the rhino trackers in Namibia (see caption, p. 80), you could try making a tracking bed. The idea is that when there is no soft substrate for a passing animal to leave its tracks in, you simply create your own. One use for this is to find out whether or not a burrow or hole is occupied. By smoothing the surface of the soil outside a fox earth or badger sett, which is usually fairly fine in texture anyway, you can, on return visits, tell when an animal has been in and out, and what it was. Then you can use a hand rake or a twiggy branch to wipe the prints out and start again. Obviously you should keep disturbance to a minimum, as it would defeat the object if your presence upset the animals whose front door you were investigating.

I've been using variations on this theme for years: I once tracked an escaped snake around my house using sieved icing sugar, I located the holes mice were using to access my shed, and even found out what animals were passing through the hole in my hedge every night. Once in Uganda I discovered that a large aperture in a hotel's garden hedge had been created by a hippopotamus that came every night to graze on the lawn outside my patio doors!

I'd always thought these were smart bits of detective work on my part, but I have since seen the same idea used on a much larger scale as part of "road ecology" studies in Canada. Tracking beds of fine soil about 1 m x 50 m (3 ft x 160 ft) were created across the width of an overpass as part of a study into how many animals of which species were using it to cross a busy stretch of highway. Daily checking revealed the tracks of nearly every mammal in the area from martens and squirrels to bears, moose, elks, and wolves. A similar trick was being used down either side of a stretch of road to work out the ratios of animals of different species crossing the road successfully compared with those that were killed trying.

Tiger tracer

If time and storage space are issues or if you cannot be bothered to hump around the ingredients required to make a plaster cast, then a "tiger tracer" is for you. This consists of a notebook-size piece of acrylic on which you draw with a china marker or nonpermanent marker pen. You simply lay the acrylic over the footprint and draw around it, making notes of any points of interest. Later the print can be traced onto cellophane sheeting or paper to form a permanent, life-size record.

This technique got its name because it is used as part of tiger studies in India, where researchers have found some tiger tracks to be so distinctive in shape, size, and other features that individual animals can be identified by footprints alone. This is very useful for scientists trying to learn about the movements of secretive animals on a budget that prohibits the use of such invasive and expensive techniques as radio collars and GPS tracking. But the amateur naturalist can easily adapt it for use on a smaller scale and closer to home.

The keen amateur naturalist can use the tiger-tracing technique pioneered in India to keep records of footprints closer to home.

Splitting hairs

Deer hair and cross section

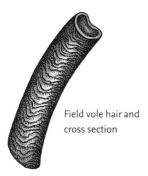

Field vole hair and cross section

Rabbit hair and cross section

Whether it is a twizzle left on barbed wire or some fur found in a pellet or scat, hair has a lot to say. It's easy enough with the naked eye to tell the difference between the coarse, banded guard hairs of a badger and the soft, fluffy hairs of a rabbit, but under a microscope, the surface texture, color, length, and cross section of each hair are very distinctive. This is usually seen as a specialist area of study, but if you want to take it further there are microscopic field guides, mostly aimed at a professional, academic market, that will tell you all you need to know.

The hairs that are of most use are the larger guard hairs. Under a microscope it is possible to see the cells and their arrangement in the pith, or medulla, of the hair. The scale pattern on the outside of the hair, the cuticula, is just as useful, but hard to see without a specialized staining technique. This obstacle can be got around if you take a gelatine impression of the hair and look at this instead.

You will need:
- a microscope with 400x or greater magnification
- microscope slides
- a small quantity of gelatine dissolved in 10 ml (2 tsp) hot water
- a pair of fine tweezers

1 Paint the gelatine solution onto a microscope slide, then leave it to cool and solidify for 10 minutes or so.

2 Using the tweezers, place the hairs across the gelatine film and leave them in position for 30 minutes as the gelatine sets.

3 Carefully peel the hairs up and off the film and look through the microscope at the impression they have left.

The rough stuff
the fascinating world of excrement

Scats, feces, dung, spraints, whitewash, mutes – call them what you like, these are all terms used to name the waste products of digestion that have passed through an animal's gut and been excreted. Specific terms are often associated with certain species.

The smell of some droppings is essential to identification – even though they can look similar, the spraint of an otter (shown here) smells of "summer meadows," whereas that of a mink lies at the other end of the olfactory spectrum, somewhere between repulsive and repugnant! Just don't inhale too deeply and don't get too close.

✳ Safety tip

There is a very good reason why humans are repelled by the odor of the excrement of many mammal species – survival. Excrement can harbor serious illness and all manner of bacteria and parasites, and so do not handle the droppings of any animal with bare hands if you can help it. Use rubber gloves or an inverted plastic bag to collect them and use a stick to explore them. (Remember which end you used, if you are going to pick it up again!) If you do come into contact with a dropping, wash your hands thoroughly with soap and water.

Droppings contain lots of information about diet and, in those species that use their droppings as "signposts," about what the animal was up to: Was it patrolling territorial boundaries during the breeding season? Was it passing through quickly and leaving a little and often? The study of dung is an eye-opener when you are dealing with the shy, elusive, and nocturnal, and in many cases, it's as close as you are going to get.

I will never forget the look of shock on my mother's and brother's faces when they first found me facedown on the front lawn poking around in a fox's dropping with a stick. They simply did not understand, despite my very enthusiastic speech, that I now had a greater insight into the diet of our garden's regular nocturnal visitor and, what's more, I knew where all the raspberries were going!

Obviously the contents of droppings can give you clues as to what animal "did it," but they vary so much in color, texture, and length, depending on what the animal has been eating, that this is not always enough. Size is an important guide, and the critical measurement is the width at the widest part. Specific animals have specific exit-hole dimensions! Identifying a small mammal species by its dropping alone is a little tricky. The droppings of insectivorous bats are superficially very similar to those of small rodents but are usually dry enough to crumble between the fingertips. Unlike those of rodents they have no real odor, either.

Location is often a big help, as is a combination of other signs – a large, pellet-shaped dropping combined with greasy smears on vertical surfaces next to runs suggests brown rat (*Rattus norvegicus*), while neat little piles of smaller pellets, near water and combined with runs and clipped vegetation are more likely to be those of a water vole (*Arvicola terrestris*).

Bait marking

When scientist Hans Kruuk was working with brown hyenas (*Hyaena brunnea*) in Africa he noticed that these enterprising beasts had been scavenging the dead bodies of local tribespeople, who wore brightly colored beads on their clothes and ornaments. The beads were turning up in the hyenas' droppings and accidentally yielding information on the territory boundaries and movements of the hyenas themselves. This observation was later artificially re-created and used in a technique that has since been called bait marking.

Bait marking works really well with a communally living beast such as the badger (*Meles meles*). Begin by mapping your study area. Critical are locations of the burrows or setts, normally at the center of a territory, and of latrines. In the world of badgers, latrines are more than just holes dug for defecation – they are scented signposts with territorial significance, positioned at key points such as near setts, along territory boundaries, at places where the badgers' well-worn paths cross natural boundaries such as hedges, and near any other important resource. A latrine can be anything from the odd single hole to a huge aggregation of pits on a boundary between two clans, where individuals from both sides make their presence known.

Once you have marked these key features on your map, you need a quantity of inert-colored plastic beads (though I have used finely chopped-up colored plastic bags equally effectively). Take a number of beads of one color, let's say red, and mix them up with unsalted peanuts and molasses or treacle. Then lug buckets of this heavy but badger-irresistible fodder to what appears to be the major sett in the area. Deposit dollops of your goo around the sett, if possible hiding it from other creatures by covering it with leaves or a rock or log. (Badgers are strong animals who will not let such obstacles come between them and a good meal.) Now simply wait for a few days before starting regular tours of all the known badger latrines to see where your red beads turn up.

Every time they do, draw a straight red line on your map from the place where you left the food to the latrine. Over time you will get a star shape on your map which will represent the territory of the animals that live

The sett is at the center of a badger clan's activities and so is a good place to start your mapping.

A badger territory map showing the extent of two territories. You can make it as simple or ornate as you like.

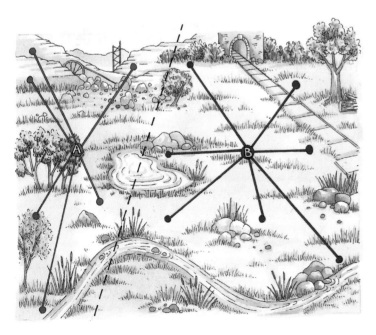

in the sett you marked with the red beads. You can then repeat the experiment by leaving, say, blue beads at a neighboring sett. This will enable you to map out the next-door clan's territory and where red and blue beads appear in close proximity, you will be able to identify the boundaries. It is an excellent way of getting a graphic image of badger territorial life.

You can use a similar technique with small mammals such as mice, substituting food dye for the plastic beads that would give these creatures indigestion. Small mammals tend to defecate when they are feeding, a "bad" habit that the naturalist can tap into. Put your dyed bait (rolled oats are ideal) in a shallow tray and place this near a hole or a run. Then arrange other feeding trays with noncolored bait in a grid-like system within the habitat. Cover each with a board or stone supported at the corners, leaving a big enough gap underneath for the animal to pass – this will help it feel comfortable while at the same time protecting your bait trays from wind, rain, and thieving.

Check the trays after a day or so to see where the colored droppings turn up, and you will begin to get an idea of territory size of the small mammals in your patch. Repeat with different colors in neighbouring habitats and territories, and plot your observations on a map as for large mammals.

A badger feeding

Feeding signs

Evidence of eating is yet another sign to be interpreted by the naturalist in the field. It's like looking at a plate at the end of a meal. You would be able to tell whether the human had a T-bone or a take-out burger; well, the same goes for animals. Some are very tidy eaters and their feeding signs are hard to pick up; others would be easier to miss if the animal itself stood there with a big placard pointing the way!

The beaver is the largest rodent in North America. A beaver family can fell as many as 300 trees in a single winter, and a pair can gnaw through a branch that is 10 cm (4 in) thick in 15 minutes. Bark is the mainstay of their diet.

Herbivores – nibblers and gnawers

By definition, many herbivorous animals spend a lot of their time taking chunks out of plants, whether chewing shoots and buds or stripping bark from saplings and tree trunks. They have individual table manners and have utensils and ways of wielding them.

Starting with the champion of chiselers, there is no creature quite like the North American beaver (*Castor canadensis*). The teeth marks it leaves on twigs and branches are distinctive, having been made by a larger rodent than most, but it is the general modification of the environment that really gives the beaver away: Tree stumps and heavy-duty felling are about as extreme as feeding evidence can be!

The feeding evidence at other end of the spectrum, though more widespread, takes rather more interpreting. Imagine trying to chew bark off a tree with your upper teeth missing. Why? Because that is what sheep and deer do – they have incisors only in the lower jaw and use these to remove bark by gouging at it. It is more of a scraping action than chewing or nibbling, and the result is fairly rough and ragged. (Incidentally, do not confuse deer feeding damage with deer "fraying," an equally destructive act that leaves a tree denuded of its bark. Wih fraying, the motivation isn't a meal but either removal of "velvet" from newly grown antlers or, in the case of a buck roe deer, territorial – leaving a visual and scent flag.)

The same job attempted by rabbits and hares produces a much smoother result as they tidily nip away at the bark, leaving distinctive-size teeth marks with little or no fraying. Rabbits' and hares' teeth are so similar in size that they are hard to distinguish by measurement alone. But the hare's upper incisors have a notch halfway along their cutting edge, so each bite leaves two raised strips and looks as if it was made by an animal with four upper incisors rather than two.

Guide to teeth mark dimensions

Species	Distance across all incisors
Mice & voles	2.2 mm (1⁄12 in)
Water voles & rats	3.5–4.5 mm (1⁄7–1⁄6 in)
Rabbits & hares	6–10 mm (1⁄4–2⁄5 in)
Beavers & porcupines	10 mm (2⁄5 in)
Sheep & deer	10–30 mm (2⁄5–1 in)

Bank voles (*Clethrionomys glareolus*) are very neat nibblers and will often nibble their way round a trunk at ground level (a process known as ringbarking), killing the tree in the process. In a "good" vole year it can be hard to believe that the huge amounts of die-off seen in woodland are caused by these small rodents. They are also excellent climbers and will often sit in the V of a branch and nibble away. This sort of damage almost glows white when it is fresh, though die-off at height is less common. Squirrel damage, on the other hand, is often obvious as die-off in the crowns or at the end of branches.

Look for the distinctive teeth marks of mice, voles, and squirrels on fungi, too (slugs also rasp away at fungi, but they leave a depression and no teeth marks). Red squirrels (*Sciurus vulgaris*) have a habit of taking their fungi and lodging it up high in the trees.

The same sort of logic can be applied to shoots and twigs that are chewed on by deer, rabbits, and hares. Deer can bite only so far through a stem; the rest of the action is done by tearing, leaving a frayed end. Rabbits and hares, on the other hand, bite neatly through as if they were using a pair of quality shears. So now you can tell who's been eating your roses!

Similar observations can be applied to other browsers and grazers around the world, if you have some knowledge of their anatomy and feeding behavior.

A male and fawn roe deer (*Capreolus cabreolus*) browsing

Little nutters

The smaller mammals, from mice and voles to dormice and squirrels, are real nut specialists, and their feeding remains are often encountered in the field. These become quite distinctive when you understand the mechanics of the "chiggling" techniques used by each of these nutters to extract the nutritious kernel from the hard outer casing of a nut.

Squirrel

Squirrels take a notch out of one end of the nut and then, using their lower incisors like a crowbar, they split the nut into two halves. The halves will show the odd scratch made by the upper incisor.

Mouse

Mice, with their long front limbs, hold the nut some way from their body and at an angle, with the top toward them. They nibble a hole and insert their lower incisors into it, using them to gnaw and the upper ones to grip the outside of the nut. Mice gnaw from the inside out, turning the nut as they go. This leaves a large hole at one end of the nut with distinctive incisor marks on the edge of the shell and a row of irregular scratches on the outer surface. The overall shape of the hole is often untidy, with the inner edge being lower than the outer.

Vole

Voles start in the same way, then insert their nose and upper incisors into the hole and use the lower incisors to gnaw away from the outside in. This leaves teeth marks only around the edges of the hole, which is a smoother shape than one chiggled by a mouse.

Dormouse

Dormice (*Muscardinus avellanarius*) do the tidiest job of all, leaving a very smooth lip to the edge of the nut, but a neat row of marks on the outside, as with mice.

Some of these small mammals also have a penchant for flesh – especially voles, and they use a similar technique. I often find caches of vole feeding remains containing nuts, seeds, and a quantity of neatly chiggled snail shells! A rodent chewing on a snail shell tends to concentrate on the coils, unlike birds such as thrushes, which smash the shells into smithereens.

Voles and rabbits commonly eat grass, too. Look for field vole runs under and around rough, tussocky grass – you will notice patches of neatly close-cropped grass, along with clippings and distinctive droppings. Water voles leave similar traces on banks close to water. Rabbits are the famous creators of "lawns" near their warrens which they habitually graze.

Pine, spruce, and fir cones are another staple diet of many creatures. Their seeds are very rich in fats and oils, making them a particularly valuable resource in the buildup to winter. Climbers such as squirrels and voles will harvest them directly from the trees, while terrestrial species rely on those that fall to the ground or are missed at the dining table.

Squirrelled cones are the most obvious feeding signs when you walk through a coniferous wood. Squirrels hold the cone at an angle, with the base up, and systematically work their way down the stem, removing the scales to get at the seeds. The fibrous remains of the scales give the leftover spindle a hairy appearance, with the last few scales often left undamaged; a clean cut through the stem is also usually evident, where the cone was bitten from the twig. You can even tell whether a squirrel is right- or left-handed by the way it has handled the cone!

A similar cone worked on by a mouse or a vole is much smoother, the base often nibbled into a rounded shape, and the evidence tucked away under cover, with the removed scales piled up near the scene of dining.

Several animals are able to prize the seeds out of pine cones for food. Squirrels are excellent at this, chewing the cone down to the core.

You might find the remains of cones that have been fed on by birds, too. Crossbills (*Loxia curvirostra*) do not remove the scales; they split each scale lengthways and twist and loosen the seed. The result is a tattered-looking cone, with the split scales being obvious trademarks. Woodpeckers just seem to batter the cone until it gives them what they want. A certain amount of splitting occurs here, but nothing as systematic as with the crossbill's technique. The situation in which the cones are discovered also bears witness to the species concerned. Woodpeckers often jam cones into crevices in bark before attacking them, and only discard the old cone when they have a new one to work on – hence the cones and debris that may pile up beneath a popular "forge."

Teeth
little miracles of design

Found in the jaws of mammals, reptiles, and fish, teeth are wonderful devices whose form fits precisely with the function they evolved to perform. They help you to ascertain a lot about the owner, especially if they are still attached to its skull. Not only can you make a good guess at the identity of the animal by working out its diet and way of life, but you can also in some instances age a mammal by its dental records alone.

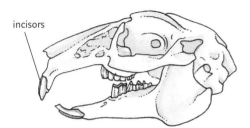

incisors

Rabbit jaw showing prominent incisors

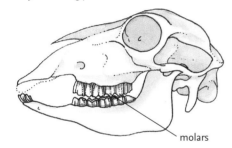

molars

Sheep jaw, with no upper incisors

canines

Dog jaw, with the sharp carnassials typical of carnivores, used for shearing through meat

Incisors are the cutting teeth at the front of the jaw. The incisors of mammals such as rodents and lagomorphs (rabbits and hares) grow constantly through their lives and have to be kept in check by chewing and gnawing. In profile, incisors look like chisels. This is no accident, because the front face of the tooth is made of a harder material than the back, which means that the back and front wear at a different rate, resulting in a formidable set of self-sharpening blades that never go blunt. Rabbits and hares have a second set of tiny incisors behind the main cutting ones, a very good way of separating them from rodents by teeth alone.

Deer and sheep have no incisors in the upper jaw, just a bony plate, but the lower jaw shows four pairs, rather than the regular three (the fourth are really modified canines).

Bats have tiny, much reduced incisors. Not a lot of call for cutting teeth in these mammals, and they just get in the way of echolocating, and so they have been scaled down.

Canines are the grasping, holding, ripping, and gripping teeth. Also known as eye teeth, they are the four big, pointed teeth most visible in the jaws of carnivores. Certain deer and pig species and, of course, elephants, have these teeth enlarged for specialist feeding or combat. Rodents and lagomorphs have no canines and a distinctive gap in their place known as a diastema.

Molars and premolars are the cheek teeth, and their design depends on whether the diet is plant- or meat-based. In carnivores the cheek teeth are known as carnassials; they look like blades in profile and act like pairs of meat shears. In herbivores they are flattened to form grinding surfaces like millstones.

Long in the tooth? Estimating the age of an animal by its remains

It is possible to estimate a mammal's age by looking at tooth wear, as long as you have a rough idea of what a healthy, non-worn tooth looks like. Ten per cent wear for every year of a mammal's life is a rough average, so by the time it is five years old, its teeth will be worn down to about half their original length.

Age can be gauged more accurately if you have the chance to remove a tooth from a dead animal. Soak it in a weak solution of nitric acid (obtainable from good scientific suppliers) to dissolve all the calcium, then take a thin cross-section using a piece of specialist slicing equipment known as a microtome. When stained and looked at under a microscope, this section will reveal bands of growth around the root of the tooth. These bands are a material called cementum that holds mammal teeth into their sockets and is laid down annually in the autumn or winter. So the bands can be counted in much the same way as can the growth rings of trees.

The tooth of a sperm whale (*Physeter catodon*) cut to determine the age of the animal by revealing the number of annual layers in the core. The total number of layers can be seen only if the tooth is cut vertically. The layers in the teeth of all cetaceans are conical in shape, and so do not individually extend over the entire height of the tooth.

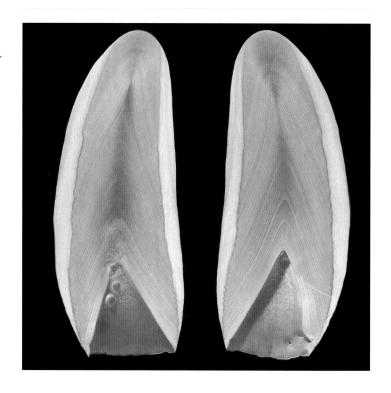

Bones – the hard bits
and what you can learn from them

Any vertebrate, be it mammal, bird, amphibian, reptile, or fish, by definition has a skeleton inside holding it up and in shape, and forming a frame to which muscles and other organs are attached. Because the skeleton is so fundamental to a creature's form and to the way it works, even fragments can yield a lot of information.

✳ Safety note

It goes without saying that handling dead bodies has an element of risk associated with it. The body may harbor disease in the form of harmful bacteria or viruses. So precautions need to be taken. Avoid handling with bare hands – wear surgical rubber gloves. Don't get your face too close to your work and keep any open wounds well covered. Always wash your hands with a good antibacterial soap immediately after handling any animal material.

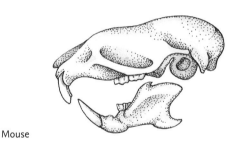

Mouse

Vole

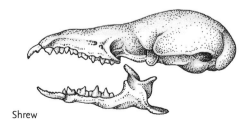

Shrew

The skull is a stunning lesson in form and function perfected. Just by glancing at one you should be able to say whether it belonged to a bird or a mammal. You can also judge the importance of the different senses. Large eye sockets obviously mean large eyes and good sight. The size of the ear bulla, though not quite as obvious, reveals the importance of hearing. Many channels for nerves and spongy bone hint at an acute sense of smell.

Other clues about the owner's way of life can also be gained from the skull. In the case of mammals, large cheek bones and a sagittal crest (a raised ridge along the top of the skull) for the attachment of powerful jaw muscles say "predator," a statement backed up by the nature of the teeth. The position of the eyes tells you how an animal perceives its world. Forward-facing eyes like ours give binocular vision, enabling us to judge distances – useful for leaping from branch to branch in a tree, for example – while eyes on the side of the head give better all-around vision.

Tooth wear is the best way of telling an animal's age, but other clues can be had from the skeleton. The dimensions of the skull are a good start, especially if you have some known references as a comparison. Hares have a bony knob on the outside edge of the front leg bone (ulna) nearest the foot, which is very obvious until the bone finishes growing when the animal is about a year old. Bony growths and wear around joints (arthritis) can point to an older animal. You can also look at the jigsaw-like joins, called sutures, between the bones in the skull. These tend to start off very obvious and then fuse and disappear as the animal grows older.

Cleaning bones

If you are going to mount and display a skeleton, you'll want the bones to be as clean as possible. Nature has its ways of dealing with this process – there is a whole task force out there, honed to perfection by millions of years of evolution, whose sole purpose is to find dead animals and eat them. If you can get hold of a supply of these creatures and provide them with optimum conditions to get on with their work, they will eventually do the rest. This is, however, a smelly and time-consuming process: Not everyone wants to keep a carcass crawling with maggots in the house, or even in the garden shed. Using chemicals is still pretty unpleasant – do it outside – but they do get the job done quickly.

1 Start with cold water and bring it to the boil *slowly*. If you put the carcass into boiling water you run the risk of toughening the flesh and making it even harder to remove. Tether the carcass or skull with string to a stick or an old pencil. It's much easier to pick up and check up on that way.

2 Add a solution of washing soda, caustic soda, or sulfurated potash. These leave the ligaments in place, which means the bones stay in order. Note, the fresher the carcass, the better this works.

3 Check progress regularly, because if you leave them too long, or if the bleach solution is too strong, the bones become brittle and teeth have a tendency to fall out. (If this happens, you can glue them back in place with clear-setting modeling glue later.)

4 Once you have removed all the flesh from the bones, rinse them and immerse them in cold water containing a small amount of bleach for a few hours to sterilize and whiten them.

5 The last stage in the cleaning process is removing the grease. Using string, a mesh bag, or a grill, suspend the bones in a degreasing agent. The specimen has to be suspended rather than left sitting in the solution so that the grease drops off and sinks to the bottom.

6 Once you are satisfied that your bones are clean, rinse them thoroughly and leave them to dry.

You will need:
- a portable camping stove
- an old pan dedicated to bone cleaning
- a chemical solution of washing soda, caustic soda, or sulfurated potash (you can obtain these from scientific suppliers)
- water
- a stick or pencil from which to suspend the bones
- string
- a degreasing agent such as household ammonia solution, gasoline, or the sort of industrial de-greaser you use on a car engine

Mounting and displaying bones
Forget plastic model-making – this is the ultimate model kit!

Carry out the mounting process before the ligaments harden up, so that they are still pliable. In a perfect situation, if you have done your macerating correctly, the connective tissue will have kept most of the bones in their original positions. But it is more than likely that there will be a little fragmentation, and so you will have use to logic and imagination to decide where all the bits go and what shape the skeleton should rest in. A specialist anatomy book will help you, and with a little practice you will be able to recognize which bone is which and how they fit together.

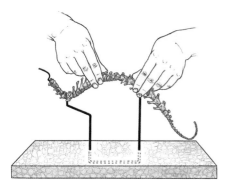

Step 1

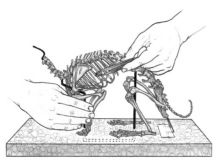

Step 2

You will need:
- wire of several thicknesses (depending on the size of the animal you are trying to mount)
- clear, quick-drying glue
- a polystyrene tile large enough to sit the whole skeleton on
- pins strong enough to hold the bones in place
- forceps

1 Start by threading the vertebrae and supporting them on an arch of wire, which will be permanently attached to the finished model.

2 Support this arch on a cradle of thicker wire and set the whole structure on the polystyrene tile.

3 Pin the limbs in position. Any missing joints or teeth can be re-created by the careful use of a dab of glue. Use forceps to lift small or delicate parts. It may help to use temporary supports to hold everything in position until the ligaments and/or glue have set firm. Then move the skeleton to its permanent display board and remove all the supports except that of the spine.

4 Attach the skull and support it on its own cradle. Label your specimen, stand back, and admire.

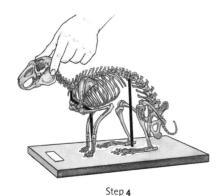

Step 3

Step 4

first trap your mouse

As we have seen throughout this chapter, you can learn a lot from the signs an animal leaves behind. But the smaller the mammal, the less likely it is to leave meaningful tracks, droppings or other evidence that is easy to find. Yet small mammals are out there and everywhere. Pretty much any ecosystem in the world supports a large number of them. In some parts of the U.K. populations of common shrews (*Sorex araneus*) are close to 50 per hectare (20 per acre). Because small mammals are important links in many food chains, studying them can shed light on the overall health of the environment on which they depend. But if they don't leave signs that you can interpret, you have to find other ways of getting close to them.

One common technique is the live small-mammal trap, which lures the subject into a trap and keeps it there until it is released. This is particularly useful for finding out what animals live where, how many there are and how they move around a habitat. Set your traps up in a grid, bait them without setting the trigger, and wait a week to allow even the more timid individuals to familiarize themselves with them.

Once you have caught an animal, you need to mark it. Grip it firmly with gloved hands (even a mouse can turn into a miniature chainsaw when it thinks its life is at stake) and clip a patch of fur using fine scissors. This haircut doesn't have to be drastic, just enough to allow the individual to be identified a second time it is caught. Then release the animal and wait – with luck it will wander back into your trap again.

So how do you set about trapping? Well, what you call a small mammal trap depends on what you call a small mammal – many of the same principles can be scaled up or down to suit. I have seen a trap design used to catch wolverine work just as well with mice!

At the sophisticated end of the scale, the Longworth mammal trap is a well-engineered bit of kit that comprises two main sections: the trap mechanism itself and the nest chamber. An animal is lured into the trap by the placing of suitable bait. It hits a trip bar, which in turn trips the door mechanism. A gravity bar comes down and locks the door so that your mammal cannot escape and no others can enter.

One of the smallest terrestrial mammals in the world (*Suncus etruscus*), the Indian pygmy white-toothed shrew, having been caught in a pitfall trap (see opposite)

The Longworth trap is composed of two main sections: the trap mechanism itself and the nest chamber. The animal is lured into the trap with suitable bait and hits a trip bar. This trips the door mechanism, bringing down the gravity bar on the door and locking it.

A pitfall trap and baffle

Longworth traps are expensive and a bit fiddly to set up; they also come in only one size, which limits you to catching animals of about mouse size (though the sensitivity of the trip bar can be altered so that you can, for example, avoid catching lighter animals such as shrews). The one I pestered my mother to give me for my 11th birthday is still going, admittedly after a bit of riveting and repair, 20 years later.

The Longworth trap is made and widely used in the U.K.; the U.S. equivalent is the Sherman trap, which is used worldwide and has the advantage of coming in a variety of sizes; of folding flat and opening out so that it is easier to clean, service, and transport; and of having spare parts available via the Internet.

If you're on a tight budget, plastic traps are available from pet shops. They are mostly designed for recapturing escaped pets and catching unwanted house guests in a humane way. They work, but small mammals can chew through some of them in a matter of minutes. If you want a cheap but effective trap, I recommend making your own.

Empty traps by gently tipping the contents into a large heavy-duty transparent bag. Your captives may come out kicking and bouncing, so be prepared to close the bag quickly (making sure the animal can still breathe, of course). They can then be identified, sexed, measured, and weighed while suffering minimal stress.

☀ Trapping tips

From the moment you set out to trap an animal, its life may depend on you – a responsibility not to be taken lightly.

When baiting a trap, use a variety of food geared to the animal you want to attract. Raisins, seeds, and unsalted nuts are obvious choices, but I have heard of people using bread soaked in aniseed, peanut butter, chocolate, and cheese. Include insects, too, for the benefit of small insectivorous animals such as shrews.

Remember that most small mammals are agoraphobes – they hate open spaces or stepping far from what is familiar. In the wild, set your traps against logs, tree trunks, roots, the edges of natural paths, or anywhere under cover, among tussocky grass or a bramble patch.

Be careful. I have unwittingly released many animals before I have had a chance to look at them properly, simply by being impatient. And be alert if your trap is surprisingly heavy – you may accidentally have caught a larger and fiercer animal than you expected.

Do your homework first. Some small mammals are protected by law, and permits must be obtained in advance if you want to work with them. This applies to shrews in the U.K., for example.

Check your traps regularly, ideally twice a day, first thing in the morning and in the evening. Shrews do not do well in traps, and if you are likely to be catching them you should check every two hours or so. If you cannot find the time to do this, don't set traps.

DIY traps take a bit more effort, but you can customize them to your exact requirements. A simple wooden box with a drop-down trapdoor held in position by a piece of wire bent around a nail and attached to the bait is all you need. When the animal takes the bait, it disturbs the wire, which then stops supporting the door; this swings shut and traps the animal. Make sure the door is a good fit, because if your enterprising captive can get its paws or teeth under the door, it can lift it and escape. Put in a couple of nail stops to prevent the door being pushed open.

Pitfall traps for mammals

Pitfall traps are easy to make and set. All you need is a smooth-sided vessel with a lid. Old cookie tins, buckets, and thick plastic storage jars are ideal.

1 First punch or drill holes in the bottom for drainage, then dig a hole the size of the container and bury it so that the lip is flush with the ground.

2 Trim the lid so that it just fits inside the opening of the container; then using glue or strong tape, make a pivot out of cocktail sticks or pieces of wire. When placed on top of the trap this makes a swinging lid that will tip any small creature that walks on it into the container below.

3 Cover loosely with soil, dead leaves, and a large piece of wood or stone propped up at the corners. This makes the area attractive to small mammals, but more important it provides protection from the elements and prevents rainwater from entering the trap and making your captives cold and miserable. Wait.

The one disadvantage of pitfalls is that you may catch more than one animal. This may not sound like a bad thing, but if you trap two rival males of the same species, or if the second creature is a predator such as a weasel, the outcome could be tragic.

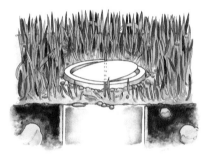

Step **1**

Step **2**

Step **3**

Creatures of the night
bats

Working with bats requires even more patience and specialist knowledge than working with terrestrial small mammals. The Chinese expression *yen yen*, which means "swallow of the night," says it all to me – in their element, the air, bats are fast. They are also small, nocturnal, shy, and protected by law. They squeak at an inaudible frequency and do not leave footprints. It's enough to make the naturalist give up on them and do something easy like go on safari.

But the fact that they are seemingly impossible to study makes them irresistible to the curious. Armed with the latest technologies, there is nothing to stop a "Batman" or "Batwoman" making some real discoveries – this is a frontier science.

Bats are highly successful creatures. They have been around in a recognizable form for over 50 million years, and during that time they have diversified to fill numerous niches. There are somewhere between 850 and 950 different species – nearly a quarter of the world's mammals – ranging in size from certain flying foxes that have a near 2m (6 ft 6 in) wingspan and weigh 1.6kg (3 ½ lb), to the world's smallest mammal, a bumblebee, or Kitti's hog-nosed bat (*Craseonycteris thonglongyai*), with a wingspan of 15–16 cm (about 6 in) and a weight of a mere 1.7 g (¹⁄₁₆ oz)!

Flying foxes (*Pteropus giganteus*) – an example of the Megachiroptera group of bats

Horseshoe bat (*Rhinolophus spp.*) in stages of flight

The family Chiroptera, to which all bats belong, is divided into two suborders: the Megachiroptera, a tropical supergroup of what we commonly call fruit bats, or flying foxes; and the highly diverse and wide-ranging Microchiroptera, which are found pretty much anywhere that there are insects for them to feed on. Here we will concern ourselves with the Microchiroptera, because unless you live in the Arctic or Antarctic, the chances are you have some living near you.

Most people's first experience of bats is seeing them…well not exactly seeing, but catching a quick movement out of the corner of the eye, a flicker by a light, maybe a fast zipping silhouette high above the head – a far from satisfactory experience for those wishing to know more.

My own introduction to bats involved a dead one – a pipistrelle (*Pipistrellus pipistrellus*) that I found on my patio as a kid. I remember being fascinated by its minuscule size and the minutiae of its features – its claws, teeth, and eyes. It was then dried and consigned to my childhood trophy collection, where it resided in a matchbox until the beetles found it. I didn't think much about bats after that until, during the twilight of one summer's evening, I noticed a few, probably pipistrelles as well, patrolling up and down a line of oak trees outside my house. I don't know what prompted me to do this, but I remember thinking about how they located their prey with echolocation, and so I casually tossed a small stone in the air and watched in amazement as one of the bats suddenly changed course, ducking down toward the stone's trajectory…. I had just interacted with an animal that was one of the biggest enigmas of the night, and that experience was quite enough to get me going "bats!"

The bat detector

Bats live in an acoustic world dominated by what is known as ultrasonic sound. It is very hard to describe – it's something like a sharp, high-frequency tick. Listen carefully next time you are out and, if bats are present, you may just pick up tiny bits of their calls. This is the lower range of the frequency of their communication; the rest we miss because our ears simply don't work at that level. Children's ears are more sensitive to these frequencies, and our ability to pick them up with the naked ear drops off quickly as we approach adulthood. But there is a readily available piece of technology that comes to the frustrated naturalist's aid: the bat detector, a simple handheld device that acts as a translator.

Available from good natural history and science suppliers, these boxes of "electrickery" unlock the door on the mysterious world of nocturnal aeronauts. They are basically sensitive microphones that pick up the bats' ultrasonic vocalizations and then reduce the frequency to within a human's normal hearing range. You can listen to the sounds via a speaker or headphones and even record them for future reference.

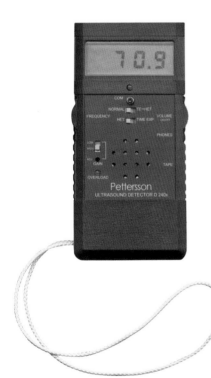

Now do not get too carried away here. Although it would be nice if each species had its own distinctive call, like birds, the bad news is that they don't. That would be far too easy! Bats produce a varied repertoire of sounds depending on what they are doing, their situation, and the weather. On top of this, each bat detector is slightly different, and not all allow for direct comparisons of calls heard.

Some bats are easier to identify than others. The greater and lesser horseshoe bats (*Rhinolophus ferrumequinum* and *R. hipposideros*) make characteristic soft, warbling calls at two totally separate frequencies on the bat-detector dial. Noctule (*Nyctalus noctula*) and Leisler's (*N. leisleri*) bats make a fairly distinctive "metallic" noise. But the rest require a lot of walking about at night, good ears, and intelligent detective work to unravel. If, however, you practice long and hard and hang out with other bat enthusiasts, you will soon get to grips with some of the more idiosyncratic sounds. A combination of the type of call and its frequency, the habitat and the behavior of the mammals in question will get you well on your way.

If you want to encourage bats into your garden, the best way is to build a kind of bat box. This is pretty much like a bird nest box, described on p. 65.

Farther afield
marine mammals

There is a whole group of mammal species which spend all or most of their lives in the world's oceans. This includes the pinnipeds (seals and sea lions), the cetaceans (whales, dolphins, and porpoises), the sirenians (manatees and dugongs), and an otter or two. Studying these animals creates its own challenges – you don't find many footprints or feeding signs. With marine mammals, it's mostly down to direct observation, and this could mean as little as a far-distant "blow" of water vapor or a glimpse of a flipper or tail. But even these can be tremendously exciting: Although I admit that the sight of a vole nibbling on a nut may leave some people cold, nobody, surely, could be unmoved by a breaching humpback!

The best way to see cetaceans is with an organized whale-watching or dolphin-watching group. Even if you normally prefer to do things on your own, a boat full of like-minded people squeezed together for the sole purpose of seeing these remarkable, smile-inducing creatures, added to the knowledge of the skipper and the usually present "expert," is a recipe for a good time. As with a lot of mammal-watching, you can be lucky or unlucky, but I am a great believer in the maxim that the more time you spend watching, the more you will see and understand. So let me tell you a story that will give you a taste of the rush you get from watching marine mammals.

It was going to take a lot of something to lift the spray-sodden spirits of the human contingent packed into this small boat. We had already been bumping and bouncing our way across the swell off the southern African coastline for an hour and a half, seemingly with nothing to look forward to but the same treatment on the way back – short of the boat actually sinking, things couldn't get much lower! But this is the way it is with cetacean-watching. Just when you think you have a round turn on things, nature throws something at you as a reward for your patience. In this case the reward was a southern right whale (*Eubalaena glacialis australis*) and her calf, lolling around about 400 m (440 yd) away with the teal-colored water breaking over the mother's distinctively encrusted, callused head.

We cut the engines and the whale drifted closer to the boat, whose human contents were nearly falling over each other and into the water in the rush for the best observation spot. It was a "Kodak moment" without a doubt, as the whale rolled over and we looked into her huge eye – not cold like that of a fish, but thoughtful – definitely that of a cognitive mammal. (If that sounds stupid, stare into any mammal's eyes next time you get the chance.) It was special, not because we hadn't seen this before – we had, maybe a hundred times in the last week. It was a combination of the intimacy, the buildup and the moment itself, very peaceful, with the silence punctuated only by the baritone exhalations of the cow and the more frequent, higher-pitched breathing of the calf.

As if to celebrate this, with all the pizzazz of a carnival, the scene was invaded by a different kind of breathing – little puffs, like air being released from a bicycle-tire valve. It all happened so fast that it took a while to realize that we had been joined by a large school of dusky dolphins (*Lagenorhynchus obscurus*) and a couple of rare Heaviside's dolphins (*Cephalorhynchus heavisidii*), speeding, leaping, and weaving all over the place, in and out between the whales and our boat. Camera motor-drives were buzzing, although all I managed to get were a few perfect shots of dolphin splashes! It didn't matter – I will never forget the moment.

A last glance of the fluke of a southern right whale (*Eubalaena glacialis australis*). There are no international rules for whale-watching and dolphin-watching, but to minimize disturbance, do not get closer than 100 m (300 ft), never approach a marine mammal head-on, and avoid changes of direction and engine tone.

Opposite: Bottle-nosed dolphins in the Caribbean (*Tursiops truncatus*)

The earth creepers
reptiles and amphibians

The herptiles, as they are sometimes known, are a group of animals that have a hard time in the world of classification. Although both groups are "cold blooded" – more accurately poikilothermic, which means that their body temperature varies according to the temperature around them – reptiles and amphibians are not closely related. The only obvious thing they have in common is that they nearly all (and even this is a generalization) have a secretive and skulking habit. Even the word herptile, derived from the Greek for "creeping thing," seems to back up our centuries-old loathing of creepy creatures. But combining the study of reptiles and amphibians under the heading of herpetology is quite handy, as many of the techniques used can be applied to both.

Above: The head of a Peringuey's viper (*Bitis peringueyi*) camouflaged in the sand in the Namib desert
Right: Painted reed frog (*Hyperolius marmoratus*) calling

What's the difference?

The 9,850-odd species of reptiles and amphibians that crawl, slide, slither, and hop over our planet's surface can be broken down into a number of smaller, more easily digestible groups. There are three orders of amphibian, numbering 4,550 or so species (see below). What makes these creatures collectively amphibians is not easy to define and there are many exceptions to the rule, but most have moist, thin, nonscaly skin and a life cycle that at some point depends on water. The majority lay eggs which hatch into larvae that breathe through gills; as they metamorphose into adults, the larvae develop lungs – a neat trick that would be a useful way of defining them if it wasn't for the fact that some salamanders never actually "grow up" and develop lungs. But, as a rule of thumb, if it hasn't got scales, but has four legs, a backbone, and no fur, it's an amphibian.

There are about 6,000 species of reptiles and it is thought that they originated from an amphibian ancestor some 350 million years ago. The vast majority (5,700 species) are snakes, lizards, and the wormlike lizards known as amphisbaenians; then there are the tortoises and turtles, the crocodilians, and two species of the lizardlike tuatara, found only in New Zealand. The main difference between reptiles and amphibians is that most reptiles are much less dependent on water. They have also evolved thicker, scaly, impermeable skin that helps them to conquer drier habitats; have, in the main, lost their legs; and either lay hard-shelled eggs or retain their eggs within the body, so are not tied to water for breeding.

Orders of Amphibians:

Anura (the frogs and toads, and some burrowing, wormlike creatures)

Caudata (the salamanders)

Gymnophiona (the caecilians)

Orders of Reptiles:

Squamata (the amphisbaenians)

Testudines (turtles and tortoises)

Crocodylia (crocodilians)

Rhynchocephalia (tuatara)

The right handful
handling reptiles and amphibians

The golden rule is not to handle *any* animal unnecessarily, as you learn so much more if it is undisturbed, and in the case of herptiles, the word "handling" implies any form of physical contact. However, there are times when it is essential if you are to identify an animal or catch and relocate it as part of a study. In these circumstances it is important to minimize the amount of discomfort and stress your subject suffers and, in the case of dangerous or venomous herptiles, to handle it as safely as possible.

Frogs are famous for their squirminess and slipperiness, and even a little one can be a real handful. Nets are ideal but still allow the frog to wriggle about or even jump out, making it difficult to establish specific details such as sex or identity. To keep hold of a frog – once you have finally *got* hold of one – cup your hands around it and then manipulate it so that the head faces out toward the gap created between the forefinger and thumb of one hand. As soon as it sees light and tries to break free, allow it to push most of its body through before clamping down gently but firmly on its hind legs – these are most frogs' "thrusters," so if you can stop it kicking and at the same time support the front part of its body, you have it secure.

If you need to hold on to your specimen for more than a few minutes – and many species do take a while to identify, especially when you are working in the frog-diverse tropics – there is a risk that it may start to dehydrate from the warmth of your hands. So thoughtful herpetologists carry small, clear freezer or Ziploc bags. Once your frog is inside the bag, you can view its features clearly and easily without either distressing it too much or inadvertently releasing it.

Gently grasping the "fiddliest" frog in the world. A small, slippery, aquatic African clawed frog (*Xenopus tropicalius*).

Toxic overload

You may think that amphibians are benign compared with famously dangerous herptiles such as snakes, but they have some surprising talents, especially when they perceive you as a life-threatening predator, and it is worth being aware of these.

The cane toad (*Bufo marinus*) showing its parotid gland, which can eject toxic spray

parotid gland

The red-backed, or reticulated poison frog (*Dendrobates reticulatus*) from Peru

Many species of toad and some frogs have noxious chemicals in glands in their skin; these are primarily designed to make them distasteful to a predator, although it has been suggested that the toxins also kill off bacteria and fungi that would presumably thrive in damp, warm conditions favored by these animals. If ingested, some of these chemicals are very toxic to humans. So, as with all animals, wear gloves or wash your hands thoroughly after handling and do not rub your eyes, nose, or mouth with your fingers. Take this warning seriously, as the secretions (bufotoxins) of some species, particularly the cane toad (*Bufo marinus*), have been known to kill humans. I have certainly heard stories from reliable sources of dogs and cats dying after just mouthing one of these animals.

When stressed, the cane toad and other species can eject a toxic creamy white spray from the parotid glands on either side of the head behind the eyes. This can travel for up to a meter (over 3 ft), and once in the eyes, nose, or mouth causes a severe burning similar to the sensation of eating raw hot chillies. I speak from experience on this one, as I was once retrieving my pet cane toad from a cozy little spot it had found beneath the television. It treated me as a predator, got me in the eyes – and there was no more watching TV that night!

I also have firsthand information which suggests that prolonged handling of some of the poison-dart frogs (*Dendrobates pumilio*) from South and Central America, even those species formerly thought of as fairly benign, can lead to some of the skin's toxic alkaloids being absorbed and causing nausea. In some species 0.00001 g (0.0000035 oz) of these substances can kill a man, making the defenses of these amphibians among the most potent in the world.

Some of the large ambush specialists, such as African bull frogs of the genus *Pyxicephalus* and the horned frogs (*Ceratophrys* spp.) of South America, have a nasty nip on them, and the fanglike protrusions in the roof of the mouth can make their bites particularly painful. A little horned frog that I once captured bit on to the end of my finger and wouldn't release its grip – it even started swallowing and making its way up toward my knuckles, despite being only the size of a Ping-Pong ball!

Vivariums
keeping reptiles and amphibians in captivity

Because of their small size and secretive nature, much of what is witnessed of the lives of reptiles and amphibians in the wild comes down to chance. Although you can substantially increase your luck by understanding your subjects' habits and being in the right place at the right time, making useful observations of anything from egg laying to mating displays is very hard in the field. The amateur herpetologist can genuinely add to the world's knowledge by keeping and observing herptiles in captivity, and because of advances in science and a growing awareness of the problems facing these previously unloved denizens of our planet, this is an exciting and burgeoning discipline.

The female surinam toad (*Pipa pipa*) carries her developing young beneath the skin on her back.

Much of what we know of these animals has been uncovered in captive situations. Brood care in the spine-headed tree frog (*Anotheca spinosa*) was systematically worked out in captivity, as was the fact that certain caecilians were loyal to the same tunnel system for long periods of time and not randomly pushing through the soil and leaf-litter like earthworms. The most famous "birth" in the amphibian world, that of baby frogs bursting out of the back of a female Surinam toad (*Pipa pipa*), was first observed in an aquarium. All these observations can be applied to the wild, helping us to piece together an understanding of herptile ecology and making us better able to preserve these animals in the future. The other positive is that keeping and studying herptiles promotes an appreciation of a group of creatures who, at the end of the day, need as many friends as they can get!

The very mention of the word captivity lets a lot of snakes out of the box, so to speak. It raises issues as to whether you should keep wild animals at all, and brings to the fore concerns about the large international trade in herptiles for the pet industry, some of which involves very questionable practices. This is an area peppered with issues that are too complicated to have a place in this book. I will confine myself to giving some basic advice intended to start you off in the right direction. More specific information is available from books and websites dedicated to herpetoculture (see Further Reading p. 281).

Because the hobby has blossomed so much in recent years, there are also frequent trade fairs and expos where you can see both the good and the bad sides of herpetoculture. It is up to you to make your mind up and wade through this maze of intrigue.

The most important consideration when keeping any animal in captivity is what it requires to keep it healthy and happy. This is especially true of reptiles and amphibians, as they are highly sensitive to subtle environmental factors. Before you collect an animal from the wild, make sure that it is not endangered and that you are not breaking the law by keeping it. Once you have finished studying it, return it to exactly the same place from which you took it. See Codes of Conduct (p. 11) for what you should and shouldn't keep and the ethics of keeping any wild animal in captivity for no matter how short a period.

Keeping these species in captivity has become much easier that it used to be – you no longer need a spirit stove and thermosiphon, as Victorian herpetologists did. Specialist dealers on most continents and on the Internet can supply you with literature and equipment. From probes for sexing snakes to computer-controlled habitat recreations, from frozen rats to carefully distilled dietary substances, it's all out there. The basic piece of equipment is called a vivarium – a broad term for any container or enclosure in which animals are kept for study. What you require depends entirely on the species you wish to keep – and on your budget. You could make your own outside setup for a couple of common lizards at the cost of a few pennies, while a complete rain forest environment with seasonal rain, thermostatic control, and living plants could set you back thousands of pounds.

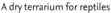
A dry terrarium for reptiles

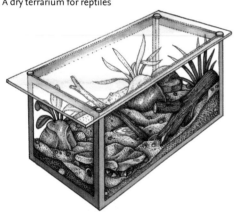
A semiaquatic vivarium for frogs and salamanders

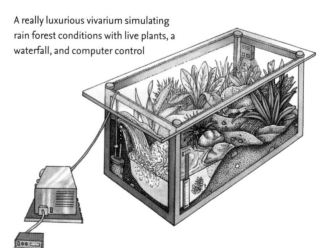
A really luxurious vivarium simulating rain forest conditions with live plants, a waterfall, and computer control

Frogging by night

The best time to see amphibians and reptiles in the wild depends, as with all creatures, on your position on the face of the planet, the season, and the weather conditions. But there are a few general tips to a happy herping trip.

The red-eyed tree frog (*Agalychnis callidryas*) is nocturnal. During the day it sits on a green leaf, eyes shut and feet tucked in, blending with the vegetation.

My best herping moments have always been at night, from the place where it all started for me – watching common smooth newts (*Triturus vulgaris*) doing their extraordinary aquatic courtship dance in my grandparents' pond and observing the incredible exodus of hundreds of tiny toadlets from the same pond – to the later experiences of finding the monstrous Goliath frog (*Conraua goliath*) in equatorial Africa and red-eyed tree frogs (*Agalychnis callidryas*) making their foam nests in the branches above a pool in Costa Rica.

The smooth, wet-skinned amphibians lose moisture readily, so it makes sense for them to be active primarily in the cool of the night. During daylight hours many hide under debris or in holes or, in the case of some tree frogs, attempt stunningly effective impressions of seemingly uninteresting foliage or bark. This means that your best bet is to go looking when they have relaxed a little and blow their own cover by going out foraging or searching for a mate (more about this later). I find head lamps handy for this – they leave your hands free for scrambling and for using other tools and books. In the tropics, where many species are a long way above you in the foliage, I cannot recommend highly enough a halogen head lamp. For me the extra range and brighter light far outweigh the disadvantages of having to replace batteries more frequently (I always use rechargeables and take spares with me just in case I end up being out all night).

One of the reasons flashlights work so well is that much of these creatures' camouflage depends on light sources coming from the predictable direction of above; at night a flashlight beam catches them on the hop, so to speak. Also, many frogs and toads have a layer of reflective cells called a tapetum behind their retinas, so when their eyes catch your flashlight they reflect it back at you. This is especially effective when the flashlight is at the same level as your eyes, and reveals the position of many nocturnal animals, from spiders to elephants!

Third, and this is probably the most important reason, a flashlight beam focuses your attention. Being visually led primates, we are easily distracted during the day. At night our sense of sight is concentrated on the little pool of artificial light just in front of us.

Cracking the croak: the art of triangulation

My frustration at the lack of nocturnal frogging skills I displayed in the Venezuelan llanos will be etched on my mind forever, as will the simple solution. It was the second night I had spent up to my waist in murky, tepid water trying to find what sounded like a herd of chihuahua-size frogs. I could not imagine how these animals could be so hard to locate when they were quacking and barking in the vegetation all around me, and by the sound of it, there were at least 50 of them scoffing at me. What made it worse was that, as I slowly waded in what I thought was the direction of my quarry, the little perishers would stop, only to start up somewhere else!

I had, it turned out in discussion the next day with a local herpetologist, made both an incorrect assumption and a foolish oversight. First, just because a frog makes a big noise doesn't mean its body is proportionally large; and second, frogs are master ventriloquists. This makes sense if you are a male frog, as your calls advertise your presence not only to the females but also to potential predators (though how the females find the males is a mystery I haven't yet cracked).

Fortunately, my friendly herpetologist suggested I make herping after dark a social thing. Not only is it a good idea to have someone with you when you are wading around in piranha- and crocodile-populated swamps after dark, but there is also a literally "sound" scientific reason for doing so. So that night there were two of us up to our thighs in the wettest swamp South America had to offer, and when the first frog croaked, I was introduced to the principle of triangulation. When you hear a call, both of you point in the direction you think it came from, then slowly move toward the spot where your bearings would cross if you were to draw a line. You keep moving closer, repeating the exercise every time your frog burps. It is a beautifully simple but effective way of working. By the way, the frog in question was only about 2 cm (less than an inch) long and, other than the moment when its throat swelled up like a barrage balloon to utter its disproportionately loud bark, it did a perfect impression of a brown reed!

When the barking tree frog (*Hyla gratiosa*) calls, it sounds like the bark of a small dog.

Jelly babies
amphibian mating

The water bounces the blazing early morning March sky back at me; things are different in this weedy ditch this morning. The water seems to defy gravity and bulge upward in the middle, with an odd lumpy texture. Every few seconds the whole reflection wobbles and shivers as something moves in the rushes at the edge, and straining my ears I can just about make out a bizarre purring noise, like a tiny electrical generator. The frogs are back.

Twenty years ago my twelve-year-old heart would have jumped into my mouth on witnessing this scene, and I would have sprinted home to find a leaky bucket to pillage some spawn for a tank, the pond, or even a bit of playground bartering. Nowadays not much has changed. I still feel that tingle of spring, but I know better than to interfere. My focus is held not so much by the inanimate spawn as by the activities of the frogs producing it.

Common frogs (*Rana temporaria*) are the earliest of British amphibians to emerge from hibernation, occasionally breeding as early as January in the warmer southwest of England. Some spend the winter in the mud or debris at the bottom of the pond in which they will mate, taking in oxygen from the water through their skin, but most hibernate on land and, like all amphibians, head back to their breeding grounds as soon as they wake up. Being in situ when the females return may improve the males' chances of mating with them, but this is a risky strategy in a shallow pond, when they may be frozen solid if the winter is a harsh one.

This stage of the frog's mating ritual is an unobtrusive one, mostly carried out under cover of darkness. If you stroll outside on a warm, wet night you are likely to spot frogs around and in the pond, but not doing much more than bobbing about. Then at some unexplained but presumably hormonally triggered cue, the pond will erupt with frogs splashing around in a frenzy of sexual activity. Mating will carry on 24 hours a day for the next one to five days, and in full swing is truly spectacular. Very little will distract a mating frog from its purpose – even if one does notice your approach and either freeze or disappear below the surface for a moment, its surging hormones will soon convince it that you are no threat and it will carry on where it left off.

Even though you will probably be totally enthralled by watching this froggy orgy, you can still practice honing your naturalist's powers of observation.

Common toads (*Bufo bufo*) and frog (*Rana temporaria*) with spawn in a breeding pond in spring

Common frogs (*Rana temporaria*) in "amplexus," the smaller male on the egg-filled female's back

The mating hug, or **amplexus**, involves the male climbing aboard the female and hanging on with his front limbs. Rough, black swellings on his thumbs, known as nuptial pads, help him to grip. You can tell a male from a female because he is generally darker and smaller, with a bluish throat, while in some populations, the female is reddish. Once the female is ready to spawn (usually at night), the male will shed sperm on the eggs as soon as they leave her body.

Sometimes, when there are more males than females in the pond, you will see literally piles of males desperately trying to clutch on to a female but in fact clinging on to each other. In extreme cases, their frenzy may be such that they smother the female and she drowns. Even if a male manages to "catch" a female, there is no guarantee that he will be able to mate – there will always be larger rivals eager to displace him.

The jelly that you see in ponds and ditches in the spring isn't all frog spawn. Common toads (*Bufo bufo*) and our three native species of newt can be found breeding at the same time (see photo on p. 121). Toads are fussier than frogs, requiring deep water, and in any particular location generally emerge from hibernation up to a couple of weeks later. Because of this they breed in fewer ponds (one toad pond to every five used by frogs). The mating activity of all the males in a colony tends to be triggered off at once, and their migrations are often large and visual affairs. Probably the best way to witness them is to contact your local wildlife trust and offer your services to their nocturnal toad road-crossing scheme, designed to protect the sex-crazed creatures from throwing themselves under the wheels of a passing vehicle in their desperation to get to their mating grounds.

Alpine newts
(*Triturus alpestris*) in full
breeding colors

Newts

Investigate a weedy pond in Europe at night, and by the light of your torch you may find any one of a variety of species of newt, smooth (*Triturus vulgaris*), palmate (*T. helveticus*), and the rare great crested (*T. cristatus*) among them. They return to water in the warm months of spring and, like their more vocal and better known relatives the frogs, they are there to mate and spawn.

What newts lack in noise, they make up for in poise, posture, and colour. The males in particular are splendidly bedecked with membranous scalloped crests running the length of their body. With the coming of spring they turn up both the contrast and the color; the flanks of all species become a rich collage of orange, blue, white, and black. If you are lucky, you may witness a newt's courtship ritual in shallow water as the male fans his tail around the female's face, flamenco-style, and literally leads her on a merry dance. His choreography has to be precise as he deposits a capsule of sperm and directs her into position to pick it up.

Crested newt eggs on
leaf (*Triturus cristatus*)

Frog farm
growing your own

Watching an amorphous blob of proteinous jelly filled with black dots turn slowly from a collection of dividing cells through animated, wriggling shreds of life to free-swimming larvae and finally four-legged frogs is one of those user-friendly miracles that can occur right before your eyes given just a few square feet of space. But although there is barely a school nature table or a ten-year-old that isn't trying to witness this miracle, many of these well-meaning attempts fail. At certain stages in the life cycle some of the tadpoles fade and die for no apparent reason.

Well, having once been a frog-fanatical schoolboy myself, with many a failed froglet to my name, I have, via a process of trial, error, and speaking to others with a similar interest, come up with the magic formula. Follow the steps below for a frog-friendly, foul-up-free, and fascinating educational experience. This advice is based on the common European frog and the common toad, which make up the bulk of my personal experience, but the principles apply equally well to other species of *Bufo* and *Rana* found all over the world.

Choose a 9–10 liter (about 2 gal) plastic tank with a vented lid (those manufactured by Hagen are excellent and very suitable for young and/or clumsy people). This a good size, neither too big nor too small, and easy to move even when full of water.

If possible, use rainwater collected from a water butt. Failing this, any natural water from a pond or stream will do. If you have to use tap water, let it stand for a couple of days to allow the chlorine used to sterilize our drinking water to dissipate naturally. Many aquarium/pet stores sell dechlorinating water treatments, but check first whether these are suitable for amphibians.

Before collecting your spawn, have your tank set up and stabilized (see pp. 142 and 144 for setting up an aquarium), with a substrate of pre-washed gravel. Add pond weed to help oxygenate the water and stabilize its pH (acid/alkaline balance). The leaves will also soon become a meadow of microscopic algae plants – useful fodder for tadpoles. Try to use native weeds but, if you are collecting from the wild, screen the weed for "predators" before introducing it to your tank – small specimens of predatory beetle larvae and dragonfly nymphs will soon become big, and with increased size comes a ferocious appetite for your tadpoles. A great diving beetle larva (*Dytiscus latissimus*) will put away as many as ten tadpoles each day!

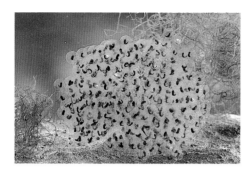

Frog spawn from the common frog in the early stages of development. With a "day" to go, the spawn shows first signs of tadpole life prior to hatching.

Resist the temptation to collect lots of spawn or tadpoles. Although you often come across huge quantities in the wild, only a few percent of it will survive. So collect a small quantity of newly laid spawn – it should be quite firm and easy to separate with your finger. Half a cupful is an ideal quantity to achieve a ratio of three to five tadpoles for every liter of water (14–22 per gallon). Remember that the more tadpoles you have, the more work you will have to do. There will be more feeding, and more cleaning out to keep the water fresh, and if you have too many in too small a space they may slow down development and even turn cannibalistic. In nature, larger tadpoles in crowded conditions produce growth inhibitors in their droppings which, when eaten by other tadpoles, stunt their growth, a common cause of failure in rearing tadpoles in captivity.

Take spawn from garden ponds wherever possible – it keeps your impact and disturbance of wild populations to a minimum. It is also good practice not to risk contaminating a habitat by introducing spawn, pond weed, or any other form of life that you have collected elsewhere. This is commonsense herpetological hygiene. Frogs in particular suffer from contagious diseases that may be spread unnecessarily in this way.

Collect your spawn with some pond water in a bag. To avoid temperature shock (remember those little black dots are living!), gently acclimatize your catch by suspending the bag at the surface for a couple of hours and gently mixing the warmer water of the tank with that in the bag, before finally tipping the spawn in.

Pond dippers at work

Tank and tadpole management through the life stages

1 Freshly laid frog spawn.

2 For the first few days of their lives the tadpoles hardly move; they spend most of their time hanging from the sides and vegetation. They are not yet actively eating – they have no mouths – but are "feeding" themselves by absorbing their yolk sacs. Do not disturb them.

3 The embryos hatch and become tadpoles. They will be content micro-grazing algae off the sides of the tank and any vegetation provided.

4 Once the tadpoles have started swimming around, change about half the water by tipping it out, using a net or sieve to catch any tadpoles that stray – they can simply be popped back in the tank. Replace the water with fresh, nonchlorinated water. Do this every week or so to keep a healthy-looking tank. If the water gets cloudy, change it more frequently. Remember not to subject the tadpoles to sudden temperature changes – keep the replacement water in the same room as the tank for a day to allow it to equilibrate. As well as providing a healthy environment for your tadpoles, you will promote strong and fast growth.

5 The head and tail are now more distinctive and the tadpoles begin to grow internal gill chambers for absorbing oxygen. The external feathery gills disappear.

6 After about three weeks they start needing more substantial salad. Every few days, give them a couple of the dry pellets usually intended for herbivorous pets such as rabbits. Observe how much they eat and try not to overfeed – otherwise you will have to increase the frequency of water changes or add other herbivores such as a few pond snails to do some cleaning for you. Introduce variety to your tadpoles' diet by boiling some lettuce for five minutes and suspending it a leaf at a time from the surface.

7 As the tadpoles grow, up their food allowance. Once the rear legs start to develop, they enter their carnivorous phase and suddenly develop voracious appetites. Feed them with flaked fish foods and small pond creatures such as bloodworms and *Daphnia*, also called water fleas.

8 As they start to develop front legs, your tadpoles' mouths and tongues grow and they will develop eyelids too.

9 As their tails begin to shrink, you need to reduce their food intake. They need a supply of very small hatchling crickets, aphids, and other tiny terrestrial insects. At this time, you should also reduce the water level in the tank to just a few centimeters (about 2 inches) and provide plenty of haul-out space such as clean sponges, moss, or stones.

10 Congratulations, you have froglets! Release them in the area from which you collected the spawn. Do this after dark and in long vegetation, not back into the water.

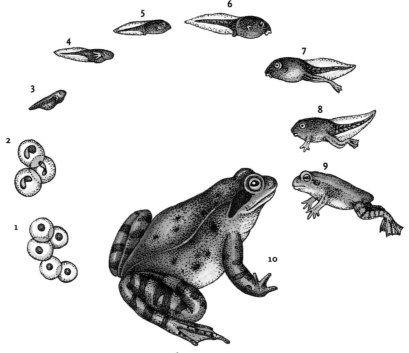

Tails and scales
for the love of lizards

Lizards are fast. Well, that's the general rule – once warm and charged up by the sun, they become invincible, solar-powered rockets. This makes studying them quite difficult, and if you go for the desirable and uninvasive option of simply watching them, the only equipment that is going to be any use is a pair of close-focusing binoculars: The more distance you can put between yourself and your highly strung subject, the more likely it is that your presence will remain undetected and you will see natural behavior rather than evasive action!

The best time to watch reptiles of any kind is when they are likely to be cold and trying to absorb solar energy. First thing in the morning is perfect, especially if the air temperature is relatively cool, the skies are clear, and the sun's heat is just beginning to warm the ground. In some cases, this is the only time during the day that these animals will be out in the open away from cover.

Female sand lizard (*Lacerta agilis*) sunbathing on a rock

As a general rule, the bigger the lizard, the bigger its brain, confidence, and ability to override natural caution when faced with humans in the wild. How tame and tolerant it is depends on such factors as whether or not it is hunted, persecuted, or regularly fed or exposed to people. I have spent days trying to watch and get a good photograph of water monitor lizards (*Varanus salvator*) in a national park in Borneo, where they were as elusive and wary as you might expect a big cat to be, never giving up much more than a length of tail or a blinking, suspicious eye. But at a resort just around the peninsula, the same species was being fed on buckets of kitchen scraps tipped into the Malaysian equivalent of a duck pond. The place was crawling with humongous, hand-tame lizards lolling about in the open. Some were even making bold approaches, too close for comfort in some cases – one of them lunged at my flip-flopped feet!

Turn rustles into reptiles

Smaller lizard species are often overlooked simply because they are small. Although the world is aware of the giant crocs and the monitor lizards, the really cool flying lizard (*Draco* spp.) or basilisk (*Basiliscus* spp.) is sitting close by, just as wild and beautiful but unnoticed. In fact, many of the smaller reptiles catch your eye only when they skip off at your approach. If your senses are alert as you walk along a heathland path or a rain forest trail, you may well become aware of a rustle in the leaf litter a step or two ahead. Rather than ignoring it and striding on, it often pays to stop, make yourself comfortable, and wait. Defocus your eyes, look in the direction of the noise and more often than not the perpetrator of the rustle – a lizard or even a small snake – will make a cautious return to its basking spot at the edge of the path, where if you remain stock still, you will be able to observe unnoticed.

Flying dragon, its rib cage providing struts for its "gliding" wings

Lasso me a lizard

As I stress throughout this book, direct physical contact with any living creature should be avoided unless strictly necessary. Sometimes, however, it is the only way of obtaining information. For example, I was recently exploring among the aromatic creosote bushes and rocky crevices of a gully in the Sonora Desert in Arizona. This place is a herpetologist's dream; everywhere you look the landscape has a heartbeat, despite the seemingly impossible heat. Now, stumble across a rattlesnake or a gila monster in an environment like this and it is relatively easy to identify – as recognizable to the herpetologist as an ostrich or a kiwi would be to a birdwatcher. The challenge comes with the reptile equivalent of the ornithologist's little brown job or LBJ. All about me, small lizards skipped and scuttled between the boulders, and with a little practice, I could tell different families apart. But according to my field guide, to distinguish some species I had to check the ridges running down their back, count their scales, or even observe the color of their belly scales – tasks that are next to impossible from any distance, even with the aid of close-focus binoculars. For these, you have to take up noosing.

Noosing a lizard

The idea of noosing is simple. Mastering the technique, on the other hand, is as patience-testing as the construction is straightforward. Because there are no lizard predators out there that hunt with pieces of string tied to the end of sticks, the normally nervous beasts seem no more than a bit bemused as you slip the open noose over their heads. The skill lies in getting to this stage without first unwittingly spooking your quarry, which can be done in more ways than you might think possible – snagging your noose in the vegetation or letting it blow about in the breeze, getting the shakes, or simply throwing a shadow and bumbling your approach are just a few of the frustrations. But with practice you will grow deft with your new tool.

The right kind of "string" is important too. It has to be light enough not to be too noticeable by the lizard, but not so light that it blows around in the slightest breeze and hasn't enough stiffness or shape-retaining qualities to form a proper loop. It also needs to slip over itself very easily. Waxed dental floss is ideal – it is readily obtainable, can be carried around in your pocket, and, before you ask, as far as I can tell, it doesn't matter what flavor you use!

You will need:
- a long pole (a child's telescopic fishing pole is good, cheap, and versatile
- a length of fine cord
- a second pole and a white tissue or rag

1 Attach the cord to the end of the pole, fashion it into a noose by tying a loose slip knot, and you have a perfect lizard-bagging device.

2 If necessary, you can distract your subject by attaching the tissue or rag to the end of your other stick and "twitch" it nearby. This should hold the lizard's attention long enough for you to position and tighten your noose.

3 Slip the noose over the lizard's head, carefully avoiding all the pitfalls mentioned above.

4 Close the noose around the lizard's neck with a fast but gentle flick of the wrist directed up and back toward its tail. Restrain the animal in your hands as quickly as possible, trying to avoid a prolonged and messy struggle.

Step 1

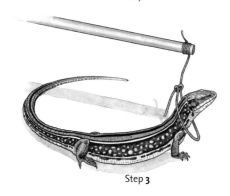

Step 2

Step 3

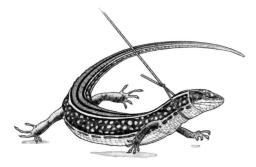

Step 4

Many lizards (and some snakes) engage in a somewhat distressing, self-mutilating survival strategy known as autotomy. When attacked, the lizard "throws" its own tail, which will writhe in a rather gruesome way for some minutes, holding the predator's gaze long enough for the tail's former owner to slink off under cover and live to grow another. A lizard with a blunt, shiny-ended tail or different colors to portions of it has probably survived such an encounter. The reason for the different appearance is that when the tail regrows the bones inside do not, so once a tail has been lost once it cannot be shed again. When you are working with nervous lizards, autotomy can happen almost instantly with little provocation, but it is more likely to be avoided if you minimize stress to the animal, handle it as gently as possible, and do not grasp the tail directly.

Tickling lizards: getting them down

This capture technique works particularly well with small tree-living lizards, especially those tricky, color-changing, lightning-reflexed geckos that frequent hotel rooms throughout the tropics. It is also a handy little trick for performing the service that is often required of a naturalist – removing the said geckos from the apartments of less tolerant people! Often the act itself takes so long that you have plenty of time to persuade the occupants that leaving the animal in position will be better for all concerned. You can catch your lizard in a buttefly net, or something similar.

Tickling requires nothing more than a long, thin piece of wire or even a length of robust grass or palm leaf and a small ball of kapok or cotton wool. Twizzle and tease the wool fiber around the tip of the "tickling stick" so that it is firmly attached; then wiggle this conspicuous bit of fluff on the ceiling, trunk, or wall your gecko is frequenting. Try to exploit natural cover, using corners and other obstacles to your advantage.

The skill in this bizarre puppet show is to make the fluff look like an insect target. You will find that your gecko's greed is much greater than any fears or doubts it may have. More often than not it will grasp the bait in its mouth and get its teeth temporarily tangled, so you can, if you are quick, bring it down or flick it into a hand net.

You can apply the same principle by tying a small insect such as a mealworm or even a recently dead fly to some thin fishing line. The lizards can literally be fished for – a great alternative to noosing!

'Road Riding'

There are limited ways in which automobiles can be used in a positive way – as opposed to causing undue disturbance – when watching wildlife, so you may be surprised to learn that they can be very useful when looking for reptiles, and snakes in particular, at night. In hot countries where most animal activity takes place after dark, our asphalt runways become a focal point. Why is a good question, and I have heard many theories. Some say that snake food such as mice and other small mammals occurs in higher concentrations here, perhaps because better marginal vegetation or edible scraps thrown out of cars attract it; others say the heat radiated back from the black surface of the highway raises a reptile's body temperature and therefore hunting ability. Whatever the reason, any self-respecting snake enthusiast should try road riding!

The best approach is to find a few quiet back roads that go through good habitat. Drive slowly along them a couple of hours after dusk, using the light of the headlights to watch for animals at the side of the road or on the road itself. Keep a head lamp on your brow and your handling tools (see p.133) at the ready, because you do not know what is literally around the next corner.

Obviously if the roads you have chosen are public highways, you are going to have to make some compromises. Just because you have seen a coral snake on the verge and jammed on your anchors, do not assume the car behind you will do the same! I have heard of some horrific near-death experiences caused by this sort of behavior, so here are a few more golden rules:

Always be aware of other road users.
Give way to other cars.
Do not make sudden maneuvers.
Always pull over in a safe place, avoid stopping on corners or bends, and avoid busy times.
Use your flashers when stopped.
Don't point flashlights directly at other drivers.

A safe alternative and something I have done in Tucson, Arizona, is to befriend the local golf-course owner and persuade him to let you borrow a golf cart. The roads on golf courses are fantastic places to pick up nocturnal animals, as by nature they contain or adjoin semi-wild habitat and are often a source of unseasonal water and productivity. Here you can safely and at your own speed go whizzing about to your heart's content.

Snakes that pack a punch

All snakes, from an angry cobra to a grass snake you have just hooked out of the pond, are capable of inflicting a bite that will at best be painful, at worst can lead to agony and even death. I tend to treat all wild snakes in the same way – with oodles of respect and caution. A friend and experienced herpetologist who was bitten by his pet python had fragments of the snake's teeth stuck in his hand for months afterward and the wound was slow to heal due to infection. Even small, seemingly inoffensive species such as rat snakes (*Elaphe* spp.) could have been eating rodents that themselves were carrying a nasty disease. So the way you secure, hold, and support a snake is pretty much the same whether it is venomous or nonvenomous.

There is a worrying trend in the popular media to show and glamorize the activities of "reptile wrestlers" and "fang fiends." These people are certainly very knowledgeable and skilled at what they do – well, obviously, if they weren't they'd be dead! If you are tempted to emulate these iconic figures, remember that you may be putting yourself, and more important the animals, at risk. Having said that, my stance is to give as much responsible information as possible and let people make up their own minds – after all, it was early exciting experiences with adders and grass snakes that led to my lifelong fascination with snakes in general.

Indian cobra (*Naja naja*). Carefully does it…never handle reptiles unless you are certain you know what you are doing! A mistake could be your last.

Notes on handling the small and the venomous

Nearly all snakebite-caused fatalities are the result of people trying to handle venomous snakes and underestimating the animal's capabilities. No one, whether amateur or professional herpetologist, should ever man-handle a venomous snake – anyone who does needs his head tested. The best herpetologists are the ones who live longest and get to shout out loud to the world what fantastic creatures herptiles are. To prolong your life expectancy, it is wise to follow some golden rules.

Never, ever touch a venomous snake. Even recently dead ones need to be treated with caution.

With large and strong species, be aware that the animal may try to loop its body around itself and form a slip knot which it will use to push your hand off its head. Pay attention and be ready to twist away before this becomes a problem.

Avoid complacency at all costs. Do not lose concentration or ease up your firm pressure, as however subdued a snake may seem it can suddenly spring into action and catch an unwary handler out.

For normal study there is no need to touch a snake's body. You can purchase numerous tools from specialist dealers on the Internet or simply manufacture them at home: These include all manner of hooks, grips, and tongs and are designed to maximize the safety of both animal and handler. I really recommend using these, although they can be expensive.

I recently spent some time with the Irula tribe in India, who, for the purpose of venom extraction, handled kraits, cobras, and saw-scaled vipers on a daily basis. These masters of snake work used nothing but their bare hands and an iron pole to dig the animals out of their holes. Working alongside them with all my specialized tongs and hooks made me feel a bit stupid, but having said that, it is better to stick with what you are used to.

Hooks and snake sticks tend to be more gentle and sensitive if used correctly and are among the most useful and wonderfully simple tools a herpetologist can have. But, in the hands of an excitable and inexperienced person they may grip the snake too tightly and cause internal damage, breaking ribs and damaging nerves. To reduce this risk, glue foam-rubber pads to the inside of the jaws of the tongs, or purchase one of the more expensive "gentle" types. Whenever possible, grasp the snake halfway down the length of its body and **never** grab it behind the head or even support it like this for the briefest time, as you may kill it.

Hooks and sticks come in a variety of sizes from telescopic, pen-size ones (which frankly are of limited use, but are handy for

Grab sticks and tongs are mechanical devices that act as an extension of your arm, complete with "thumb and forefinger" for gripping the snake's body. These are particularly useful when you are working in dense bush and need time to unravel the snake, which has almost certainly wound itself tightly around any vegetation present. I like to use a grab stick in conjunction with a hook, enabling me to grasp the animal gently and manipulate its position at the same time.

Useful though they are, these tools do have limitations. When you grab a snake with tongs, it will feel very threatened and will almost certainly struggle and bite in its efforts to defend itself.

Here, a cobra is about to be "milked" for its venom for use in antivenom, being produced for the Irula tribe in India.

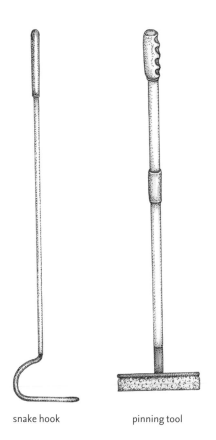

snake hook   pinning tool

poking around in dark crevices if you are looking for scorpions and spiders – see p. 170) to huge unwieldy poles that need two hands to operate them and are designed for use with large pythons and constrictors in captivity. Hooks with a longer "flat" at 90 degrees to the handle are the most useful for pinning and tailing. If you are going to be lifting snakes up, you need a hook with a "neck" that bends away from the main shaft at approximately a 45-degree angle.

Commercial snake sticks consist of a length of tempered steel with a golfing grip at the other end; and for the traveling naturalist collapsible telescopic ones are very useful. The type and size you need depends on what you are going to use it for and what species you are likely to encounter. The stick should be at least 30 cm (12 in) longer than the longest strike range of the snake you are dealing with (that is at least half the body length for most species, although some can launch themselves almost the entire length of their body, so, as always, expect the worst and be supercautious). Longer sticks can be awkward to maneuver, especially in the close confines of vegetation. Using two at the same time, like a kind of simplified Edward Scissorhands, is often the way around this problem, and with faster, nonvenomous species a hook can also be used in conjunction with the "tailing" technique shown below.

Making your own snake stick

If you are on a budget, you can create a very workable and usable set of snake hooks by bending and modifying various diameters of welding rods, or even a section of a thick wire coat hanger. Note, however, that handmade snake sticks are too flimsy for pinning or lifting heavy species. For such purposes use a thick gauge wire instead.

You will need:
- a suitable piece of metal
- a length of wooden dowel

1 Hammer the tip of your metal flat and round it to make it easier to slide under the animal's body.

2 For smaller hooks use a bit of coat hanger (one of the straight bits, not the hook itself) and secure it firmly to a length of wooden dowel.

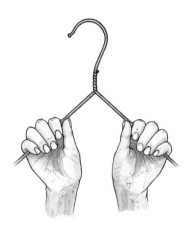

Step **1**

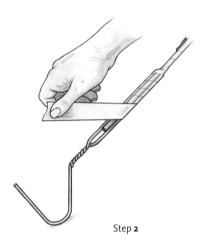

Step **2**

Using a snake hook or stick

There is no substitute for experience when it comes to using a snake hook, so practice on the smaller, slower, nonvenomous species. For terrestrial species, those that live most of their lives with their bellies hugging the ground, slide the hook under the snake's body at the halfway point and gently lift it up. This is usually all you need to do, as most snakes have a reflex response to height and the possibility of falling; they will freeze and grip the hook as best they can. As long as you keep the hook high enough for the snake to feel it cannot crawl down, it will stay put. Be careful not to lift the snake higher than your gripping hand, as this encourages it to move toward you; and be aware that although the snake isn't going anywhere, it may well feel threatened and strike out – keep a sphere of safety around the snake and be aware of the position of any other people, too. Heavier snakes, particularly Gabon vipers (*Bitis gabonica*), puff adders (*B. arietans*), and other big-bodied vipers, can be injured by their own weight pressing on the hook; supporting them with two hooks distributes the weight better.

For faster colubrids and other nonvenomous snakes, using a snake stick is an art form akin to juggling spaghetti with chopsticks! At the same time as you pin the snake with the stick, you want to make a confident grab at the tail. This is known as "tailing" and it relies on holding the snake by the rear end of its body while supporting and/or controlling the front end, which in most cases will be either trying to get away at all costs or coming back at you. Those that crawl up the sticks (particularly arboreal species) or try to get away are best dealt with by using two sticks. These "runny" snakes usually settle down after they have passed back and forth several times; those that don't, need to be restrained by being "tailed."

Pinning sticks are something you shouldn't need to use. Pinning is a way of restraining an animal so that it can be picked up while gentle pressure is exerted on its jaws to prevent it from biting. This technique is mostly used in laboratories where snakes are manipulated in order to extract venom. For the amateur, it is just asking to be bitten.

A quick word on transporting snakes

For everything from big anacondas to the tiniest of colubrids, the best way of transporting a snake is in a cloth bag of an appropriate size – those cloth laundry bags available from the top drawer in posh hotels are great because they come with a built-in drawstring, but a pillow case or cloth sack will do fine. Place or drop the snake into the bag, use your hook to squeeze it gently toward the closed end, twist the neck of the bag together, and tie it back on itself. The snake is now safely trapped in the dark, soft confines of the bag. Do not be complacent, though: Just because the snake is out of your sight doesn't mean that you are out of its sight or bite! It may be able to see you through the weave. Long-fanged species especially can and will strike out at shadows, and being bitten through a bag is no laughing matter. Cloth bags don't give their occupants much physical protection, so place the bag in a bucket, tub, or more robust bag while the snake is in transit.

Rules of engagement

❉ If you have doubts about the identity of the animal or your ability to handle it, leave well enough alone.

❉ Never handle large or venomous reptiles if under the influence of intoxicating substances. Always have your wits about you.

❉ Never directly handle or pin a venomous snake.

❉ Know your limits and do not be afraid of admitting them – when it comes to safety, leave your ego at home.

❉ Never work with potentially dangerous reptiles alone. Always "buddy" up with someone reliable.

Fish Fantastic

It's a shame, but unless they are dangling off the end of a baited line or nestling on a bed of greasy fries, most of us tend to ignore fish. We certainly rarely make the effort to get to know them as we do other, more obviously charismatic life forms. But there are ways in which we can enter their watery realm, if not exactly on equal terms, at least in such a way as to begin to understand a little about what makes them tick.

Apart from the fact that we find it hard to extract oxygen from water, the other thing that leaves fish swimming against the current of interest is that they are often regarded as stupid, uninteresting things. When faced with this in conversation, I tend casually to bring up swimming with a great white shark (*Carcharodon carcharias*) in the cool teal waters of South Africa or sharing space with the second largest fish in the world, the rare and mysterious basking shark (*Cetorhinus maximus*). For me, these two experiences knock polar bears and mountain gorillas into a hat – they're the biggest adrenaline trips I have ever had, and both are undeniably fishy ones! Whether we are talking toothy top predators or the smallest of small fry, fish are quite simply fascinating.

Above: Barracuda shoal
Right: Shark skin detail

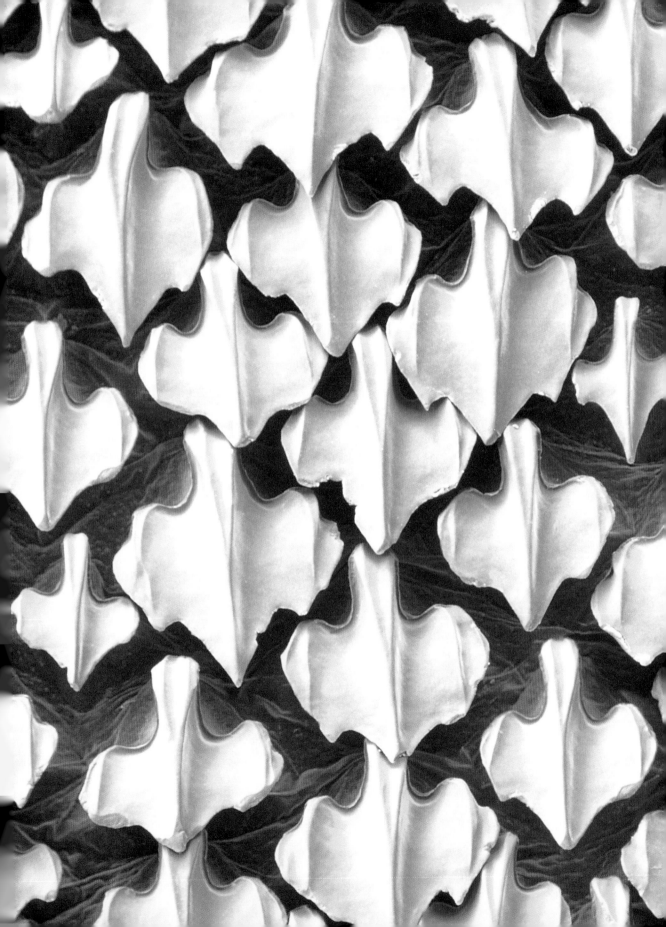

Fish, fishing, and figuring it out

My introduction to the world of fish came from fishing trips with my father. It dawned on me very quickly that to be a successful angler I had to understand not only where the fish were but why they were there. Even that wasn't enough for me; I wanted to learn about the fish themselves. I wanted to see them doing what my father described to me. I longed to see the perch (*Perca fluviatilis*) hanging under the moored boat, sun dappling their tiger-striped backs, maintaining their position by the lazy flicking of red fins. I needed to see a trout (*Salmo trutta*) waiting patiently, like a leopard, in the shadows by the eddy, picking off the occasional stray minnow (*Phoxinus phoxinus*), and of course I hungered to see the minnows themselves. Catching the fish, ripping them out of their world, lifting them through their sky into ours, soon started to lose its magic, just as the fish, flipping around in my hands, gasping and asphyxiating in the air, lost theirs like a wet pebble drying.

The deciding moment came one day when I was staring at my float, watching it bob and swerve on the surface, knowing that every twitch and ripple had an equivalent action, caused by the fish just below the surface. If I stretched out my fingers I could touch it, but it remained invisible, cloaked from my view by the turbidity of the water and the play of light on the surface. It was both frustrating and tantalizing for a young boy. Wouldn't it be great, I thought, to be able to relate what my float was doing to the behavior of my quarry under the surface? The question in my mind was how.

It was then that I stopped catching and eating fish and started keeping them.

All tanked up

As a naturalist, you will quickly find that you become a connoisseur of containers, vessels, and canisters. Few containers are as useful as a transparent tank. Homemade or store-bought, they are very handy and versatile things. Fill them with water and they are aquariums, keep them dry and they become vivariums for terrestrial animals (see p. 118). When it comes to materials, the most common question is "plastic or glass?" Both have their advantages and disadvantages, as you can see in the table below.

Choosing plastic or glass

	Glass	Plastic
Cost	Tends to be more expensive.	Cheaper if bought new.
Weight	Heavy and awkward.	Light and portable.
Clarity	Tends to stay looking good for longer and is harder to scratch.	Can become opaque with time, and is a nightmare to clean without scratching. Even if you are very, very careful, this will happen.
Repairs	A leaky aquarium can be repaired more often than not with clear silicone sealant.	Forget it. Slightly cracked ones that once contained water can be reincarnated as dry vivariums, but attempts at repair are usually futile!
Fragility	Chips easily and can crack if placed on an uneven surface or exposed to temperature extremes. Watch out especially when cleaning with hot water – never make it too hot.	Tends to get brittle with age but is fairly robust. Some types of plastic will melt if you put heat mats under them.

Setting up an aquarium

There are four basic types of aquarium: salt water, fresh water, tropical, and cold. Fresh water is the easiest to set up, and I suggest you stick to this until you are confident of what you are doing. There are loads of different kinds of tank available in many different sizes. Choose the biggest you can easily maintain. You can have too small a tank, but rarely one that is too big for its inhabitants. There isn't room here for instructions on keeping individual species of fish, so check the back of this book for further reading and supplies.

You will need:
- a tank with a close-fitting lid
- clean natural water (see "A word on water" p. 144)
- an old toothbrush
- enough pea gravel to cover the bottom of the tank with a layer 2–3 cm (about 1 in) deep
- a bucket to wash the gravel in
- "furniture" (rocks and/or wood)
- enough polystyrene tiles to form a base for your tank
- old paper, cardboard, or a plastic bag
- filter (optional)
- pond weed and inhabitants

1 New or old, give your tank a good wash – you never know what contaminants, dust, vapor, or disease it may have been in contact with and it is best not to take any chances. Use an old toothbrush to clean out the awkward corners.

2 Wash and scrub the pea gravel by placing it in a bucket of clean water and swilling, scrunching, and rubbing it. Discard the water and repeat the process until the water runs clean. Clean and sterilize any other equipment or "furniture" you may be placing in the tank. There are various chemical sterilizers on the market that are harmless to pond life, but I find using boiling water straight from the kettle effective enough.

Step **1**

Step **2**

Step **3**

3 Place the tank where you intend it to stay, as a tank full of rocks, water, and living things is heavy, awkward, and fragile; moving it will also cause unnecessary stress to those ensconced. If you are not using an artificial light source, choose a light position out of direct sunlight, as temperatures can soar and spell certain death to your fish; algae can also become a problem. Place the tank on a level surface. I find polystyrene tiles (available from hardware stores and pet shops) very useful here – they act as a cushion, leveling the bottom of the tank and minimizing stress on the glass that can cause it to fracture when full. (Believe me, I talk from experience when I say it is no fun to have even a little tank burst in the middle of the night and to find yourself tiptoeing around in bare feet on a soggy carpet, trying to avoid shards of glass and rescue the unhappy pond life that has been unceremoniously dumped on the shag pile.)

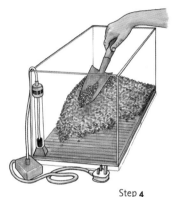
Step **4**

4 If you are using an under-gravel filter, place the tray and associated pieces into position as per the instructions that came with it. Otherwise gently scoop the gravel into the tank, landscaping it so that it slopes down toward the front. This makes it easier to clean and simply looks better.

Step **5**

5 Arrange the furniture, filters, and other equipment, but do not plug in or turn on yet. Place the paper, cardboard, or plastic bag inside the tank and pour water onto it; this way the turbulence created doesn't disturb the gravel or any leftover silt or debris that might cloud the water. Don't fill the tank to the brim – leave a little space at the top to help prevent things jumping out. Remove the lining material.

6 Now add the plants. These take up waste nutrients produced by other life in the water and recycle it; they also help aerate the water by producing oxygen – plus they look fantastic and provide good shelter and living furniture for the creatures you are planning to keep.

Step **6**

A box of water – aquariums

I began taking some of the fish I caught home to study. Keeping them in the most natural conditions I could create, I was able to find out about living fish in their own environment. To start with I even fished in my own aquarium – without hooks, I hasten to add – just so that I could relate the movements of the fish to those of the float. But soon the fish themselves took the lead. Their movements and their jewel-like quality in the clear water became intoxicating and, like anyone who has ever stared into the fish tank in the dentist's waiting room, I found myself, well, hooked!

Top tank tips

❊ Put on a tank top. Many pond insects can fly – that's how they colonize new watery habitats – and some fish and frogs can accidentally flip themselves out of the water or simply do a Houdini as part of their natural explorations. Make sure you fit a good lid and that escape is impossible. As I write, a snapping turtle in a tank next to me has just lifted a heavy metal and glass lid weighed down with bricks!

❊ Make sure your tank is out of reach of troublesome dogs, cats, and kids. I have had curious cats spend the afternoon systematically fishing out every unfortunate tadpole, leaving them lined up on a windowsill, a pathetic little death row of dried bodies. Also, a large and thirsty basset hound once drank a whole tank of water along with most of the occupants. Both these events could have been avoided by positioning the tank more carefully, and they illustrate the importance of a good, tight-fitting lid.

❊ A word on water. Natural rainwater is always best – collect it in a water butt. If you have to use tap water, put it in the tank and let it settle for a week or so before adding any animals. Alternatively, use one of the many water conditioners and dechlorinating solutions available from specialist aquarium suppliers, including most pet shops, and follow the manufacturer's instructions.

❊ Electricity and water do not mix. Always turn off electrical elements such as pumps, filters, aerators, and water heaters before placing your hands in the water. That way you do not risk electrocution. Putting a circuit breaker on the mains supply is an added precaution. Also try to avoid the mains power supply being directly below the tank.

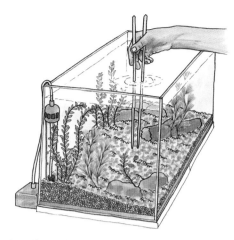

long chopsticks

siphon tubing

✺ **Use long chopsticks** or make some long tweezers out of split garden canes to move things around with minimum disturbance. Turkey basters are useful for sucking up small, offending articles from an established tank.

✺ **Do the housework.** Look at your tank as a kind of aquatic window box. Just as you need to weed your pansies and petunias, your tank will also need a little gardening in your tank from time to time. It is perfectly natural for debris to accumulate on the floor of the tank, but it can be kept under control by regular vacuuming. The easiest way to do this is to siphon it up through a length of clear rubber tubing. Place one end in the water with the other end at a lower level, outside the tank. Give a short, sharp suck on this end until you see the water coming down the tube, then very quickly take the siphon out of your mouth and direct it into a bucket or similar receptacle. Now you can direct the other end around the tank, sucking up sediment. You may get an occasional mouthful of water to start off with but, since this water can taste pretty bad, you soon learn to avoid it! On a serious note, though, certain aquatic reptiles and other creatures carry germs which at best can leave a foul taste in your mouth and at worst make you very sick. Cheats can spend top dollar on a custom-made siphon, which has a flexible bulb on the end and alleviates the need to suck. Or you could modify the bulb off a turkey baster.

✺ Get in the flow by re-creating conditions in the wild. Bear in mind that many species live in flowing water and will die of suffocation in a matter of hours in still water. To overcome this you *must* provide a pump and aeration. If this is too specialized for you or you simply cannot afford it, stick to still-water species.

The 'jilly' jar

I have absolutely no idea where the name of this fish-catching technique came from – all I know is that a bunch of my school friends and I would get together every Saturday morning to go "jilly-jarring." Maybe we invented the term? Maybe it has some colloquial origin deep in the backwoods of East Sussex? Who knows and, as long as it works, who cares? The size of the jar doesn't really matter – a bigger jar doesn't necessarily catch more fish, and the extra weight of water the string has to support when you pull it out may be a problem.

Step 1

You will need:
- a screw-top jam jar with ridges round the neck
- a long piece of string
- bait (stale bread crumbs soaked in water work well)

1 Tie the string tightly around the neck of the jar so that it doesn't slip off. Tie a support brace around the bottom of the jar for extra security.

2 Fill the jar with water and place some presoaked breadcrumbs inside. For a deluxe trap, glue a little net bag to the bottom of the jar and put the bait in that. Lower the jar into shallow water where you can see lots of small fish activity and wait.

Step 2

3 The idea is that curious fish will start to assemble around the jar, bumping it from all angles and soon finding their way around to its mouth. Once they have entered the jar, simply hoist it – water, fish, and all – as quickly as you can to the surface. Once you have observed your catch, return it to where it came from.

This is all very well, you may be thinking, but why go to all this trouble when you could just push a net into the water and scoop them up? Well, there are several answers to this. First, small, open-water fish are not all easy to catch with a net – most have quite a turn of speed and the acceleration of a Ferrari! And they take some serious outwitting, especially when there is no cover. Second, jilly-jarring trains the amateur naturalist in the arts of observation and patience. Sitting quietly by a stream side waiting and watching the fishes' behavior allows you to understand them better. And third, it is less destructive to the underwater habitat than even the most carefully wielded net.

Step 3

Fish-watching

Unless you get into the realms of huge amounts of money and expertise, aquariums have their limitations. For a much more complete experience, full of surprises, adrenaline buzzes and genuine discovery, try fish-watching. This can be as varied a pastime as the fish themselves: sitting on a cliff trying to spy the 1.5 m (5 ft) dorsal fin of a basking shark, wandering rock pools to find fish stranded by the tides, watching minnows dashing in the shallows of a brook, chumming for sharks, or donning the latest scuba gear and entering their realm.

Reading the ripples – passive fish-watching

Because they inhabit what to us is such a strange world, fish can seem very distant. Although we pass them every time we walk along a river, canal, pond, or beach, we are rarely aware of them. But, like all wildlife, fish do occasionally give clues to their whereabouts, whether it is a splash, ripple, or rise. So begin your fish-watching by using your ears.

An old Irish proverb, "Listen to the sound of the river and you will get a trout," says it all to me, conjuring up a placid summer's evening listening to the soft kiss of trout rising to take emerging mayflies from the water's surface. At the other end of the spectrum, fish can also produce a surprising amount of noise. Take my experience in Guyana with a fish known as a grunter. To this day I wouldn't know a grunter from a guppy, but I will never forget the sound – like a pig chewing pellets – that came up through the bottom of my aluminum canoe that day – an introduction to the acoustic world of fish.

Making water babies: fish lose inhibitions

Brown trout (*Salmo trutta*) development

Having said that fish tend to remain hidden in their secret world, at certain times of the year some species are so taken by the urge to breed that they lose their usual caution and drift closer to the interface between water and air. Procreation is top of their agenda. On a still spring day, look out for the violently thrashing water that signals the spawning orgies of common carp (*Cyprinus carpio*) – with other things on their mind, these normally timid fish become tolerant of human viewers approaching close, and what you see can be spectacular. The water around reedbeds fizzes with small cyprinids such as roach (*Rutilus rutilus*) and rudd (*Scardinius erythrophthalmus*) as males chase males and pair with females.

In the mating season, the schoolboy's "tiddler," the minnow, and its relatives go through a metamorphosis, with the males developing white tubercles on the head and gills and their bellies flushing pink, while the breeding females swell with their bodies full of eggs soon to be strewn on pebbles and stones on the streambed. These frisky little fish seek the spring-warmed shallows; look for them congregating in large shoals for spawning. You can get good views of them if the water is clear and calm, but this is where a neat trick known as a "jilly jar" (see p. 146) can show you what pretty fish they are, with a variety of different colors from bronze to white with dark banding.

Lift stones from the streambed, and it is not uncommon to come across a mass of pink eggs attached to the stones themselves or to the riverbed. Nearby, unless it has been disturbed, will be an attentive male bullhead, or miller's thumb (*Cottus gobio*). This is a small, secretive but common European river fish which seems to be known only to members of the angling fraternity, who occasionally snag one by mistake, or to kids who dabble with nets in fast and stony sections of stream or river.

Another doting father who is not prepared to leave his pride and joy to fate is one of our most stunning sea fish: the lumpsucker (*Cyclopterus lumpus*). Some may argue that it is also one of the ugliest. This fish is large – some 40 cm (16 in) or so from head to tail tip, and rather rotund – which adds to the experience. The male is most likely to be found in shallow water among the kelp zone, where he has a brief rendezvous with the dull-colored female before she leaves him to guard and ventilate the clutch of 30,000-odd eggs. While performing his loyal paternal duties, he may be caught out by very low spring tides and stranded, as he will not abandon his brood.

Whatever you think of the lumpsucker in the looks department, there is no denying that, if you bump into the brick-red bellied male while he guards his brood of eggs, you will never forget the moment.

One of the most bizarre fish, which has close relatives all around the world, is the Cornish sucker, or clingfish (*Lepadogaster lepadogaster*). This little rock-hugging creature, only 7 cm (3 in) long and extravagantly colored in reds and greens, with two large blue eye spots and a mouth prolonged into a snout, can sometimes be found at low tide guarding its batch of yellow, Skittlelike eggs, which are stuck to the underside of rocks. The best way to see it is to use a mirror mounted on a stick; this allows

The Cornish sucker or clingfish

you to view the undersides of rocks and ledges, the sort of places these animals like to hide out.

The Cornish sucker's real claim to fame is the device that enables it to live in the wave-battered world of the rocky shore – a suction disk on its belly formed from fused pelvic fins. This really works. If you catch one and try to pick it out of your net, it will sometimes stick to your palm and, no matter how vigorously you try and shake it off, it won't budge.

Of all the small fish spawnings, probably the most mysterious and bizarre are the writhing spaghetti masses of brook lampreys (*Lampetra planeri*) found in shallow, stony rivers and streams in the spring. A lamprey looks a bit like an alien mutant eel, with a long, sinuous body, a sucker disk of a mouth, and seven gill holes that make you think it's been spiked in the head with a fork. The spawning is the culmination of a five-year life cycle. The gang of juveniles, known as a pride, vacuum the streambed for detritus; then, as they turn into adults in the autumn, their guts dissolve and their last action before they fade out is this mass spawning.

Dummying fish

I cannot make my mind up on this one. Is it fish-watching or fish-catching? Actually I guess it is somewhere between the two – it is angling without the intention of catching anything! Dummying is a way of instigating spectacular feeding behavior from a fish, just enough to learn something before they wise up and let go. It can be tried with many different species. I have used fishing flies with the hooks taken off to encourage a trout to strike at the surface and rise. Dragging a decoy rubber fish or even a dead one past a pike's lair will sometimes attract the interest of the resident and you will, by performing a bizarre puppet show, be able to witness the slow, "I'm not really a predator" stalking behavior as the animal almost imperceptibly leans toward its prey before snapping.

Feeding the fish – using baits as lures

A few bolder – or should that read greedier? – fish species can
be attracted to baits and provide a refreshing addition to the
fish-watcher's repertoire. Starting with the smaller fry and working
up to the big stuff, you can liven up many a rock-pool ramble by tying
a piece of bacon or ham to the end of a fishing line and jiggling it to
entice residents from their homely crevices. I have used this
particularly successfully with the universal family of blennies, or
shannies (*Blennius pholis*), as these aggressive little intertidal
scavengers are always up for an easy meal. You may even be able to
pull them out of the water as they latch on to the bait with their many
sharp teeth. They can be very territorial, so keep an eye open for
interaction between competing individuals.

   I have used similar methods with other fish species too.
Red-bellied piranhas (*Serrasalmus nattereri*) in the tropics of South
America can be lured to some meat on a piece of string, and I have
been able to witness the efficiency of their infamous teeth and jaws.
A bunch of lettuce leaves on a string can be used to tempt vegetarian
marine damselfish out into the open. Tying a bundle of worms
together on the end of a piece of string, a practice known as patting,
is a great way to attract and even catch eels, as is tying a small
mammal carcass such as a rabbit to some rocks in the clear shallows,
sinking it into the water, and returning after dark with a flashlight.

Shanny, or blenny, as it's
also known

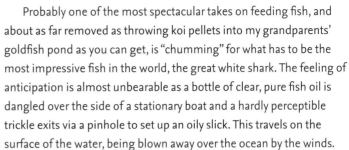

A great white shark viewed in the wild from an underwater observation cage

Probably one of the most spectacular takes on feeding fish, and about as far removed as throwing koi pellets into my grandparents' goldfish pond as you can get, is "chumming" for what has to be the most impressive fish in the world, the great white shark. The feeling of anticipation is almost unbearable as a bottle of clear, pure fish oil is dangled over the side of a stationary boat and a hardly perceptible trickle exits via a pinhole to set up an oily slick. This travels on the surface of the water, being blown away over the ocean by the winds.

To the sharks, not averse to a bit of scavenging, the slick suggests that there is food in the water. They pick up on almost impossibly small concentrations of the oil and, like dogs following the scent of a rabbit upwind, work their way along the trail, hoping to get an easy meal. Of course, feeding on a regular basis a fish that already has enough of an image problem and doesn't need to learn to associate boats with food is not a good thing, so those on board got to see our largest predatory fish swim a couple of cautious laps around the boat before vanishing as quickly as it arrived, leaving the dumbstruck fish-watchers with a sense of mystery and awe. The experience was not *Jaws*, but something far more lasting.

Using this sort of practice as an occasional embellishment to your fish-watching will probably have little long-term impact on the creatures or their environment. You should be aware, however, that feeding any wildlife continually may have complicated repercussions. The regular feeding of fish on coral reefs and at certain shark-watching and diving sites has already thrown up many questions and is frowned upon by some scientists. Use your discretion and bait wisely.

Reading the rings – aging fish by their scales

Look closely at a fish scale and you will see its rings of growth. This is just one way to estimte a fish's age.

The 13th-century Holy Roman Emperor Frederick II had the right idea. He had a pike which he "tagged" by threading a ring through its gill covers. The fish was then released – and caught again in 1497, some 267 years later! The legend goes that it was a monster of some 1350 kg (3000 lb) and almost 6 m (19 ft) long. All this sounds rather fantastical and a bit of a "big fish story," but recent advances in science suggest that there may be an element of truth in it.

Identifying individual fish is possible. The big scales on a mirror carp, the bars on the flank of a pike, the blotches on a koi carp, and the spots on a trout are all as particular to that fish as a fingerprint is to us. This fact, combined with observations on captive animals and pets, has given us a basic awareness of what ages fish can attain. It is known that certain species can live for a long time; there is an unconfirmed (and questionable) report of a koi carp (*Cyprinus carpio*) reaching a stately 228 years; spiny dogfish (*Squalus acanthias*) can certainly live for 40 years, maybe up to a hundred; lake sturgeon (*Acipenser fulvescens*) have been recorded at 82; and there is an official record of a female European eel (*Anguilla anguilla*) that reached 88 years of age!

But what if you want to tell the age of a fish that you haven't known all its or your life? Well, there are various ways. Depending on the species, otoliths (ear stones), fin rays, and opercula (the bony flaps covering the gills) can be used, but for the most part your fish needs to be dead to deliver the required information. With living fish it is generally the scales that provide the answer.

Most fish keep growing throughout their lives. They also have scales that coat and protect their bodies, a little like a suit of chain-mail armor. Now the useful thing is that the pattern and number of these scales remain the same throughout the fish's life, so as the fish grows the scales have to grow too in order to maintain total body coverage.

The scale-based technique for aging a fish assumes that growth is not constant throughout the year; it works particularly well if there is a seasonal aspect to the water temperature and hence to fish activity. Scales tend to grow fastest during the spring and summer, as the fish are feeding and the water is relatively warm. In winter the opposite is true and growth slows down. By looking at a fish scale under a microscope you can count the number of growth checks in very much the same way as you can count the rings on a saw-cut tree trunk: One check represented by a line or ring represents one year of age. What is also handy for ichthyologists (fish scientists) is that you can remove a scale and it will grow back with little or no negative long-term effect on the fish.

To scope a shark

A telescope isn't just a great investment for birdwatchers; it is also handy for watching fish – admittedly big ones! The basking shark (*Cetorhinus maximus*) is often best seen using a telescope (see equipment p. 27). The technique is simple: Find a piece of land that juts out into the sea as in the west or north of Britain, and sit on it. You increase your chances considerably if you choose a calm day, as this creates the "millpond" effect on the ocean that sea-watchers love.

Just sitting and watching makes for a thoroughly pleasant day, as even if the fish don't show there are usually loads of plants attracting large numbers of insects, and you are also in a good position to witness seabird movements or to catch a glimpse of the blue bullet form of a peregrine. Headlands and bays seem to create excellent conditions for plankton, either carried to the surface by water welling up from the deep or enjoying the shelter and warmer water these areas provide. Plankton is fodder for anything from a 10 m (33 ft) basking shark to the smaller fish, which in turn attract marine mammals that are worth looking out for at the same time.

Pondering over the sea requires concentration, as it is easy to become hypnotized or daunted by the sheer volume of water stretched out in front of you. But a careful combination of scanning with the naked eye and with binoculars or a telescope, should enable you to pick up any discrepancy in the smooth ocean surface caused by a shark's fin. It is important to keep a wide view at this point, as it is not unknown to be gazing intently out toward the horizon while a family of bottle-nosed dolphins plays unobserved at the bottom of the cliff below you. You are looking for clues such as a shining flank catching the light or what looks like a wave breaking or even heading in the opposite direction to the current. Watch the bows of boats for dolphins riding the pressure waves and large "snowdrift" flocks of seabirds such as kittiwakes or gannets, which often indicate fish near the surface and a good focal point for dolphins or harbor porpoises.

A basking shark, as you would be likely to see it when shark-watching

Superfish

It is rare that a wild fish attracts a crowd of interested bystanders, but there they all were, locals out for a Sunday constitutional, dog walkers and dogs, screaming children in strollers; suggesting that whatever it was they were watching out for was either deaf or so engrossed in what it was doing that it simply wasn't going to be disturbed by all this racket. And this turned out to be true, because what the people were watching were fish – Atlantic salmon (*Salmo salar*), called by some the "king of fish" – taking part in one of the most ambitious odysseys in the animal kingdom.

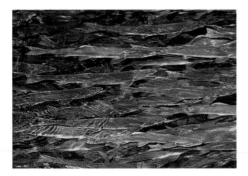

Salmon (*Salmo salar*)
migrating back from the
sea to spawning grounds

By the time they reach the estuary that was the scene of all this excitement, the fish have already come a long way, traveling downriver from their spawning grounds and out to sea, where they spent several years fattening up on the ocean's bounty. Then on some cue known only to themselves, they head back to the mouth of that same river – a journey that has already involved finning several thousand kilometers! This is the last stretch, the home strait as it were, when the fish leave the relative obscurity of the sea and embark on a hormonally driven dash to the gravely, well-oxygenated headwaters that are their spawning grounds. In fresh water they become ecological superheroes, supporting hugely important fisheries and sport for humans, and nourishing the many animals that prey on them, from bears to bald eagles. They have even been described as river fertilizer, as their bodies break down in the aftermath of their orgy and animals that drag their carcasses from the stream also provide a forestry service, enriching the soils in the river catchment areas.

The best thing about the salmon spectacle is that is very observer-friendly and relatively easy to predict. First you need to find a salmon river with a good, healthy population. Some rivers support a spring or autumn salmon run; others manage both. The conditions the fish are waiting for occur shortly after heavy rain or when the snow melts in spring and the river goes into spate. The salmon will have been queuing in the lower reaches for the seasonal freshets or spates to lift water levels high enough to carry them over obstacles, smoothing out the harsh rapids, weirs, and waterfalls where the best fish-watching is to be had. Here, the power of these fish, which are sometimes 1 m (3 ft) long, provides some remarkable athletic feats as they fight against the rushing currents. Rises in river levels may, however, be short-lived, and so progress upstream may consist of lots of stops and starts.

Where to look? Apart from weirs and waterfalls, any bottleneck in the river's flow is good. On quieter days the salmon can be seen sitting in pools below such obstacles waiting for the water to rise; they often stack up in slow, fin-flicking holding patterns, conserving energy until it is really needed and then unleashing it against the flow of the river. The best way to view them in these pools is to steal a technique from the angling fraternity and wear Polaroid sunglasses, which cut out the reflections and allow you to see "through" the surface of the water.

Depending on where you are watching your salmon and how fast they are making their journey, they will seem very different in appearance; those that have just left the ocean will be silvery in color, but as they head upstream many physical and physiological changes take place. These are most obvious in the cock fish – not only do they stop feeding, but they also take on battle dress; their flanks blush with all the colors of the rainbow and their jaws distort into a hideously warped war club to be used against other males: The jawbones lengthen to form a hook, known as a kype, and the teeth grow longer. At the same time their gut shrinks and their reproductive organs develop.

Although watching salmon leap up 3 m (10 ft) waterfalls is spectacular, the best bit for me is following them right up to their final destination, the culmination of all this effort – the gravel beds where the spawning occurs. Here the water is clear and alive even when the land is locked in the frosts of winter; you can watch the cocks jockeying for females and position with much splashing and foaming of water, and then see them "chaperone" their chosen mates, jealously guarding them from the attentions of any other males. The females then start thrashing the gravel with their bodies, scooping out the nest, or redd or hollow in which they lay their thousands of eggs. All this action takes place in water that can be so shallow the fishes' backs break the surface, and the charges of the males who have not yet attached themselves to a female can be so vigorous that some individuals get carried away and run aground. To watch the very end and beginning of this iconic fish's life cycle is well worth any effort involved in getting to the site.

Salmon eggs and young,
still with their egg sacs

Hot flush – spring time

The robust and feisty three-spined stickleback (*Gasterosteus aculeatus*) can be found in salt, brackish, and freshwater habitats pretty much throughout the Northern Hemisphere. It grows no more than 10 cm (4 in) long, but what it lacks in stature it makes up for in intrigue.

Male sticklebacks become very territorial in the spring when they feel the surge of their hormones; they blush with a crimson belly, and the normally silvery eye turns bright sky blue. Set up a 60 cm (2 ft) aquarium and let it settle down for a week (see p. 142). Provide plenty of detritus in the form of pond weed, dead leaves, and a little sediment, preferably from the pond from which you will be sourcing your sticklebacks.

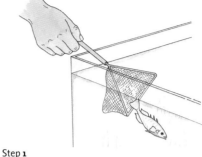

Step **1**

You will need:
- A small fishing net
- Male and female sticklebacks
- An aquarium already set up
- Mirror
- Cardboard
- Scissors

Step **2**

1 Find a male stickleback by fishing in a pond with a net on a warm spring day, and put him into your aquarium. Leave him for a week to settle in, feeding him on small pond creatures or bloodworms, available from most aquarium and pet stores.

2 Before too long you should see the fish sucking up mouthfuls of mud and arranging weed and detritus on the bottom of the tank. He is building a nest and will fuss over it with great attention to detail.

Step **3**

3 Place a mirror against the glass, and your fish should go into an aggressive display, thinking the reflection is a rival male in his part of the pond. He will attack it with his mouth open and spines erect.

4 Cut out three stickleback outlines from cardboard. Leave one white, color one red, and give the third just a red belly. Place these against the glass. Which one does your stickleback attack most vigorously?

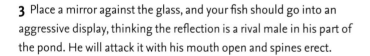
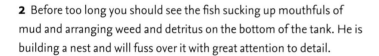
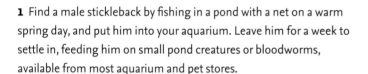

Step **4**

Step **5**

Step **6**

5 Then go out and catch a fat female stickleback who is full of eggs. The females look like the males but are an olive green color and lack the blue eyes. Introduce her to the tank and, assuming you have got it right, you will see a zigzag courting dance. If you are lucky, the female will be suitably impressed and the male will lead her into the nest. Here she will lay her eggs and he will fertilize them with his milt.

6 When all this is over, remove the female and in a few weeks the doting male will fan, aerate, and guard the eggs, before becoming a proud father before your very eyes. Remember, when you have learned as much as you want from your fish, you should release them in the water from which they came.

Red and you're dead

Male three-spined stickleback in breeding colors

The world-famous Dutch ethologist and 1973 Nobel Prize winner Nikolaas Tinbergen kept a fish tank like the one described above in his laboratory. One spring he noticed that, at a certain time every day, his captive male stickleback would start swimming in an excited manner and attacking the glass of his home. It didn't take the astute Tinbergen long to make the association between his agitated fish and the movements of the red postal van that drove past his window every day at the same time. The fish was responding to the color of the van, which was the same as the belly of a rival male. This association between what are called sign stimuli and the resulting behavioral reflexes of the fish led to a series of very neat and beautifully simple experiments, on which the above project is based.

In certain lakes in North America, some male three-spined sticklebacks have a black belly and throat instead of the normal bright red one. It has been found that, although they have a little more difficulty impressing the ladies, they live longer, as their black throat doesn't attract predators in the same way as the red.

Looking through the mirror

One of the problems of being a terrestrial animal trying to peer into the underwater world is that the interface between the two – the surface of the water – reflects light. In fact it does this in more than one direction; anything but the smoothest, stillest water has a surface that is being interfered with, rippled, tugged, torn, and pulled in all directions by the wind and currents below. This means that light bounces in all directions, so that no matter how clear the water is, looking through it can be difficult, if not plain impossible.

Fishermen get around this problem and reduce the glare on bright days by donning polarizing sunglasses. These have a special coating that reduces the amount of reflected light. As light comes down from the sun, hits the water surface and bounces in all directions, the light that is flung off in the horizontal plane is what is known as "glare." Polarizing glasses cancel out this glare, leaving just the ambient light and allowing the wearer to see through the surface. It's as simple as that. When I was little, the only good polarizing sunglasses were huge and made you look like Elvis, but nowadays they come in a variety of styles ideal for the fashion-conscious fish-watcher!

Underwater viewer

Another way to see beyond the confusion of the surface is to use this simple device, which is equally effective in salt and fresh water. It works on the principle of pressing a clear window against the water, cutting out ripples, while a baffle cuts down the glare and improves viewing. The beauty of the design is that, if the window is damaged, you can replace it very easily.

You will need:
• an ice-cream tub with a close-fitting lid
• scissors or a knife that will cut through the tub
• plastic waterproof paint – black
• plastic wrap or clear cellophane

Step 1

1 Cut the bottom out of the tub and the center out of the lid, leaving the edge with the seal to act as a frame.

2 Paint the insides of the tub to eliminate glare.

3 Stretch the clear film over the top of the tub.

4 Put on the lid to fasten the film in place, press the plastic wrap against the surface of the water, and start viewing.

Step 2

Step 3

Step 4

Total immersion technique
try snorkeling

My first experience of this ultimate underwater-viewing experience was lying on the rocks with my face encased in a mask immersed in the shallow water of an intertidal pool. It was just a matter of time before I cast off my land ties and started experiencing the freedom of getting as close to being a fish as a human can.

All you need to get started are the regular mask, snorkel, and fins, but a wet suit is a good idea in temperate zones, as the cold can really put the kibosh on your enjoyment and limit your time in the water. Once you are kitted out, a whole new vista opens up. Animals that cannot tolerate the intertidal zone are just a fin stroke away, and the diversity of life to be seen is extraordinary. I remember being totally blown away by the colors and the curious creatures that I hadn't even heard of, and that was just below the surface off a pier in a south-of-England holiday resort.

A fresh approach to fresh water

It's a strange thing, but although most of us wouldn't think twice about dressing up in fins, mask, and snorkel at the seaside, donning the same gear in the course of a riverside walk seems tantamount to social suicide. This is a shame, because river snorkeling can be every bit as rewarding as ocean snorkeling. The only real differences are that your buoyancy is less in fresh water; and in some rivers, where there may be obstacles and little space for maneuvering, fins become more of a hindrance than a help.

Maybe the reason river snorkeling hasn't caught on is that it is just too extrovert. Don't be surprised if you are greeted by a crowd of less enlightened observers. Most are just curious about what you are doing; those with richer imaginations may think you are a police diver looking for a body. I remember feeling a little self-conscious the first time I put on my suit of black crushed neoprene and slipped into my local river. But after a few minutes observing trout lying up in the eddies behind rocks, hearing the constant fizz and bubble of the moving water in my ears, watching frisky minnows chasing each other in the shallows, and even being allowed in the deeper water to hold court with the king of fish, the salmon, any embarrassment about what

I was doing or looked like dissolved into the watery world in which I was immersed. The experience is so addictive that I often leave the water after an hour or so, having lost most of the feeling in my extremities, just one short shiver away from hypothermia. But never mind that – this is the only way really to enter the underwater world. There are no words to describe what it's like – I just want to encourage everyone to share it. Come on in, the water's lovely.

A few safety tips

I do not want to scaremonger here, but entering any underwater environment is potentially hazardous. As is crossing the road, of course, but we take those rules for granted, as we have known them all our lives. And with the water, as with the road, the precautions are just common sense once you think about them.

☀ Take a class, even if you are not intending to use scuba equipment. Snorkeling and scuba diving share many skills and techniques, and scuba diving in itself is a very useful skill for the naturalist, but if this feels like overkill, there are professionally run classes that focus on snorkeling. Make sure you can snorkel in a controlled environment before taking the plunge into wild water.

☀ Choose your water wisely and avoid swimming in fast-flowing water, locations that are subject to strong currents or flash floods, or anywhere upstream from a weir, rapid, or waterfall. It is all too easy to be swept away.

☀ Buddy up. An experience shared is an experience doubled, as they say. It is also sensible to swim with a partner in case one of you gets into difficulties. It is twice as easy for two to get out of trouble as one.

☀ Keep a lookout for predators in the ocean and in some freshwater habitats, especially in the tropics and subtropics. I realize that getting close to wild animals is what it's all about, but there are some where a little distance is preferable. I have been surprised a couple of times by a crocodile as I have tinkered around in rivers in Africa and South America, forgetting that I'm not at home in England, where such precautions are unnecessary. So do your homework first.

Spineless wonders
invertebrates

An alien returning to its spaceship after a visit to Earth would report back to its leader that Earth isn't populated by a race of clever apes bent on self-destruction but by a huge number of strange, spineless creatures that are found in places as extreme as the skull-crushing depths of the oceans, the peaks of the highest mountains, the burning deserts, and the frigid polar regions. The report would put these creatures as the most important organisms on Earth and, like it or not, it would be right. The invertebrates rule the planet, not once upon a time, not after a nuclear holocaust, but now, today.

The invertebrates have been doing what they do for a very long time. The first arthropods were scuttling around on the planet's surface around 500 million to 600 million years ago, and the soft worm and jellyfish-like ancestors were oozing around the oceans and wet places well before that. Over eons of time these animals have perfected their craft, becoming highly specialized, integral cogs in the machinery of every ecosystem on Earth.

Above: Coconut crab
(*Birgus lattro*)
Right: Snails

Jargon busting
what is an invertebrate?

Calling these creatures bugs, mini-beasts or creepy-crawlies is all very well in its way, but because there are so many of them, learning some of the names and classifications can help to avoid confusion. Put simply, an invertebrate is any living animal without a backbone. The majority of these belong to groups with legs, including a group called the arthropods, which means "jointed legs." What they have in common is an exoskeleton – a skeleton on the outside of the body – and they achieve flexibility a bit like a human in a suit of armor: Their limbs and bodies, as you might guess from the name, are jointed and segmented. The arthropods make up the majority of living creatures – recent estimates have suggested that there are between 25 million and 30 million species in the world, most of them yet to be discovered. It would obviously be impossible to cover all of them within these pages, and so here is a brief introduction to those most commonly encountered by the naturalist.

millipede

Millipedes, centipedes, and allies (Subphylum Myriapoda): there are around 15,000 species of these, split into four further classes, the most frequently encountered of which are the millipedes (Class Diplopoda) and centipedes (Class Chilopoda). One thing they all have in common is an elongated body with many legs running along its length.

mole cricket

Insects and allies (Subphylum Hexapoda): the majority of the million or so species that have been described in this group are insects. They are further broken down into 28 orders, some of which we will look at in greater detail in the next chapter. All the hexapods have six legs, their bodies are divided into three parts – head, thorax, and abdomen – and they have a breathing system that comprises a network of hollow tubes called trachea.

Florida jumping spider

The eight-legged ones (Class Arachnida): about 80,000 of these species regularly scare humans for no better reason than that they are "spidery." The arachnids contain 11 subclasses, which range from huge Goliath bird-eating spiders (*Theraphosa leblondi*) and fearsome scorpions to the smallest of mites and ticks.

edible crab

Crabs and allies (Phylum Crustacea) are primarily based in the world's oceans and fresh waters, although among their 30,000 or so species there are a few that have managed to invade the land.

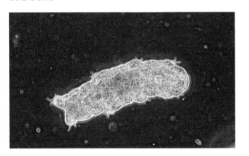
water bear

Velvet worms (Phylum Onychophora), tongue worms (Phlyum Pentastomida), and water bears (Phylum Tardigrada) are some of the more oddball arthropods. The velvet worms in particular seem to represent a "missing link" between worms and arthropods, whereas the tardigrades are a must-see for anyone with a microscope and the time to look closely at the surface of moss leaves.

garden snail

The nonarthropod invertebrates are mainly soft-bodied creatures with no true skeleton and include molluscs, true worms, echinoderms, flatworms, nematodes, bryozoans, sponges, jellyfish, and anemones. Examples of these can be found in many habitats from the seashore to the bottom of the garden. As there are so many species of insects, I am devoting all the next chapter to them, and will deal with my favorites among the other invertebrates here.

Arachnids
eight-legged miracles

The arachnids are forever being lumped together with insects, a misconception that isn't helped by the fact that many insect field guides have a section on spiders at the back. But there is a simple rule here – anything with more than six legs is not an insect, and that applies to all the arachnids.

The Goliath bird-eating spider, measuring 20 cm (8 in) across at full stretch, is the biggest of the spiderkind.

Although it sometimes seems as if the whole world is suffering from what I think of as "Miss Muffet syndrome" and what other people call arachnophobia, there is really no reason to fear spiders as a whole. Of the 35,000 species in the world, only 20 to 30 are dangerously toxic to humans. On the other hand, there are thousands of reasons for liking them. For a start, their diversity is stunning – they are a truly versatile bunch with a mind-boggling variety of strategies for getting through life. Some spiders spin elaborate traps, some jump, some parachute, some scavenge from the kills of other spiders, and some notoriously eat their partners once mating is over. But they all have certain things in common, and the best way to starting getting to know them is to look at those features.

Know your way around a spider

The best way to learn about their anatomy is to catch one and investigate it using a hand lens and a bug restrainer (see pp. 33 and 39), as most species are very active and will not give you much observation time before deciding to put those eight legs to good use. If you can't restrain a live spider, you should be able to find a molted exoskeleton in a neglected corner among the old spiders' webs – try the cupboard under the stairs or a dark corner of the garden shed. This will give you a good idea of how a spider is put together without having to deal with the living beast scuttling around.

The main things that all arachnids have in common are a body divided into two main parts – a cephalothorax (which means 'head chest') and an abdomen – plus four pairs of walking legs, a pair of pedipalps (which look like legs in spiders and are the pincers in scorpions), and chelicerae (the piercing fangs of spiders and micro-pincers of scorpions).

Pedipalps or palps: leglike appendages that sit either side of the mouth and point forward. They are rich in tactile sensory hairs and chemoreceptors, allowing the spider to "feel" its way around in much the same way as an insect uses its antennae.

Eyes: usually eight; fewer in some species. The position of the eyes is a useful pointer in spider identification.

Legs: are covered in the same sensory hairs as the palps and other parts of the body, so that the spider can "feel" its environment as it walks along.

Mouth: consists of a set of appendages that process its prey as it passes through them, as if they were different stages on a factory production line.

Chelicerae, or fangs: These are a versatile feature, used for spearing prey, defense, picking things up, winding silk, digging, carrying eggs around, and even, in some species, for rubbing together to make a noise.

Cephalothorax: contains most of the sensory organs, the mouth, stomach, and the muscles that power the legs, all enclosed in a hard exoskeleton.

Abdomen: it's soft and contains the heart, breathing apparatus, sex organs, and silk glands. It can be podgy plump, slim, or withered and shriveled depending on the species, sex, and stage of development.

Carapace: the shell-like capsule on top of the body. Look underneath, and you will see the ridges to which the muscles are attached.

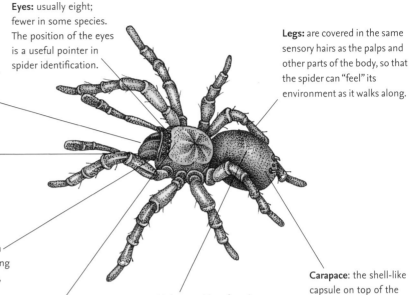

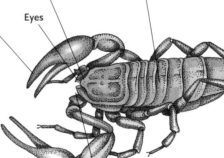

Eyes

Legs

Pedipalps or palps

Jumping spider showing its chelicerae, or fangs, and large eyes – all the better for hunting

Versatile hairs

A spider's hairs perform a multitude of functions, from camouflage to grooming. It's hair that enables spiders to crawl up walls and stroll across ceilings. The specialized hairs on its feet are called scopulae and are divided into hundreds of even smaller extensions, each with a flattened paddlelike tip. Like a coaster sticking to the bottom of a wet glass, each paddle "grips" by using the surface tension of the microscopic film of water found on most objects.

The larger and more obvious hairs are sensory in their function, for example, to tell a spider whether or not an object is moving. Other very fine, feathery hairs act as ears: They are blown by the tiniest vibration or breeze and can literally tell a spider where its next meal is coming from. Some species have hairs on their legs which comb the silk that makes a web to produce the right texture. Water spiders (*Argyroneta aquatica*) use the hairs on their bodies to trap a layer of air, allowing them to breathe.

Some wolf spiders (*Lycosa* and *Pardosa* spp.) use their palps as part of the courtship ritual, to make sure that a female knows what their intentions are and is prepared to reciprocate – a useful precaution if an unwilling female may literally bite your head off.

Spider silk

Silk, which is produced from a spider's abdomen, is the main reason for their incredible success as a life form. It makes both a home and a hunting ground, and at the end of the day, if everything goes wrong it can be rolled up, moved on, and recycled in a more congenial spot.

This crab spider is pretending to be dead to protect itself from predators. An arachnid's legs work by being full of blood under high pressure; when the animal dies, there is no blood to keep the legs extended, which is why you find a corpse with the legs tucked up into the body. One of the easiest ways to tell the sex of an adult spider is to look at the tips of its palps: if it is a male it will look as if it has boxing gloves on! These large, bulbous tips are used like miniature turkey basters to inject sperm into the female.

You can see the spinnerets of this black widow spider (*Latrodectus*). Silk flows out of the tiny nozzle at the tip of each spinneret. It starts off as a liquid soup of protein in the abdomen, then hardens and stretches when it comes into contact with air.

There are nearly as many designs of web as there are types of spider; they range from the simple tangles you expect to walk into in a haunted house to the last word in silk technology, the orb web. I have had many moments of utter amazement with spiders, but one that summed up the awesome qualities of silk took place in Mexico, when I was coming back to camp after a nocturnal tarantula hunt and had turned off my head lamp. I was stumbling along when I found myself caught up in what I knew was spider silk; on turning on my flashlight I was confronted by a wonderful tangle of golden threads all around me. The spinner of this glorious structure was dangling inches from the end of my nose. It was a member of the genus of golden orb web spiders (*Nephila*), a real beauty of a beast some 8 cm (3 in) across its leg span, with a web among the strongest of all spider creations. As I was trying to extricate myself from this horror movie scene, I noticed another creature in a similar predicament. A lizard had fallen foul of the same trap and was suspended in the silk next to me.

As if this wasn't enough evidence of the qualities of spider silk, the webs of other golden orb spiders are apparently used as fishing nets by indigenous peoples in South America and New Guinea. A web is collected in a hoop of vegetation, lowered into a stream and drawn up again when it makes a catch. Any holes created by overenthusiastic fish are simply darned up with a needle in the same way a fisherman would repair a regular net.

Luring an arachnid from its den

Many spiders rarely leave their silken palaces unless it's to find a mate or to grab a passing snack. Digging a spider from its burrow is a destructive and invasive thing to do, and so you need to lure them out instead. Look on dry banks and especially walls with crumbly mortar, and you will see tiny burrows that show up white, being reinforced by a dense weave of silk. The entrance of a hole that is occupied will be neat and there will usually be no spoil heap.

Wolf spiders and tarantulas sit in the mouths of their holes at night, awaiting unsuspecting prey items. But these animals are incredibly sensitive to vibrations or airborne disturbances such as might be caused by an eager naturalist, and they will rapidly retreat to the safety of their lairs. Pour fresh water into the entrance of the burrow and any resident spider will come rapidly to the surface. Quickly block its retreat, place a cup over it, and secure it for identification, then as soon as you have finished and the burrow has dried out, let it go. This may seem a bit brutal, but the spider suffers little and its home remains intact.

Alternatively, lure a spider by persuading it that you are a meal. Strike a tuning fork, gently touch one of the silk strands across the doorway of a spider's home with it, and the spider should dash out to investigate. The web is there to catch the spider's dinner, and it will think your musical contribution is an insect tripping over its trap. You may even hear its palps striking the metal of the fork, which is an eerie sound. If you can't get hold of a tuning fork, try a party blower with a piece of grass taped to the end – unravel the tube, hold the grass against one of the threads, and blow.

Handling venomous arachnids

Scorpions can be caught using a modification of this technique. Locate a lair – usually an elongated keyhole-type affair if it is in exposed soil – gently poke a twig or blade of grass into it, and jiggle it around. If the scorpion is hungry, it will grab on and will be too stubborn to let go. Use a pair of "soft" forceps (ordinary forceps or tweezers with foam rubber or a pad of parcel tape wound around the tips) on either side of its sting to stop it retreating once it has realized its error.

The orb web is made from the minimum of materials: Less than 500 mg (⅟₆₀ oz) of silk is used for an average-size web, although if you were to unwind it it could be over 20 m (70 ft) in length! Each web is spun using touch alone and only takes about 20 to 30 minutes to complete. It really is a miracle of silknology.

Luring a Kenyan wolf spider from its hole

Some scorpions pack their main punch with big pincers; others have weak and narrow pincers but shoot venom out of their other end. So it is a wise precaution to treat all of them with respect and not touch them with bare hands. The same applies to poisonous spiders.

So given that any archnid you stumble across will promptly try to make a dash for it, how do you get close enough to have a good look? The trick is to stop it briefly in its tracks by simply popping a container over it. This can be a cup, a net, a hat, or a scarf – it doesn't have to hold the creature for long, just long enough to give you time to think.

What you do next depends on the species and the nature of the terrain. If you are on level ground, slip a piece of cardboard under the cup to trap your quarry, or gently coerce it to walk into a specimen pot – with a scorpion, I would again recommend the use of "soft" forceps so that the grip doesn't damage the animal.

This treatment is too rough for spiders, which are particularly fragile. If – and only if – you know what you are doing, you can pick a large spider up by gripping it gently but confidently on either side of the cephalothorax. This sort of spider has two main defence strategies and the one it chooses depends largely on which part of the world it is in. American theraphosids rely on a collection of urticating hairs, which under the microscope look like a collection of barbed spears, and are attached to the spider's abdomen by a weak pedicel. When threatened, these animals kick their legs against their abdomens and send forth a cloud of hairs, which when they get in your eyes, nose, mouth, or soft skin can ruin your day. Learning which species "kick up" like this comes with experience. So, if in doubt, treat them all as having the potential to do it. The rest of the world's tarantulas do not have this ability, but they defend themselves with their "fangs."

The black-light phenomenon

Many invertebrates are out and about at night and are hard to spot, even with the aid of a torch, because they are a similar color to their backgrounds. This is where a "black light" comes in. These are small, portable, and widely available in the sort of shop that sells tie-dye shirts and crystals. Buy as powerful a one as you can. When out at night scorpion-hunting, wave the light about in front of you, and pretty much every scorpion you come across will take on an unearthly quality, glowing a weird kind of bright green in the uv light and making it very easy to watch. No one really knows why this phenomenon occurs, but it is very useful for the nocturnal naturalist.

The world wide web

Although the very fragility of a spider's web is part of its attraction, it is a shame to think that these phenomenal feats of design and construction rarely last longer than a day. However, if you find a web without a spider in residence, it is possible to collect and preserve one of these fabulous structures. Choose a still day and make sure the web is dry, with no droplets of dew.

Step 1

You will need:
- the most gorgeous orb web you can find
- a sheet of newspaper
- a can of white or black spray paint
- a can of artist's fixative (available at art shops) or hair spray
- a sheet of cardboard large enough to fit the web on and in a color that contrasts well with the paint
- scissors

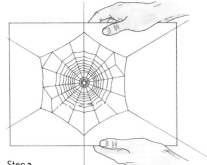

1 Position the newspaper behind the web so that you don't get paint all over whatever is behind it, then spray the web evenly and lightly on both sides from a distance of about 40 cm (16 in) – much closer and the pressure of the paint will damage the web. Leave it to dry for a while and repeat.

Step 3

2 Once the web is dry for the second time, spray it on both sides with the artist's fixative or hair spray to make it sticky.

3 Before it dries, carefully line the cardboard up with the web and push it against the silk. This is the most delicate part of the operation – you have to get it right the first time or you will end up with a sticky mess when what you want is a perfect web stuck to the card.

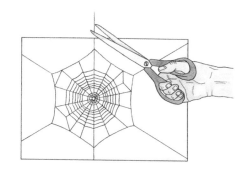

Step 4

4 Cut the supporting strands with scissors to release the web from its surroundings. Spray it with another coat of fixative to make sure it is firmly in place.

5 Hang the card on your wall and consider starting a collection of the orbs of different species.

Crustaceans
arthropod rulers of the ocean and a few damp places

Familiar to anyone who has gone poking around in rock pools and crevices down by the shore, these are some of the first creatures a young protonaturalist will learn to catch and carry home in a bucket. They are commercially important – we eat them – and I have even had a leather wallet stolen by one! I'm referring to the crustaceans, a primarily aquatic group, some of whom have taken on the insects and found a niche for themselves on dry land.

Woodlice

Woodlice are probably the most familiar of land-dwelling crustaceans, but flip one over, and you may get a surprise. Toward the back end, behind seven pairs of legs fighting to turn the body the right way up again, is an area of what look like pale scales but are actually gills.

Gills are the devices that enable animals to breathe in water. They are designed to absorb oxygen from the water and to get rid of waste gases, a process that works more efficiently if the skin covering the gills is thin and the blood flows as close to the surface as possible.

Though the woodlouse is armor-plated on top, the plates underneath are very thin, with the gills near the surface. They can absorb oxygen from the air, but only in the presence of water, in which the oxygen can dissolve. This is why you find woodlice lurking in damp places – if they dry out, they don't just dehydrate, they suffocate.

The secret of land invasion – a woodlouse and its gills

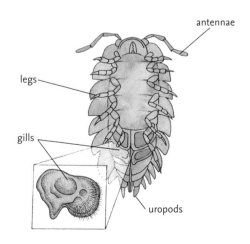

antennae

legs

gills

uropods

What woodlice like

In the absence of their beloved dark and damp conditions, woodlice feel uncomfortable and keep moving, which is why if you see a woodlouse away from cover on a sunny day, it will be stepping out purposefully. Once it finds a suitable habitat, it will take a few turns around it to pick the perfect spot, then simply stop. This experiment will give you some insight into its approach to life.

You will need:
- a board or tabletop about 30 cm (12 in) square
- a sheet of acrylic the same size as the board
- plasticine
- black cardboard or paper
- cotton balls
- a water-based marker pen
- 10 woodlice

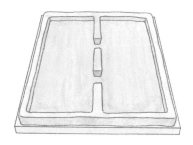

Step **1**

1 Roll out the plasticine to form long sausage shapes and use these to make a wall around the table or board. This is your arena.

2 Use three smaller strips of plasticine to divide the arena in half, leaving gaps between them so that you have two chambers with two "doorways" between them.

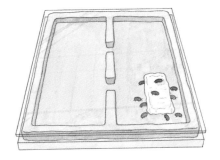

Step **2**

3 Put a piece of damp cotton wool in one side of the arena and introduce five woodlice into each compartment. Put the acrylic lid on quickly to keep the woodlice in.

4 Check after an hour or so, and you will see that all the woodlice have been attracted to the damp environment of the cotton wool.

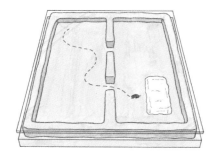

Step **3**

5 Repeat the experiment using a single woodlouse. Put it in the dry half of the arena and trace its movements with a marker pen – once it gets wind of the cotton wool, these become much more focused as it tries to make a "beeline" for the damp.

6 For phase 2 of the experiment, remove the cotton balls and allow the area to dry out. Then cover half the arena with the black cardboard and watch as the woodlice scuttle toward the dark areas they prefer.

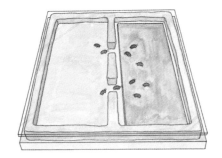

Step **4**

The robber, or coconut, crab is a land-living crab, but it still breathes through gills, which are surrounded by spongy tissue to keep them moist.

Where have crabs put them?

We all know that crabs live in water, so why don't they have gills? Well, the fact is that they do – it's just that they're hidden away inside the body. Next time you're at the beach, lift a crab out of the water. Many shore crabs can tolerate this for a while – they're used to it because of the daily ebb and flow of the tide. A crab out of water will probably start blowing bubbles from around its mouth, which is your clue to how it breathes. Blowing bubbles is how it ventilates its gills, but because the limbs used for this in other crustaceans are not present in crabs, the job is done by the base plate of the mouth parts. This wafts water into the cavities on either side of the body, under the carapace. Once the water has passed over these, it is left to "leak" out through pores between the crab's legs. To demonstrate this, squirt food dye from a pipette into the area in front of a living crab in a tank of seawater: You will see how the liquid gets sucked in and where it leaves the body, too.

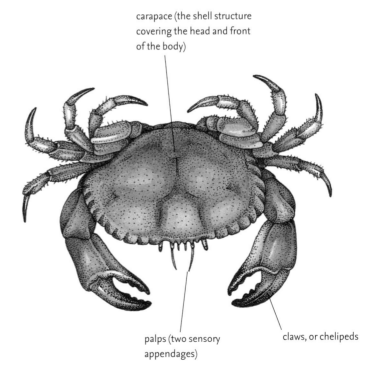

carapace (the shell structure covering the head and front of the body)

palps (two sensory appendages)

claws, or chelipeds

House swap

Hermit crabs (the common British species is *Pagurus berhardus*) are not true crabs, but they are familiar to anyone who has stared into a rock pool for long enough and been surprised when a usually sedate mollusc gets up and sprints off! Although they have a carapace, it doesn't cover their soft abdomens, and so almost all hermit crabs require the extra protection of an old mollusk shell. For land hermit crabs, these shells give their residents protection against the elements, too, with many tropical beaches looking like a caravan park in the summer holidays as hundreds of these comical-looking creatures trundle around in all but the hottest weather, when they burrow into the sand or seek the shade of bushes.

The biggest hermit crab is worth a mention here, as it is also the largest land-based arthropod in the world, the spectacular and now sadly endangered robber, or coconut, crab. These animals use a mollusk shell only for their initial tentative steps onto land. Later they take up residence deep within cracks and crevices, emerging at night to scavenge. Incidentally, it was a robber crab that made off with my wallet on an island in the Indian Ocean!

Looking for a new pad. A hermit crab measures up a new shell using its pincers as a caliper.

Some hermit crabs, especially in the tropics, have invaded the land, turning beaches into crustacean caravan parks.

As a hermit crab grows and the confines of the mollusk shell become too close for comfort, it has to look out for new accommodation. You may be lucky enough to observe one moving house if you keep it in a vivarium or aquarium (depending – obviously – on whether it is a land- or water-dwelling species) and provide a variety of different-size gastropod mollusk shells for it to consider. Persuading your crab to leave its house is easier than it sounds. Many can be extracted by gently pulling on the front limbs; this can turn into something like a tug-of-war as the crab often grips the inside of the shell with special modified limbs, but keep up the pressure and you should get there in the end. Blowing on them works well with land-based species.

Once you have extracted your crab, have a good look at the back end of its body: It is a floppy, soft, and vulnerable sack, and you can also see the limbs that have turned into grippers. Now put it back into its tank and watch it scuttle around, measuring the shells for size with its legs and using the large pincer like a caliper. When it selects its "des res," it rapidly reverses inside. Panic over.

In the wild the changeover is equally rapid and nervously performed, but usually the animal will have preselected a shell, and the changeover is rather like a bashful person swapping underpants.

Just a word on shell collecting here. In most places this is a harmless thing to do but, as ever, take only what you need. In some tropical nature reserves, particularly on islands that support populations of land hermit crabs, collecting shells may contribute to a housing crisis denying crabs homes. Find someone in authority and check out the position before you start gathering.

Catching your crustaceans

One easy but effective way to find members of this diverse group is simply to look for them, flipping and turning over stones and seaweed to expose whatever is living underneath. You will discover a plethora of barnacles, sea slaters, and other rock-pool creatures in this way – just remember the golden rule of returning anything you have moved to its original position after you have looked. Attaching an old shaving mirror to a stick and using this to look underneath ledges and into cracks and crevices is especially useful if the rocks are too big to move; the mirror illuminates these dark hidey-holes by reflecting sunlight too.

The "original" woodlouse, the sea slater is a little more water tolerant than its truly terrestrial counterparts.

A stout pole is another useful tool – not only does it act as a handy third leg while you negotiate slippery weed and rocks, but also certain shallow-water species of lobster can be observed by prodding gently into likely looking crevices and lairs. If a lobster is in residence, it will usually defend its corner by grabbing the intrusive stick with its pincers, allowing you to lift it out of its lair. The chances of success increase if you look around rocks at the lowest tides.

Many of the free-moving crustaceans such as crabs and lobsters are scavengers, and so you can lure them in with dead animal material. As a kid during my summer holidays, I used to bait rock pools with scraps begged from the butcher or fishmonger or with the contents of my ham sandwich. Crabs of many kinds would come scuttling from all corners, some even leaving the water to skip over into neighboring rock pools. They would congregate around the bait like hyenas at a kill, to be joined by smaller hermit crabs and the prawns that were actually my intended target.

This was my first lesson in what a good sense of smell these little carnivores have. Since then I have used numerous variations of a baited trap: a large bamboo stem or log to catch freshwater crayfish in Australia; home-made wooden boxes crudely nailed together and drilled out to the rough specifications of a lobster pot; and modified plastic drink bottles weighted down so that they don't wash away. They all use the same principle and can all be effective.

Burrowing species such as the true shrimps can be collected in a flat-bottomed net, available at any seaside resort or from a specialist netmaker or natural history supplier. For the free-swimming and larval stages, try a plankton net – a long, tapered net with a collection vessel at the end that can be towed slowly behind a boat. All the marine crustaceans have a larval stage, so there is an enormous number of little creatures floating about out there: the great drifting masses that help to feed the rest of the food chain. In fact, by catching your

Rock pools provide habitats for a whole host of marine life. Starfish and urchins are likely to be found in rock pools at low tide, and you will probably also find small crustaceans, worms, and even a few fish.

crustaceans in a plankton net, you are imitating the feeding habits of the filter-feeding baleen whales and sharks.

Once you have gathered up your crustaceans, the single most useful piece of equipment you can have is a tank. Forget your bucket and spade; this is *the* essential for anyone visiting a beach. A tank can be anything that holds water and has transparent sides to it. Plastic is better than glass, because there is less chance of it getting broken, although it may be scratched in the course of your rambles over a rocky shore.

As soon as you lift an aquatic animal out of its realm, its beauty is compromised – all sorts of bits that are usually supported by the water flop. Creatures that live in shells shut up shop when feeling threatened, and little mechanisms such as the feeding motions of a barnacle or the breathing or burrowing of a prawn cease to function if the animal is divorced from the medium in which it is designed to function. But pop any of these creatures into a tank of water, and sooner or later they relax and carry on with their lives, leaving you in the privileged position of being able to watch. Mussels open up and show you their siphons; a blob of shapeless jelly becomes egg cases or anemones; a section of seaweed stem reveals itself as a pipefish, and the starfish that looked dead a moment ago starts gliding around at a surprising speed.

Collecting the crusts

Probably the simplest way of making a collection of crustaceans is to gather discarded crab carapaces from the shore. Walk along any strand line, and you will find evidence of these animals in some form or another. Sometimes it will just be the odd limb or fragment of shell; at others, especially at certain seasons, after storms or when many animals are molting, a strand line can become a breaker's yard of empty husks and fragments of carapace – twisted, tangled wreckage of many species. Because of the fragile nature of these cast-offs, the shore-scouring naturalist can be pretty sure that they have not traveled far and that species represented in this way are to be found in nearby waters.

One of the great natural spectacles – king, or horseshoe, crabs (*Limulus polyphemus*) coming ashore to breed and lay eggs.

Collecting the carapaces of a common species can tell you a lot. For a start, no two are the same – they show huge variation in color and pattern, both at different stages of their lives (they shed their exoskeletons in the same way as all the other arthropods) and between individuals. A display of the carapaces of common green shore crabs (*Carcinus maenas*) or blue crabs (*Callinectes sapidus*) is an impressive sight, especially if you can gather a range of sizes, from juvenile to adult. If you come across the fresh cast of one of these crabs, you will be able to see how it escaped from its own skin by popping the carapace off the top: It's a bit like opening the hood of a car and crawling out of the split between this and the underside of the body. The difference between a molted exoskeleton and a dead crab can easily be ascertained by passing the remains under your nose. A shed skin will be less upsetting to your sense of smell. It will also have pale, hollow-looking eye stalks, because when an animal molts, everything is removed from the old skin – even fine details such as the eyes and gills are part of the exoskeleton.

If you find a cast like this in a rock pool, it is worth looking around and even turning over a few stones – you may find the freshly

Like a car wrecker's yard, a strandline can tell the shore naturalist a lot about the local resident crustaceans.

molted crab, or "'peeler," itself, still soft, pale, and defenseless, its new exoskeleton not having hardened up yet. Investigate the old skin carefully, and you will also be able to see how the crab's discarded "tail," or "apron," resembles a lobster's or a shrimp's but has been curled up beneath its body. Inside you will also be able to see the fluffy gill filaments that are usually hidden away from view within the protective armor of the carapace.

In the course of your rambles you may also stumble upon the husk of a freshly molted prawn or shrimp floating in a rock pool or even bits of the carapace of lobsters washed up by the tide. Sadly, these are rarely complete – they are too fragile to survive even the shortest journey. It is worth combing any shore after a severe storm, as interesting flotsam and jetsam may be kicked up. Get there as soon as possible, as nature's beachcombers will also be quick to mobilize – the gulls, vultures, and other scavengers are as keen to get to any animal material as you are. Storms have the unfortunate habit of tearing from their safe holes and crevices many species that would otherwise give themselves up only reluctantly – and not just crustaceans either. I have seen the strand line resemble a white stripe as far as the eye could see, thanks to the anaemic-looking bodies of thousands of masked crabs (*Corystes cassivelaunus*), a species that is rarely seen, as it spends its life buried under the sand. Other sand residents, such as clams, as well as ocean drifters and sedentary creatures such as goose barnacles (*Lepas anatifera*), may all be stranded by rough weather and become rich pickings for the shore naturalist.

The softies
mollusks

The name "mollusk" is derived from the Latin word *mollis*, which means soft, and once you have got through to the living animal – often encased in a not-so-soft shell – this is one thing every member of this group has in common. Among their 10,000-or-so-strong number is found so much variety, both on land and in water, that it may be hard to believe they all belong to the same phylum. At one end of the scale is the slow and unprepossessing slug, while the other are the cognitive, intelligent, and active cephalopods: the octopuses, cuttlefish, and squid, which have abilities that begin to compare with vertebrates'. I will never forget an octopus that slithered from an old drink can that had been its home onto the deck of a boat I was on. When I popped it in a tank for further study, it changed color from red to a ghostly bleached white and looked at me with an eye so soulful that I immediately felt guilty and released it. The same couldn't be said for its lowly brethren the clams that I ate for supper the same day!

As a group, their huge diversity of form may have something to do with the fact that they have had plenty of time to work on it – these animals first came creeping into being some 600 million years ago, and since then they have come up with every possible body design, ranging from chitons, clams, nudibranchs (sea slugs), and snails to octopus and squid. They can be found in most ecological systems, from the deepest ocean trenches to the tops of mountains, from lakes and streams to barren deserts. There are seven different kinds:

Aplacophora, the marine mud-dwelling "wormlike" mollusks.
Polyplacophora, chitons, which have "chain mail" shells.
Monoplacophora, primitive marine creatures such as limpets.
Scaphopoda, the tusk or tooth shells.
Gastropoda, snails and shell-less slugs.
Bivalves, including scallops, mussels, and cockles, which have two halves to their shells.
Cephalopoda, the squids, cuttlefish, and octopuses.

But look closely at their diverse soft forms and you will find a few things they all have in common.

Most have an **internal or external shell** made of calcium. The hard shell in the snails and bivalve mollusks is relatively large and serves to protect the animal. In the fast-swimming squid, however, it is reduced to a small, internal pen-shaped structure, while in octopuses, nudibranchs, and some of the land-living slugs, it has been lost totally.

Mantle: one or more lobes or folds in the body wall that lines the shell. It contains glands which secrete the materials that form the shell.

Muscular foot: used for moving around, digging into sand or mud, or clinging onto hard, rocky surfaces so tightly that even the roughest sea cannot shift them. In the squid and octopus, the single foot has evolved to become a number of arms or tentacles.

Unsegmented soft body: it has to be kept moist to stay alive.

Belly feet: the gastropods

"Snail trails"

Slugs and snails are, in fact, much the same thing, except that most snails have a hard shell they can crawl into whereas most slugs do not. Both are gastropods, or "belly foots," a term that describes them well, as they get around on a single, large, muscular foot that sits underneath their whole body. Like so many invertebrates, they have a bit of an image problem, combining a reputation as pests with moist and slimy habits that a lot of people find repugnant. However, as an open-minded naturalist you will soon find that sliminess is a practical solution to many of the challenges facing a thin-skinned animal out of water. The slime, secreted by tiny glands that cover the exposed part of a snail or slug's body, reduces water loss, binding the molecules together in much the same way as adding gelatine to water makes jelly. Because they do not have a shell, slugs are more vulnerable to desiccation than snails, so they have thicker slime.

A snail's shell is an additional protection against desiccation, which is the main reason why you find snails in drier habitats than slugs. In extreme cold or heat a snail retreats into its shell and seals off the entrance with thick mucus, which dries to form a waterproof seal called an epiphragm..

You can clearly see the growth rings on the shell of this wandering snail (*Lymnaea* sp).

Unlike many invertebrates, snails do not need to shed their shells to grow. Instead, they lay down two layers of new material at the mouth of the shell – a horny outer layer that provides a waterproof covering for the tough chalky layer beneath. Snails have growth spurts when times are good (spring and summer) and slow down when the going gets tough (winter). So a bit like tree rings, a snail's shell may have little wrinkles or slightly different patches of color that show the boundaries between periods of growth.

A terrestrial gastropod breathes through a hole in the mantle called a breathing pore, which the snail can open and close. It leads to a chamber called the mantle cavity. Blood vessels in the snail's skin can pick up all the oxygen it needs from the air that finds its way in. Some water-dwelling snails, including the great pond snail (*Lymnaea stagnalis*), breathe this way too – keep a few in a jar and you will hear a popping noise as they come to the surface and open their breathing pore. Other water snails breathe through gills, or use a combination of both techniques. Land snails and slugs can also to a certain extent breathe through their skin.

Land snails and slugs have four tentacles that stick out of the head and are used to feel the way around. Each tentacle has an eyespot at the tip, but their sight isn't up to much – they can do little more than distinguish between light and dark. Nevertheless, this is enough to tell a snail when daylight is fading, so that it can emerge from its daytime retreat to feed in the safety of the night. The tentacles are also covered in taste buds that are extremely sensitive to the taste and smell of food, in some cases up to 50 cm (20 in) away.

These tentacles are so important that mollusks protect them by cutting off the blood supply, turning them inside out and sucking them back into their bodies. When the danger has passed, they roll them out again. And if the worst comes to the worst and a tentacle is badly damaged, a mollusk simply grows a new one!

Rather surprising intercourse. See the passionate and bizarre mating rituals of common garden snails in a herbaceous border near you.

Part of their courtship ritual involves each stabbing the other with a calcified spine.

Snail and slug sex

Snails and slugs are hermaphrodite, which means each animal is both male and female. This is said to be a body layout that has evolved to double the efficiency of potential reproductive encounters between these slow and vulnerable animals. Despite having two sets of sexual organs, they need to mate, but once the deed is done, both animals will have been fertilized and can crawl away happily to get on with the business of laying eggs.

Their eggs look like clusters of anything between ten and a hundred miniature, translucent white Ping-Pong balls, and you will find them underground in crevices and under stones or bark, where they are not going to dry out. Having laid the eggs, the adult takes no further parental responsibility, and the young hatch a few weeks later. Snails are born with miniature shells called protoconches, which are built up while they are still in the egg.

The eggs of aquatic mollusks show much more imagination and diversity of form. The easiest to find and identify are those jelly masses that are the egg clusters of water snails, which you can come across under lily pad leaves, submerged stones, and pond weed. In a rock pool or along the strand line, look out for the pale yellow, spongy egg masses known as sea-wash balls – these are the eggs of common and red whelks (*Buccinum undatum* and *B. antiqua*). Each of the pods contains ten or more eggs, but only one will ever survive to adulthood, as the first to hatch eats its developing siblings.

Defense strategies of the softies

They may have soft bodies under their hard shells, but even the shell-less mollusks are far from defenseless. Many shells come with spines and bristles and a retractable front door called an operculum, making the impenetrable fortress that little bit more impenetrable. Pick up and prod a garden snail and it will reward you by covering you in a thick, green, bubbly ooze – a powerful deterrent to any would-be mollusk predator or overcurious naturalist. Various slugs will, when interfered with, produce a superviscous mucus from glands on their mantles that, when it gets on fingers, fur, or feathers, is also pretty unpleasant.

State-of-the-art mollusk sporting the latest in defense strategy – a smoke screen of ink and the ability to jet-propel itself to safety

Try catching a cephalopod and you soon realize the fantastic power of jet propulsion as it sprints for safety, at the same time emitting a puff of ink that expands rapidly to give the escaping animal a smoke screen and leaves the naturalist or the predator with nothing but a phantom image of the animal that was once there. Even small species such as the little cuttlefish that often turn up in rock pools are capable of creating this sort of confusion.

Although not famous for their speed, some of the bivalves are also capable of a trick or two. Scallops can skip or fly when they sense approaching danger, particularly from their archenemy the starfish. They create this movement by flexing their valves and squirting out a jet of water. It is kind of random in its aim, but enough to allow them to escape from their slow-moving nemesis.

The food file: the radula

A feature unique to mollusks is a filelike, rasping tool called a radula, which allows them to scrape algae and other food off rocks, to rasp away at vegetation, and, in some species, even to drill through the shells of other mollusks or to harpoon fish.

The radula is not easy to see without a good magnifying lens and a cooperative animal. Pond snails are quite obliging, as they cling to the underside of the water surface and graze the film of microscopic plants. Or you can pop one in a jam jar containing suitable food and watch it slide up the glass, its radula moving back and forth like a jaw.

Encourage any gastropod to walk on glass, and you may be lucky enough to see its radula in action.

You should be able to see the radula at work most clearly with a common garden snail or slug, because not only do they have relatively big mouths and therefore larger radulas, but they will also eat almost anything. A useful trick here is to "paint" a sheet of glass or acrylic with something that will whet a snail's appetite. I find that giving some lettuce a whizz in the food processor and adding a little water works well, but feel free to experiment. You need a souplike consistency, not too runny and not too thick, so that it will stay on the acrylic. Add a bit of cuttlefish bone (available from pet shops) – snails need the calcium it provides to build up their shells – and it may tempt them.

Put your snail on the baited glass or acrylic and wait for it to move. Then slowly lift the sheet into as near a vertical position as you can without the snail slipping off. Look at the snail through your magnifying lens, and with luck, you will find that it is hunched up and using its radula to scrape the food off the surface. As it eats it will move slowly along the rows of teeth on the radula, leaving zigzag marks – a pattern you often see on greenhouse windows where nocturnal slugs and snails have been feeding on the accumulated algae.

A radula at work, scraping and passing food back to the mollusc's mouth.

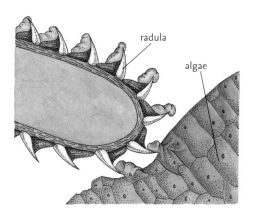

radula

algae

On the seashore
meet the bivalves

The largest of this group is the suitcase-size giant clam (*Tridacna* spp.), a kind of oceanic filter bag-cum-gardener of photosynthetic algae that it nurtures in its mantle. But this extravert is the exception. The typical bivalve mollusk is a rather unassuming creature. Most of them live secretive and enigmatic lives, lurking in the ooze of estuaries and skulking in the sands and silts. But just because you cannot see them doesn't mean they are not up to some interesting things. To get to know them just requires a bit of lateral thinking – oh, and a gardening fork and a sieve!

Secrets of the sands

Common mussels (*Mytilus edulis*) are bivalves with tight-fitting shells that keep the moisture in when the tide goes out.

To find the strange life forms that are keeping themselves safe from dehydration, temperature extremes, and predation in the damp sand, it helps to learn to read the etchings on the surface. These tend to blow the cover of the animals below, and once located the beasts can be exhumed unharmed with the deft scoop of a spade. By sifting through the sand or mud you will turn up many different kinds of creatures, not just bivalve and gastropod mollusks, but also little shrimplike crustaceans, various crabs, urchins, and starfish, a plethora of different worms, and a fish or two, all of which have adapted to the unique challenges this environment offers.

The trick to seeing the creatures themselves involves nothing more than digging gently with a fork and sifting through the sand and mud to find the beasts that live there.

The best place to see any activity is down at the water's edge, and so naturalists with any savvy will follow the retreating tide. You may spot jets of water being squirted in the air by various mollusks, which, when they detect the vibrations of a predator (that's you!), pull their often huge, trunklike siphons back so rapidly into their shells that any water left in them is forcibly ejected, straight up, as if from a water pistol.

Most of the mollusks you will find here are **bivalves**, as their shells are often streamlined to burrow easily through the sand. These creatures are like living filter units that either stick their two siphon tubes – inhalant and exhalant – out of their burrows and into the mixture of water and muddy nutrients just above it, sucking it down for processing while blowing the wastewater out of the other tube, or, slightly more proactively, use an incredibly long and mobile inhalant siphon to work systematically across the surface of the mud like a vacuum cleaner. It is these activities that give the distinctive star-shaped pattern on the surface once the tide has retreated.

Etchings of *Hydrobia*

Other species of gastropod can also be found here. The tiny spiral shells of *Hydrobia* cruise the surface of mud and sand, leaving a detailed weave of lines in their wake. These very important little gastropods make up for what they lack in dimensions (approximately 4 mm or ⅙ in long) in sheer numbers. They can exist at densities of 60,000 per sq m (50,000 per sq yd) and make rich pickings for any bird with the technique to harvest them. If you scoop up a handful of mud and water, swish it about, dump it in a shallow white tray, and leave it for just a few moments, you will find that any small animals that were present have started moving. The minuscule *Hydrobia* snails give themselves away by leaving their trails behind them.

Pretty much any indentation you investigate with your trowel will turn up a bivalve or two. One that will prove difficult to lay your hands on is the pod razorshell (*Ensis siliqua*) and its numerous allied species. Nearly all possess a particularly strong muscular foot and an elongated and very smooth pair of valves as a shell. These are the drag racers of the bivalve world, and when they perceive a predator coming, they practically sprint through the sand to get out of the way.

Keeping a foot on a rock

Among the things you will probably find when rambling along a rocky shore are the simple, inverted-cone-shaped shells of long-lived mollusks. Limpets (*Cellana* and *Patella* spp.) often etch the surface of the rock with a circular engraving that identifies their home base. You can test just how loyal they are to these bases by mapping the rock surfaces on which the limpets sit. At low tide, mark each limpet you wish to study with a different color and mark its position on your map with the same color. For obvious reasons, when marking the limpets, you should use colored correction fluid, oil-based paints, or indelible markers, not water-based pigments. When you return after the next high tide, look for your limpets. Have they moved at all? Have they returned to the same base or gone to another? What happens if you move a limpet from one place to another – does it return to its original spot? You'll probably discover that they are pretty home-loving creatures.

Common limpets (*Partella vulgata*) and barnacles (*Balanus balanoides*) in a rock pool clinging to the surface of the rock

This sort of study can be carried out over a long period of time and any patterns can be observed in animals that, to the untrained observer, might seem stationary and dull. If you do not believe that these animals move at all, have a snorkel around your study rock and you will see the individuals you are getting to know gliding across the surfaces, grazing away at the layers of microscopic algae.

You can do studies of this nature on pretty much any snail species, terrestrial or aquatic. Look for snails in your garden – you will sometimes find them huddled together in damp, sheltered locations, such as behind an ivy-infested wall, among flower pots, or in a pile of logs. Mark them in the same way and, over time, map their movements around the garden. Do they swap "roost" sites? How far do they travel? Go out at night and see if you can spot any of "your" snails. You could also try this in reverse, marking the snails you see out and about at night, then looking for their hiding places by day. The questions you can ask and answer and the discoveries you can make with this sort of study are endless. To carry out similar experiments with birds, mammals, or reptiles you would need to get into the complicated world of clipping nails, small patches of fur, or even scales. But with arthropods you just need a few spots of a nontoxic pigment on that naturalist-friendly exoskeleton and you are in business.

The critical thing with any marking experiment is to ensure that the color you use doesn't affect your subjects' survival in any way. It mustn't be so bright and obvious that it flags them up as dinner to potential predators; it must also be safe and not poison your subjects or stick their legs or wings together.

Shell collecting

Given that gastropod shells are so good at being a strong fortress throughout the owner's life, it is not surprising that many should live on long after the original resident has passed away. Building up a collection of such shells can be a useful way of getting to know your mollusk species, whether on the seashore or in the garden. Label your collection carefully, remembering to include the date and location of your find and any other interesting observations. The colors of some shells, particularly those with smoother surfaces, will show up better if you apply a coat of varnish, mimicking the wet look that they would have in life.

Shells with a long spiral can be made to reveal their internal beauty as well – use a file to grind away one side to expose the inner architecture, choosing a grade of file appropriate to the thickness of the shell. The result will be a beautiful addition to your collection and a window into the private abode of a mollusk.

The best place to find the shells of marine mollusks is the strand line – I can easily wile away a huge chunk of a day walking along the beach with eyes fixed to the wiggly line of assorted flotsam and jetsam that has been disgorged by the ocean. Keep an eye on how far you have walked, though. I have more than once walked miles and miles along a particularly interesting stretch, only to realize I'm late and have to run all the way back. Once I was even caught out by the tide and had to swim part of the way back with the pockets of my shorts full of shell ballast!

On exposed shores where there is a curve to the beach, many shells will accumulate at one end or on one side of groins or break waters, due to the combined actions of long-shore drift and the hydrodynamics of the shells. I have known the shells of different species or even the right and left halves of bivalves to be found at opposite ends of the beach, while some that are damaged in some way turn up somewhere in between.

A treasure trove of mollusk cast-offs

Worms

There is a lot of confusion about worms. We may think we know what they are – those long pinkish things we see when we dig the garden, right? But there are many kinds of worm the world over and, apart from the fact that they are found in damp environments and have a superficially similar elongated body shape, they are totally different. So before we start looking at their behavior, let's have a quick who's who.

Earthworm – multitalented and eaten by many birds

The earthworms – including the common earthworm (*Lumbricus terrestris*) with which most of us are familiar from messing around in the herbaceous border – belong to the family of true segmented worms or **annelids**, which comprises about 15,000 species and also includes the leeches and the bristleworms.

To qualify as a true worm, that creature wriggling around in your net has to show some sign of segmentation, both internal and external. True worms have well-developed nervous, digestive, and circulatory systems and most have bristles called setae along the length of their bellies which can be used for a multitude of functions, from traction to breathing.

Flatworm – one of the terrestrial species, found in damp places

Flatworms or platyhelminths are not worms at all, really. Shaped like flattened tubes and with no segmentation, they simply glide around like micro-slugs. They each have a saclike gut and no bristles, and turn up mostly in aquatic environments. Flatworms belong to the class Tubellaria, whose other members are parasites such as flukes and tapeworms, best known for making us ill.

You can catch flatworms by tying a piece of raw liver to some string and dangling it in a pond overnight. Any flatworms present will congregate on your bait and you can transfer them to a petri dish to observe them under a microscope or hand lens.

Roundworms or nematodes (Nematoda) comprise 12,000 described species, but this is probably only a very small fraction of the total. They turn up everywhere, but are so small that they mostly go unnoticed. However, spread a little soil or a drop of pond water under a light microscope and I guarantee an introduction to some of these animals.

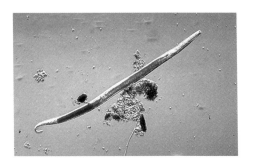

Roundworm – probably one of the most numerous creatures in the world

Ribbonworm – a marine worm only by name

Ribbon worms are worth a mention because they are easy to find on rocky shores. I remember lifting a rock on the west coast of Scotland to be confronted by a large red blob of what looked like strawberry jam. As I got closer, it started almost imperceptibly to shift; the movement was noticeable only because of the glistening of its surface. When I investigated further, the blob unraveled itself to form a slightly animate ribbon that, when stretched out on the sand, was about 5 m (16 ft) long (and this was apparently a small one)! Again, this is a worm in name only; mine was a member of the appropriately named species *Lineus longissimus*, of the phylum Nemertea.

The other two phylums of wormlike creatures are really in the realms of the specialist: These are the peanut worms, Sipuncula, and the acorn worms, Echiura, both of which feed on detritus and live in sediment and under rocks.

'Intestines of the soil': the earthworms

Earthworms are very, very successful animals: As the fossil record proves, they have been making burrows and holes in our planet for some 120 million years. This makes them incredibly important to the health of our gardens and other ecosystems, and in the past many iconic figures – from Charles Darwin to Aristotle, from whom I stole the subtitle above – have sung their praises. This is because all that burrowing is vital to the health of the soil, and when the soil is in good condition, so are the plants and the animals that eat worms.

Part of the reason earthworms are so influential boils down to their numbers. A hectare of grassland can contain up to 7.5 million of them (that's 3 million per acre), and between them they will turn over some 10 tonnes of soil each year and excavate over 5,000 km (3,000 miles) of burrows! In the process, they aerate the soil, neutralize acidity or alkalinity, and digest dead and decaying matter, breaking it down into humus a lot more efficiently than any garden appliance. Humus is the miracle worker of healthy soil, enabling it to retain water and providing lots of the nutrients that help plants to grow.

Earthworm burrowing

The ins and outs of a worm

If you look closely at an earthworm you can see its 250 or so segments quite clearly. Less visible are the ring-shaped muscles that run around the body and the long ones that run along it, all of which the worm can control with great precision. Add to this the fact that a worm's body is 70 percent to 95 percent water, and you have the recipe both for its flexibility and for its great tunneling ability. Water can't be squashed (try it with a balloon filled with water – if you press it in at one point, it bulges out at another), so when a worm is squeezing its way through soil or vegetation, all those muscles push the water forward and propel the worm by means of a wave of contractions called peristaltic motion. The process is made all the more efficient by a thick, slimy mucus secreted from glands on the skin. This acts as a lubricant, enabling the worm to slide through tiny spaces while at the same time stopping it from losing too much water through the skin in dry weather, and binding loose soil particles together.

You may think that 250 segments is quite a lot for an average-size worm, but wait till you hear about its "taste buds." There are vast numbers of these – perhaps 70,000 per sq cm (more than 450,000 per sq in) – and they enable it to find food despite its lack of eyes. Both the taste buds and the setae are sensitive to touch and vibration, telling the worm all it needs to know about the world around it. Earthworms do have some light-sensitive cells, but like many nocturnal animals they cannot see red, so covering a flashlight with red cellophane is a good trick for watching them at night.

Another of the functions of the setae is to help the worm fight back when a bird is trying to pull it from its burrow under your lawn. You may have wondered how such a tiny creature can turn this apparently one-sided battle into a hotly contested tug-of-war. Well, it's all about bristle power. These tiny hairs can grip the walls of a burrow so tightly that even a huge predator such as a blackbird doesn't win every time.

Saddle or clitellum: – a pale segment found two-thirds of the way down the body in adults – the point of contact between mating worms.

Tail: the flatter, paddle-like bit at the other end!

Head: the thin, round end and the bit at the front when the worm is moving. Otherwise difficult to identify because it lacks eyes, ears, or an obvious nose.

Mouth: the only real "feature" on an earthworm's head, just under the tip of the snout.

Worms don't get together often, but when they do, both end up fertilized and able to lay eggs.

The private life of Lumbricus

Like snails and slugs, earthworms are hermaphrodite, which means that each adult has both male and female sexual organs but still needs to mate in order to reproduce. And, also like snails and slugs, they have probably evolved this strategy in order to maximize breeding potential – earthworms do not get together very often, but when they do, you end up with two fertilized adults for the price of one mating. Take your red-cellophane-covered flashlight out on a warm, wet summer's night and tread very gently so as not to disturb them.

The key to successful earthworm mating is the pale saddlelike segment called a clitellum, found about two-thirds of the way down the body. This produces a blanket of thick mucus that binds two worms together in a sticky embrace. A mating pair lies side by side, with the head of one facing the tail of the other. The long setae on their bellies turn the embrace into a bear hug, holding the pair tightly together for two or three hours as they exchange sperm.

Over the next few days, the saddle keeps producing mucus, which the worm passes along its body. As it flows over the male and female organs, the mucus gathers up a quota of sperm and eggs and carries on along the body until it literally rolls off over the head, just as if the worm were pulling off a sweater. The mucus seals over the sperm and eggs to form a small, lemon-shaped cocoon that remains in the soil for two to three weeks. There may be up to 20 eggs inside it, but usually only a few baby worms hatch.

Making a wormery

One of the problems of studying worms is that they will insist on doing most of what they do underground. Keeping a few in a wormery will fool them into thinking they are still hidden away in the soil, while giving you the chance to observe them as they go about their daily lives.

You will need:
- 1 piece of wood 115 cm (46 in) long and 2 x 2 cm (just under an inch) in cross section
- 2 x 30 cm (12 in) squares of clear acrylic
- 14 small wood screws
- 1 strip of wood 30 cm (12 in) long
- elastic bands
- a selection of different-colored soils (garden soil, sand, potting compost)
- a few leaves
- 5 or 6 worms
- 2 pieces of black cardboard 30 cm (12 in) square
- a screwdriver, drill, and scissors

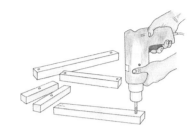

Step **1**

Step **2**

1 Cut the wood into 5 pieces: 2 x 30 cm (12 in), 1 x 25 cm (10 in) and 2 x 15 cm (6 in) long. Drill two holes a few centimeters (an inch or so) from the corners at either end of each of the three longer pieces and one hole in each of the short pieces.

2 Place the pieces of wood together to form a sort of upside-down goalpost. The medium-sized piece runs at right angles to the two short ones to form the base, with the long pieces as uprights. Sandwich the two uprights between the sheets of acrylic, making sure they are flush at the edges, and screw everything together, leaving the 'feet' till last.

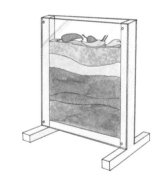

Step **3**

3 Pour the soils in alternating layers into the space between the sheets of acrylic, top with the leaves and water lightly.

4 Introduce the worms and put the strip of wood on top, holding it in place with the elastic bands to stop the worms escaping.

5 Put the paper or cardboard against the sides to act as blinds, and keep your wormery in a cool place. Check it every day to make sure the soil is damp but not soggy, removing the blinds when you want to observe the worms.

Step **4**

A diet for worms

It may not sound very appetizing, but worms actually eat the soil as they burrow through it. That is, they eat the soft part of it – the rich organic humus, produced by plants and animals that have died and rotted away. Worms have an inefficient digestive system: Something like two-thirds of what they excrete is still humus. They absorb what they need and pass on the rest, helping the process of decomposition, which is what releases the nutrients, without greatly depleting the wealth of the soil.

The vast quantity of humus that passes through their bodies is what turns up in holes in your lawn looking like wriggling white cigars. These are called casts, and they are almost entirely the responsibility of two species of worm, *Allolobophora longa* and *A. nocturna*, which are the ones that most commonly cast their casts, as it were, away from their burrows. You may not relish having your lawn covered in worm dung, but as I say, this is actually two-thirds organic matter and as such doesn't differ that much from rich, crumbly soil. Don't be tempted to put chemicals down to poison the worms – lawns are hard enough to maintain as it is, without having to do all the spiking and aerating and fertilizing yourself. If you leave the worms to get on with it, they will happily do all this work for you.

Lawn manure. Earthworm casts are the soil every gardener should love, and the holes made by worms will aerate the turf, too.

Six-legged mini-beasts
insects

Insects have to be the most successful life form on the planet, with well over a million known species and possibly as many as ten million that have yet to be identified. This means there is an awful lot of discovering still to be done, so with over a thousand million insects per hectare of normal grassland (400,000,000 per acre), if you look in the right places at the right time, you could easily discover something that has never been known before!

At first glance, a flower bed may look just like a flower bed, but look closer, take your time, concentrate, and you will soon come to recognize the wealth of weird and wonderful life that is going on before your very eyes. Those tiny bite-size pieces missing from the edge of a rose leaf mean that an aphid has been chomping away. That in turn could mean there are ladybug larvae about, chomping on the aphids in their turn. Look underneath the leaf of a stinging nettle in the spring and you may find the eggs of a small tortoiseshell or peacock butterfly; come back a few weeks later and see if the caterpillars have hatched. It's all out there – it's just a matter of looking.

Above: 7-spot ladybug
Right: Purple emperor wing

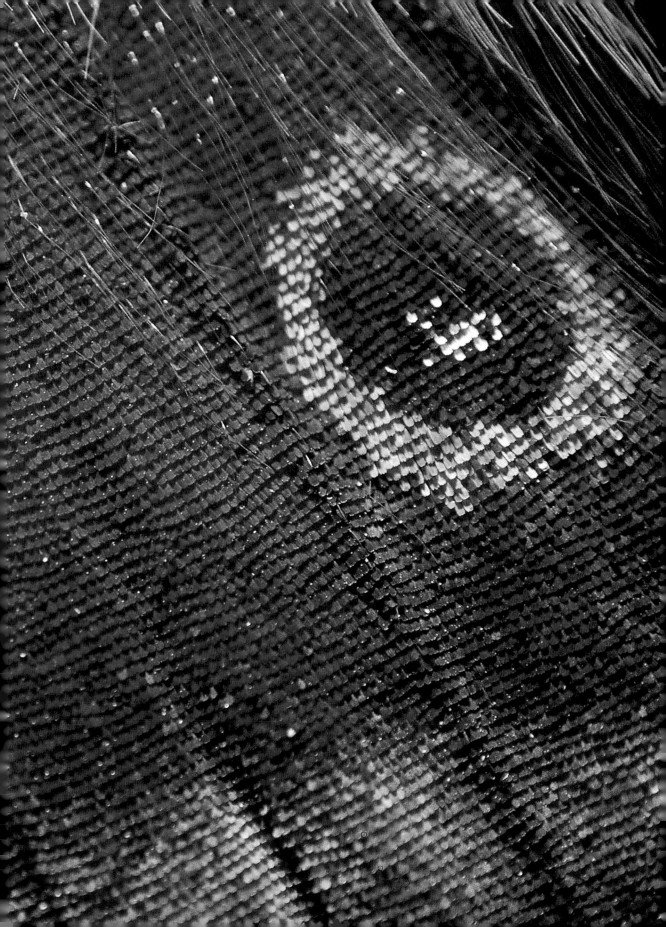

So what exactly is an insect?

A creepy-crawly with wings is the simplest answer to that question, although it's not a 100 percent accurate one. Insects are certainly the only invertebrates that can fly, but not all the adults and none of the larval stages have the power of flight. Other defining characteristics are six legs and a characteristic body structure made up of three sections – head, thorax, and abdomen.

Mouth: may be in a variety of shapes and structures, or not there at all. Some moths simply don't have a functioning mouth – they are too busy breeding to bother about eating. With other insects, it depends on their diet: Mouths can be designed to crush seeds, slice meat, or shear through leaves. As well as taking in food, many insects also use their mouths to excrete compounds such as caterpillar silk, toxins, venoms, and digestive juices.

Head: boxlike in shape, this is where most of the senses are found.

Antennae: are the organs not only of touch but also of taste, scent, and vibration.

Eyes: may be simple or complex, capable of detecting little more than the difference between light and dark or discerning not only all the colors that we can see, but also ultraviolet. A dragonfly's compound eye has thousands of lenses, is sensitive to movement, and probably sees the world in pretty clear detail.

Thorax: is a hard box that carries the legs and wings on the outside, and on the inside, the mechanism to drive them.

Legs: used, of course, for walking, but various insects have modified theirs to jump, swim, dig, and do battle with. Some legs also have sensitive hairs that tell their owners about what's going on around them.

Wings: where these exist there are always two pairs, though in beetles and true bugs, the forewings are modified into a protective covering for the rear ones, which do the flying.

Spiracles: the tiny holes down the side of the insect's body that enable it to breathe, taking the air into lots of little tubes called trachea. The insect can open and close its spiracles to minimize water loss, but "breathing" is no more than a passive wafting in and out of air. It's not as efficient as having lungs, but it works for them.

Feet: they have the same sensory devices as the legs, but they also have hooks for gripping and spikes, bristles, and hooks for grooming.

Abdomen: this may seem a funny place to keep the heart, but that is what insects do. The digestive organs and fat storage are here too.

The essential bug-hunting kit

As we have seen throughout this book, observation is the key to being a successful naturalist, whatever beast or plant it is that catches your fancy. And this is truer with insects than it is with anything else, for the simple reason that so many of them are so minute. So your first step on the path to being a successful entomologist (insect expert) is to train your eyes to take in what they see around them.

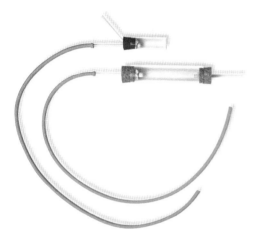

Short, sharp sucks are best – you can hurt a soft insect if you suck it too violently. Don't pooter anything sticky, like a slug, or with long, fragile legs like a daddy longlegs. They'll get stuck and may be injured. Keep the collection jar dry (and that means not accidentally blowing into it, as the moisture from your breath is enough to make the jar uncomfortably humid for some insects). And don't collect too many insects at a time, as you may find that one of them ends up eating the rest!

That said, there are a number of pieces of equipment that will be useful to you. Picking up insects is the first challenge, as many of them are tiny and can be crushed by tweezers, however carefully you use them The answer is a **pooter**. You can buy one from a specialist supplier or make your own using a small jar with a plastic lid with two holes in it. (Make the holes by heating a meat skewer over a candle or a gas element on the stove, then poking it through the plastic.) Cut two lengths of plastic tubing (the kind you get in winemaking kits), one 20 cm (8 in) and one 30 cm (12 in) long, and push them through the lid so that they come halfway down the jar. Place the free end of the long tube over an insect, suck (very carefully) on the short tube, and, hey presto, you will vacuum up your specimen and be able to deposit it gently in your jar.

One of the frustrations of studying creepy-crawlies is that they creep and crawl – and most of them do it extraordinarily fast! So you need what I call a **bug restrainer**. Any sort of clear jar is OK for this purpose, but you can restrain your specimen gently and get even closer if you use two see-through plastic cups, one inside the other. Keep them dry or your subject may stick to them. Cut the base out of one cup and cover the hole with plastic wrap; stick a circle of white polystyrene to the base of the other. Pop your bug into the plastic wrap cup and gently push the polystyrene cup in on top of it – the polystyrene gives you a bright, plain backdrop against which to view your specimen. Work quickly, and once you've done all the observing and identifying you want, release your bug back where you found it. Again, be wary of larger insects – don't restrain something like a daddy longlegs or a spider that will be bigger than the base of the cup when it stretches its legs.

Another useful tool for catching small animals is a specially adapted pair of barbecue tongs. The adaptation comes in the form of a tea strainer attached to each end of the tongs, so that they form a mesh cage when they close together. I call these **cricket tongs**, but they are equally handy for capturing grasshoppers and anything else that sits on foliage and is likely to bolt before you can sneak up on it.

Stick insects
forest phantoms

Properly known as the *Phasmida*, those schoolkids' favorites the stick and leaf insects are very much part of a young naturalist's life. Almost anyone interested in insects will at some time have kept an Indian, or laboratory, stick insect (*Carausius morosus*), feeding it on privet, bramble, or ivy. These are a fascinating introduction to the world of insects, and also have a bizarre reproductive life. All individuals are females, producing fertile eggs without the need for a male – a phenomenon known as parthenogenesis, and a useful strategy if you need to colonize a new habitat rapidly. But the main reason stick and leaf insects fascinate us is that they are masters of disguise and show this survival trick in its most elaborate form. Just look at a leaf insect of the genus *Phyllidae* – it looks so like a leaf that you expect to see a caterpillar feeding on it.

A master of disguise, a stick insect spends the day in stick mode, confing movement to the hours of darkness.

Like many insects, especially those that rely on camouflage for protection, these are active mainly after dark, so going out at night to catch them moving about is the best way to find them. Otherwise you will spend a long time trying to beat them in a game of hide-and-seek that they have been perfecting for millions of years.

Stick insects are easy to keep in captivity, which is a great way to learn about them if you are unlikely to travel to the tropics, where most of them exist in the wild. Having said that, you need to be sure exactly which species you are keeping and give it the specific conditions it needs – ventilation, humidity, and temperature are all critical and vary significantly from one species to another. *C. morosus* is easiest for the beginner and can be the subject of an interesting experiment. You need at least three insects, so that you can rear them in three different environments. Surround one with light colors – of both box and food – to match its own coloration. Give another dark colors, and rear a third in the dark. What happens? Those that are on the light leaves stay the same color, because they are perfectly camouflaged by it. Those in the dark stay the same too, while the ones that have been able to see that their environment is different change color to blend in with it.

Butterflies and moths

This is a group that needs no introduction. The scientific name for the order is Lepidoptera, meaning "scale wing," and refers to the tiny overlapping scales that cover the wings of both butterflies and moths, determining their patterns and colors. I think of them as the PR agents of the insect world, and with something like 180,000 to 200,000 species to choose from, you must admit they do a pretty good job. There is very little in nature more incredible than a chrysalis rupturing to reveal a crumpled canvas, the wings of a butterfly to be; or a greater pleasure than watching the first butterfly of the year enjoying the spring sunshine. And although I'm not going to attempt to detract from the obvious beauty of a butterfly, I do suggest that you look closely at the "face" of the next one you see – stare it straight between the compound eyes. Then you will see that, despite its captivating wings and glamorous reputation, this gorgeous creature is every bit as alien looking as any other invertebrate.

Monarch butterflies and a magpie moth. Most butterflies rest with their wings vertically above their body. Most moths rest with their wings flat out.

So what makes a butterfly a butterfly? Or a moth a moth? Well, although they have traditionally been split into two groups, they are pretty much the same thing. Butterflies fly by day, are colorful, have little knobs, or clubs, on their antennae, and rest with their wings held vertically above their bodies. Moths fly by night, are dull looking, have no knobs on their antennae, and rest with their wings flat out. Both have hairlike scales on their bodies, which tend to be more pronounced in night-flying moths, providing better insulation against cool air and making the bodies look bigger. As with everything in nature, there are exceptions, and the more you learn, the more complicated it gets, but these rough guidelines will apply to most situations.

Like many insects, butterflies and moths have an unusual way of growing up. The change between a caterpillar and an adult butterfly is so complete that, if you didn't know better, you wouldn't think the two could be related. So let's have a look at the stages they pass through.

The egg

There are as many different kinds of egg as there are species of butterfly and moth. They may be laid singly or in groups, all together or scattered far and wide. This means that there are no hard and fast rules for where and how to find them, but as ever, there are a few tips that will help you on your way.

With butterflies that are active by day, watching them is the best way to find their eggs. A good field guide will help you establish which species feeds on which plants, but if you use your eyes, you will soon learn to recognize the signs of a female butterfly looking for somewhere to lay her eggs – she moves from plant to plant, flying low over the leaves, checking them out with her sensitive feet to see if they meet her requirements. Sunny, nettle-ridden corners of fields are good places to watch for small tortoiseshells (*Aglais urticae*) and peacocks (*Inachis io*), whereas the cabbage patch – or a clump of nasturtiums in the flower bed – will feed the large or small whites (*Pieris brassicae* and *P. rapae*, commonly known as cabbage whites).

When the female has chosen her plant, she curls her abdomen under the leaf and may flutter her wings as she lays. Watch from a safe distance so as not to disturb her and take a mental note of her exact position. As soon as she flies away, check the underside of the leaves of the plant and you should find a cluster of green, glassy-looking eggs.

The larvae of the large white butterfly (*Pieris brassicae*) emerging from their eggs to begin a life of eating

Eating for dear life: caterpillars

A few weeks after the eggs have been laid, the caterpillars emerge – the length of time varies enormously from species to species. Breaking the rule that defines most invertebrates, caterpillars don't have a hard, external skeleton – their bodies are supported by the body fluid inside, kept at pressure. These soft, sometimes hairy babies may look defenseless but are spectacularly well equipped for their two functions in life – eating and staying alive long enough to proceed to the next stage. Caterpillars are little more than stomachs on legs. They are born on their food plants, and all they have to do is eat, building up the raw materials that they will need when they turn into butterflies or moths.

Defense is the key to a caterpillar's survival. Some go in for the sort of camouflage that would make a stick insect look to its laurels. But others have bright colors that positively advertise their presence – the caterpillar of the cinnabar moth (*Tyria jacobaeae*) looks as if it is wearing a striped rugby jersey, and you can't get much less subtle than that.

What these colors are saying is "Keep off. I'm poisonous, or at least pretty nasty tasting." Birds or other predators who try eating such a caterpillar soon learn their lesson and leave others of its kind alone.

The caterpillars of peacock and small tortoiseshell butterflies have a whole barrage of defensive tricks. When they are young, they feed as a group, giving them safety in numbers, and if a predator approaches, they hunch up together, to make themselves look larger and presumably fiercer; they are also covered in spines, making them hard to handle and swallow. As a last resort, they simply roll off the leaf and camouflage themselves at the base of the nettles. Lots of other caterpillars use this trick too, so if you want to have a look at one, hold a spoon underneath them to catch them before they escape.

Many caterpillars are nocturnal, emerging to feed only after predators have packed it in for the night. Go out into the garden with a flashlight, and you'll be amazed at what you see. Artificial light seems to blow a lot of caterpillars' cover, particularly if it comes from below or from the side, because their camouflage colors and disruptive patterns are designed to work against natural sunlight, which, of course, comes from above.

Check out the needles of Scots pine and Norway spruce in late summer for the pine hawkmoth caterpillar (*Hyloicus pinastri*). Using a flashlight at night will help to blow its cover.

Nighttime is a good time to locate the secretive caterpillars of common brown butterflies, such as the meadow brown (*Maniola jurtina*) and gatekeeper (*Pyronia tithonus*). Find some long grass at the edge of a field or under a hedge, get down to its level, and shine your flashlight into it from the side. With a bit of luck you will pick out the shapes of small caterpillars that have emerged from their daytime position deep among the grass blades.

While you are observing caterpillars, you may notice that they have rather more than the six legs that are standard issue for insects. Fourteen, in fact. So what is this all about? Well, they found that six legs just weren't enough, so they evolved a few more. They still have six *true* legs clustered near the head, which are made of hard material, have joints, and are used for walking. Toward the back end they have four pairs of soft pro-legs, at the end of each of which there are Velcro-like hooks that enable them to cling to leaves.

Pupation – the amazing change from caterpillar to casket, inside which the old body dissolves and a new one is created, in this case, a monarch butterfly

A newly emerged small tortoiseshell butterfly drying its wings and pumping blood into its veins

After a couple of days, caterpillars start to spin a little pad of silk to which they attach their back legs. They become very still and may change color as they prepare to molt for the first time. When they are ready they simply walk out of their skin, which remains attached to the silk, and carry on feeding. Because the skin isn't complicated by the addition of wings and the like, it doesn't take too much energy to produce, which means that a caterpillar can grow quickly and shed its skin as soon as it gets too small for comfort. Growing quickly is another of a caterpillar's defense mechanisms, because lacking that protective outer skeleton, it is potentially an easy snack for a lot of ever hungry predators. It sheds its skins something like five times in the course of its caterpillar life, before embarking on the final molt that will change it beyond recognition.

All change – the pupa stage

When the big moment arrives, caterpillars do give us clues that something important is happening. Some change color, becoming duller than before. Some stop eating and start charging around looking for the right place to turn into a pupa or chrysalis. Some bury themselves in soil, others dangle from a stick or branch. The small tortoiseshell hangs upside down, curling its head up in a J shape, whereas a cabbage white remains head up, but spins a little waist harness around its middle.

When everything is set, the caterpillar's head capsule pops off – yes, really – and the skin splits and is shrugged off for the last time, revealing the casket that is going to accomplish one of the great transformations in the living world. At this point most of them have no features to speak of, and if the pupa didn't twitch occasionally you would be hard pushed to recognize that it was alive.

What is extraordinary about the transformation from a caterpillar to a butterfly or moth is that it is not a gradual process. A mammal embryo develops into a baby through recognizable stages, but the caterpillar's body literally dissolves and then rebuilds itself, producing something as completely different from the original as you could imagine. When the pupa splits, after anything from two to twenty-four weeks, depending on the species, the adult emerges – and at first sight is a bit of a disappointment. Where are those beautiful wings, you may ask, looking at this scrunched-up creature that appears to be all eyes and antennae, with six ungainly legs that don't seem to be designed for walking? But be patient. Watch as this newly emerged creature drags itself somewhere it can hang freely and pumps blood into the veins in its wings. The wings expand, the blood sets, and your ugly duckling turns into a beautiful, elegant butterfly.

Butterfly wings

We tend to look at butterfly wings in a superficial way, as if they were the petals that transformed the insects into living, mobile flowery things. When you see a butterfly sitting still with its wings open, you might think it is doing nothing, but in fact it is likely to be using those wings like solar panels or radiators. Butterflies need to get their body temperature up to around 30°C (86°F) to be active. Held open they expose a large surface area to the sun's rays, warming the blood in the wings and taking that warmth back to the insect's body. This is not always done by holding the wings flat, either; first thing in the morning, the grayling (*Hipparchia semele*) leans toward the sun with wings shut, to capture the rays, but by midday will angle its wings edge-on to the sun to reduce the surface area and so avoid overheating.

Those dazzling colors often seen on the wings of day-flying butterflies and moths are species-specific badges to be flashed around as they fly or even used in elaborate displays to others of the same species – particularly useful when trying to find a mate.

As soon as the sun sets, color plays a less important role, and the brilliance of diurnal butterflies and moths is replaced in the night-flying species by gorgeous lines and textures designed to enable the insect to blend into a natural background when it is at rest during the daylight hours. Any bright colors found on these insects are often hidden until required as a startling technique. If you watch butterflies long enough you will notice how they use their wings: Some will flick and flash their wings, especially females that do not want to be bothered. Female "white" butterflies commonly flick their wings down and raise their abdomen to put off overly keen males!

Many moths and butterflies use hidden surprise colors and markings to confuse a predator. A suddenly revealed eyespot is usually enough to send a small mammal scurrying, and many of the satyrid butterflies, buckeyes (*Junonia coenia*), and the European peacock (pictured here) use this device. The peacock combines it with a hissing sound produced by the wings.

Here you can see a moth's wing scales (the "dust" that rubs off) and struts (the veins). The color patterns are formed by a mosaic of scales, some of which contain pigments, others of which create "color" by reflecting light.

Bringing up butterflies (and moths)

For a really intimate look at the life phases of a butterfly (or moth), you have to grow your own. Collect eggs or caterpillars from your local patch – that way you will know what plant they feed on, and have a ready supply of it close at hand – or buy them from a specialist supplier. The advantage of collecting eggs is that it reduces the risk of sneaky little parasitic flies and wasps having found the caterpillars before you do. If you are buying, don't be lured into choosing something exotic unless you are sure that you can get hold of the equally exotic plant that is the only thing it will eat.

1 If you are starting with eggs, keep them in a small, airtight plastic box to protect them from predators and stop them drying out or being scattered to all corners of the room by a misplaced sneeze! Don't worry about air holes, there's plenty of air in there, but open the box every other day to ventilate the eggs, and breathe on them gently to keep them moist. Keep the box at room temperature out of direct sunlight and check it every morning – caterpillars often hatch at night.

Newly hatched caterpillars are tiny – as little as 2 mm (½2 in) long. Many of them consume their own egg shells to get them into that lifelong feeding habit, so don't clear up the debris until your caterpillars have wandered away in search of other food. When this happens, line a slightly bigger plastic box with tissue paper, provide a leaf or two of the right plant, and, using a spoon and a fine paintbrush, gently transfer your babies into it. A small but thoroughly washed, grease-free margarine tub is the ideal size – in anything much bigger they run the risk of getting lost and starving to death while searching for food.

Keep checking the eggs until all have hatched, and transfer each new batch of babies as it appears. Clean the box every day, and keep the caterpillars well supplied with fresh leaves that are neither very young (which will upset their stomachs) nor old and leathery (which will be hard to chew). Caterpillars that are feeding happily will start to produce dusty droppings known as frass, which will remind you to keep changing the tissue paper.

2 Caterpillars grow fast, and in the process, as well as shedding skins, produce more and more frass and need more ventilation. Time to move them to somewhere more spacious. Anything from a larger margarine tub to a shoe box makes a good home at this stage. Provide cut stems of their food plant in a small container of water (old film canisters are ideal) and wrap tissue paper or plasticine round the stems to stop the caterpillars falling in and drowning. Replenish the food supply and clean the house every day, upgrading the accommodation whenever it looks as if it is getting too crowded.

3 After about five molts, caterpillars are ready to stop growing and turn themselves into pupae. At this stage you need to provide butterflies with sticks or twigs from which the pupae can hang. Moths, on the other hand, will either cocoon themselves in egg boxes or bury themselves in soil. If you are using soil, zap it in the microwave for ten minutes to sterilize it, leave it to cool, and then dampen it with a little water before lining the bottom of your caterpillar house with it.

4 Now you just have to wait – and wait patiently, for the next stage is a pretty unrewarding one. Move the pupae to an airy mesh cage that will be suitable for the adult butterflies or moths when they appear, and provide branches or netting for them to climb up. Spray the pupae with water every few days using one of those mist-sprayers you can buy for houseplants, and protect your treasures from predators, which can be anything from mice to earwigs.

5 When the pupa first darkens in color, then becomes semitransparent, it is time to get excited. Check every few hours, especially first thing in the morning, as the adults are likely to emerge during the night to give themselves a bit of predator-free time to sort out their new wings. Once this has happened, your successfully reared butterflies and moths can be released back into the wild.

Alternatively, if you have a pair of moths, you might like to see if you can complete the cycle by getting them to mate. The common hawk moths such as the poplar (*Laothoe populi*) and privet (*Sphinx ligustri*) are easy for the simple reason that you don't have to feed them – these are the ones that devote all their energies to breeding. So all you need to do is make sure you have both a male and a female. The clues to their sex are in the shape of the antennae and the width of the abdomen – females are fat and chunky, males are thinner. The other magic ingredient is a bit of peace and quiet (moths are very sensitive to vibration and disturbance). So place them in a cool dark room and put a "Do not disturb" notice on the door. With a bit of luck your moths will mate within a few days, and the female will lay eggs. Having cleaned out your margarine tub, you can collect the eggs and start all over again.

Attracting moths

All the flapping about that butterflies and moths do is quite energy intensive, so they need an energy-rich diet that generally comes from nectar, sap, or the sugary secretions of fermenting fruit. Preparing a cocktail like this is a great way to attract moths on a warm summer's night and will save you being up all night charging around the garden looking for them.

It doesn't much matter what you put in your cocktail as long as it is sticky, sweet, and smelly. I use a combination of sugar, molasses, fruit juices, and dark rum, heated *gently* in a big pan. Keep an eye on it and stir it constantly, adding more water *before* it sticks to the pan unless you really want to alienate the rest of the family. Getting the consistency right is important – it must be runny enough to use as a paint, but not so runny that it dribbles down to the ground and is lost. Pour it into a jam jar and apply it generously to tree trunks and fence posts using a stout paintbrush. The more different positions and habitats you paint, the more species of moth you are likely to see. Come back an hour or so later with a flashlight and see what you have lured out of the night.

An alternative is to make a runnier mixture and soak old rags in it; these can be hung up in various places to the same effect.

Like moths around a flame

It's a well-known fact that moths and other nocturnal insects are attracted to flames and lights. As a kid I would turn my bedroom into a giant moth trap by leaving the windows open and the lights on on a summer night; then I would sit up watching, collecting, and getting to know the creatures that came fluttering in. (If you want to take this aspect of your studies seriously, invest in mercury vapor lamps, as used by professional entomologists, which are apparently particularly attractive to our night-flying friends.)

Why they feel this attraction is one of nature's mysteries. One theory is that moths navigate according to the position of the moon – if the moon always lights up the same part of their field of vision, they travel in a straight line. Try it for yourself when you are out at night in the country, where there won't be too many buildings in the way. If you always keep the moon exactly to your right, say, you can't help but walk in a straight line.

Then we humans came along and introduced the concept of light bulbs, and the moths were a bit thrown. Because the distance between a moth and a light bulb is rather smaller than the distance between it and the moon, keeping the light in the same position means flapping around in ever decreasing circles. To continue your experiment, ask someone to stand in the same position, holding a flashlight. If you try to keep it in the same part of your field of vision, you'll do what the moths do and end up walking giddily into your friend.

Leaving the lights on is one way of attracting moths, but for something a little more sophisticated, suspend a white sheet on a string or frame or between trees and mount a light source above it. Choose a still night, as a high wind makes a sheet trap seriously hard to handle. Also, be prepared to sit up all night to see what happens: Although most moth activity occurs in the couple of hours after dark, there is also a peak after midnight and another before dawn. I have seen this sort of trap in action in a rain forest, and the sheet was literally covered with insects, so that none of the white cotton was visible and anyone who stood in front of the light also got smothered by insect life. It was a truly awesome demonstration of the diversity of life in the tropics.

Making a moth trap

Not all entomologists are insomniacs, so constructing a simple box trap means you can go to bed, turn the lights off, and let the moths get on with it.

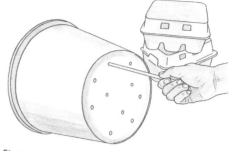

Step **1**

You will need:
- a plastic bucket
- a candle
- a meat skewer
- a few egg boxes
- a sheet of clear plastic approximately 70 cm (28 in) square (whatever size you need to make a funnel that fits into the top of the bucket)
- strong glue
- scissors
- 3 strips of wood 2 cm (1 in) square and about 30 cm (12 in) taller than the bucket
- a piece of wood 1 cm (½ in) square and 1 cm (½ in) thick
- a saw or file
- another sheet of clear plastic, approximately 20 cm (8 in) square
- a light bulb and bulb mount
- a long flex
- cable clips
- a plug
- cloth tape

Step **2**

1 Warm the tip of the skewer in the candle flame and use it to poke a few drainage holes in the bottom of the bucket. Put the egg boxes in the bucket.

2 Make the large sheet of plastic into a funnel and sit it in the bucket, using the glue and scissors to hold it together and trim it into shape – it should stick out of the top of the bucket by about 2 cm (1 in).

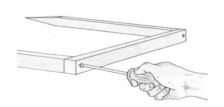

Step **3**

3 Screw the 3 strips of wood together to make a shape like football goalposts. Use the saw or file to sharpen the ends that are to go in the ground. The crossbar needs to be 20 cm (8 in) above the bucket once the posts are pushed into the ground.

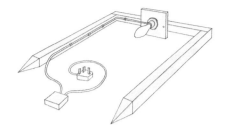

Step **4**

Step **5**

Step **6**

Step **7**

4 Set up your light fitting by wiring the flex to the bulb and screwing the mount to the smaller flat piece of wood. Attach this to the underside of the crossbar and tidy up the flex with cable clips.

5 Screw the smaller piece of plastic to the top of the structure to keep the rain off.

6 Choose a position on soft ground so that you can shove your "goalposts" into the earth and make sure it is near enough to a power point that you can plug the whole thing in. (It is a good idea to install a circuit breaker for safety – remember the combination of water and electricity can kill.) Position the bucket and funnel, then press the goalposts firmly into the ground.

7 Switch the light on at dusk and go to bed when you feel like it.

8 In the morning, turn the light off, unplug the electricity, and carefully remove the bucket. Take it to a shady place so as not to dazzle your captives and look in the egg boxes to see what you have found. This will vary a lot according to the time of year, but I have caught literally hundreds of moths this way on a warm summer's night.

Beetles

If nature was a car designer, then beetles would be the Rolls-Royces, except that nature came up with the basic format some 230 million years ago! There are over 350,000 species of beetle named so far – that's more than a quarter of all animals on the planet – and they range in size from something under ¼ mm (⅟₁₀₀ in) to the aptly named Goliath beetle at a terrifying 20 cm (8 in) long. The secrets to their success are their elytra or wing cases, which are really modified forewings, covering the rear wings with which the beetle flies. Although they are perfectly competent fliers, beetles aren't in the same league as butterflies – but on the other hand, they can go almost anywhere without worrying about damaging their wings.

They also have simple mouth parts, which means these and the rest of their body can be customized, molded, extruded, and modified depending on its choice of food and habitat. So each species of beetle out there, despite having very different appearances and lifestyles, is based on the same body plan.

A beetle life cycle – rearing ladybugs

I'm sure you know what a ladybug looks like, but you might not know that it is in fact a beetle or that it has a larva that looks a bit like a gray, warty caterpillar with yellowy-orange spots on a segmented body. When you get closer you'll notice that the ladybug larva doesn't move in the looping way a caterpillar does, but actually walks on its six spindly legs.

The larvae of the orange ladybug (*Halyzia 16-guttata*) is unusual, not only because of its color but because it feeds on the white mildew on tree leaves, especially sycamore.

All beetles go through the same sort of life cycle as butterflies and moths – egg, larva, pupa, and adult – and the ladybug is no exception. To demonstrate this, you can rear your own in a clear plastic box lined with a kitchen towel to absorb moisture. Collect a few larvae – no more than ten and as similar to each other in size as possible – in early summer to midsummer by seeking out a plant that seems to be suffering from an aphid attack, as keeping the aphid population down is what ladybug larvae do for a living. Put a few leaves of the host plant in the box to make the ladybugs feel at home.

The reason I say no more than ten is that ladybugs are fierce predators and if they get overcrowded and there aren't enough aphids to keep them happy, they are likely to turn cannibalistic and eat your experiment. Clean the box out every day, place fresh aphids on the leaves, and watch the larvae eat. You'll need a plentiful supply of aphids, because the larvae get through them at quite a rate.

The ladybug larva usually sheds its skin four times before it is ready to turn into a pupa. Then it attaches the tip of its abdomen to a surface, hunches up, and becomes quite still. About two weeks later a beetle will crawl out and possibly make you wonder what has gone wrong, because you've gone to all this trouble and produced something that looks nothing like a ladybug. Don't panic – give it a couple of days to rest and let its wings harden, and the familiar spotted coloration will emerge. Release your ladybugs where you collected the larvae, or keep a few and watch them go through the process again.

Garden friends. These 7-spot ladybug larvae (*Coccinella 7-punctata*), nearly ready to pupate, are feeding on nettle aphids. Though the adult has seven black spots, the larva has eight orange spots!

Ladybugs mating

Pond Dragons

These often brightly colored shards of insect life – the dragonflies and damselflies – are part of the essence of a summer day as they dash, dart, whizz, and skip around. Mostly they animate ponds and rivers, but they also stray considerable distances from water to feed and disperse.

The North American 12-spot skimmer dragonfly

Azure or blue damselflies (*Coenagrion puella*) mating

The biggest dragonflies are some of the most spectacular of insects. Their size, their extrovert tendencies, and the fact that there are relatively few species in most countries make them fairly easy to get to grips with. Telling dragons from damsels is more complicated, but as a rule of thumb dragonflies are bigger and more purposeful in flight, whereas damselflies, as befits their name, are delicate and fluttery. The other problem is that most are fast fliers – some dragonflies can reach speeds of 36 kph (22½ mph) – which makes following them with the naked eye, let alone getting close enough to pick out the finer details, next to impossible. So how does the would-be dragonfly-watcher and damselfly-watcher start?

Well it's a matter of learning a bit about their lifestyle. The scientific name for damsels and dragons is Odonata, which means "toothed jaws," and that tells you something important about them. These pretty, delicate creatures are voracious carnivores capable of consuming up to 20 percent of their body weight in a day. The nymphs (which is what these insects are called at their larval stage) are ambush predators, lurking in the water ready to pounce on any suitably sized tadpole, fish, or other nymph that drifts within range of their extraordinary extendible jaws. The key to this secret weapon is the lower lip, which the nymph can shoot out to stab its prey at an incredible speed.

To give yourself the best chance of observing them, go to a local pond or river. Even though dragonflies and damselflies can turn up anywhere, most of the action takes place by the water in which they live most of their lives. In addition to close-focus binoculars, a net, and a good field guide, a bamboo cane or similar length of stick from the garden is a useful thing to take with you. Shove this into a riverbank on a warm summer's day and position it so that it leans out over the water in an area where the vegetation is not too thick. Sooner or later a male dragonfly will recognize it as a vantage point and come and perch on it. He'll sit facing the water, with his back to you, so you'll get the best possible look at his wings, and you can watch him swiveling his head about as he surveys the river for prey. If you're really lucky, he will swoop out, grab a passing insect out of the air, and come back to your perch to eat it.

Hatching your own

You can rear dragonflies and damselflies in much the same way as you can butterflies, except, of course, that you need water. Collect nymphs from still water, as they are easier to provide for than those that need a fast-flowing environment. Two or three specimens are plenty for a 60 cm (2 ft) fish tank, but choose the largest you can find, as these are likely to hatch most quickly.

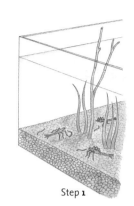

1 Set up your tank as described on p. 142, but leave the lid off. Furnish it with plenty of pond weed and smaller pond life, and include a few branches sticking out of the water so that the emerging insects can crawl up them. Position the tank in a light spot out of direct sunlight; if you have a suitable, predator-free site, put it outdoors so that the insects can fly away when the time comes. Feed the nymphs on small garden worms.

Step **1**

2 When they start hanging around near the surface of the water, you will know that they are getting ready to change into adults – their gills stop working and they start breathing oxygen through the spiracles in their sides.

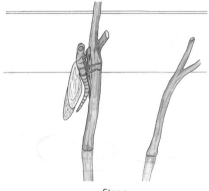

Step **2**

3 The big moment usually arrives in the early morning or evening. The nymph drags itself up one of the sticks, its skin splits open from a weak spot at the back of its head, and a brand-new dragonfly emerges from the husk. It has to be one of the most glorious sights in nature.

Step **3**

Crickets and grasshoppers

From the fields and meadows of temperate regions to the steamy tropical forests come the strident scratching and buzzing of grasshoppers and crickets. Most of them hide in thick grass, though among the world's 22,000 species there are some that live in the soil and others that inhabit caves and crevices. Although they come in a great diversity of shapes and colors, they all have the same basic body plan. So how do you tell a cricket from a grasshopper, or, to be technical, the Ensifera from the Caelifera? That's surprisingly easy for something in the insect world – look at the antennae. A cricket's are long, wispy and whip-like, almost always longer than the body, while a grasshopper's are short and thick. This is probably because crickets are largely nocturnal and use their antennae to feel for food in the dark.

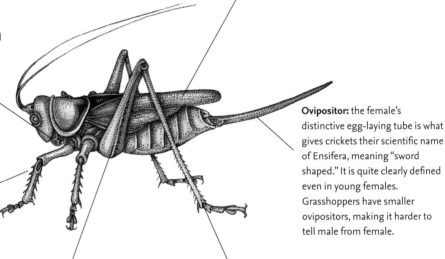

Mouth parts: these are fearsome, looking like a set of meat shears – which is pretty much what they are. The palps on either side are used for feeling for food and tasting it before the main jaws chomp it up.

Wings: the leathery front ones fold back to protect the frailer hind ones, which in adults are usually but not always as long as or longer than the body.

Ovipositor: the female's distinctive egg-laying tube is what gives crickets their scientific name of Ensifera, meaning "sword shaped." It is quite clearly defined even in young females. Grasshoppers have smaller ovipositors, making it harder to tell male from female.

Ears: if you get close enough to a cricket you will see a pair of holes on the front pair of legs, just below the knees. Believe it or not, these are its ears – well, strictly speaking, tympanal organs, which work rather like the human eardrum. In grasshoppers these holes are at the base and sides of the abdomen, usually hidden by the wings.

Stridulating organs: the bits that make the noise. Grasshoppers "fiddle" using their hind legs as a "bow." A set of pegs on the inside of the leg is rubbed against a raised vein on the forewing. Crickets rub a serrated rib of one wing against a similar rib on another wing. On most crickets' wings you can see a clear, rounded area called a mirror that amplifies the sound. Making a noise is about staking out a territory and finding a mate. Not surprisingly, then, males are much more vocal than females!

Legs: the back legs are large and muscular to facilitate jumping. In bush crickets the front legs are covered with spines and spikes, which they use to pin down their prey.

Mini adults

Grasshoppers and crickets differ from butterflies and beetles in that they do not have a four-stage life cycle. Instead, they go through a process called **incomplete metamorphosis**, which basically means they miss out on the caterpillar and pupa bits. From the moment they hatch from the egg, they look like a miniature version of the adult insect; they then go through a series of molts that enables them to grow to full size, developing wings and sexual organs as they go.

If you want to rear grasshoppers and crickets, collect a few nymphs in spring or early summer and keep them in a plastic aquarium with a fine mesh on the top. Introduce "sunshine" by mounting a 60 watt bulb on the inside of the tank or put a desk lamp with a timer switch over the tank so that it provides roughly the same amount of sunlight as is available in the wild. Don't try to use the real thing instead of this artificial sunlight – the tank and its inhabitants will get dangerously overheated if you put them on a sunny windowsill.

Grasshoppers are fussy about what they eat. They like grass but need a selection. Tie a variety of grasses into a bundle, leaving enough loose string to allow you to dangle the bundle into the tank. Raise a corner of the mesh, being careful not to let any grasshoppers jump out, and lower the fresh food. Once the grasshoppers realize what it is, they will move over to it, allowing you to lift out yesterday's leftovers. Crickets are pretty much omnivorous: They eat grass, but they like lots of other things, too – bread soaked in honey, flowers, fish food flakes, fruit, live insects, and blowflies (which you can buy from fishing shops).

This common field grasshopper (*Chorthippus brunneus*) – note the short antennae – has huge back legs enabling it to make impressive defensive leaps.

If you come across a grasshopper nymph like this one in a field of long grass, its back will give you the best clue as to its age – the more developed the wing buds or pads (in this case, tiny), the more mature the insect.

The other things you need to provide are some sturdy twigs propped up against the side of the tank so that the insects can cling to them and hang upside down without bashing their heads on the bottom when they molt. This is quite a sight: A molting caterpillar crawls out of its skin without any hassle, but a grasshopper or cricket has its legs and antennae to worry about. The skin splits open along the back of the neck and the "new" insect – hanging upside down, remember – has to struggle to get all its appendages free and emerge as a perfect and slightly larger version of its former self.

The socialites
ants, bees, and friends

Members of this order crop up in every habitat on Earth that isn't frozen solid. From the window box outside an office in deepest Manhattan to the rain forests of Brazil and the plains of Africa, the Hymenoptera, which means "membrane wings," are doing what they do best – keeping busy. In many places they are the most numerous living thing other than the plants themselves; the ants and termites alone in a given area of rain forest would outweigh all the other animals and birds put together – including the humans. There are over 280,000 species in all, ranging from the large and showy wasps and bees to the secret workforce slaving away underground, in dead wood and between the cracks in the paving slabs.

The sting in the tail

When you mention these insects, most people understandably get hung up on the sharp, pointy bit that sticks out the back. This is actually an egg-laying tube, or ovipositor, designed to pierce an animal or object to allow the female to lay her eggs. Only the social wasps, bees, and some ants have modified it into a sting. Most use the sting in defense, though a few solitary wasps also use it in hunting, to paralyze their prey. The bad news is that, although it is only the female who carries a sting, almost all ants, honeybees, bumblebees, and social wasps are female – because of the way their lives work, males exist only at certain limited times of the year. The good news is that it is expensive for any insect to use its sting, so it would never do so without a good reason. Wasps manufacture venom inside a special venom sac, and using it unnecessarily is like running three times around a football field for no reason – it's just a waste of energy. If a honeybee stings anything other than another insect, the sting is left in the victim and the process of stinging injures the bee, which will probably die a slow death as a result. So don't worry too much about being stung – unless you provoke a bee, wasp, or ant into defending itself, it isn't going to happen.

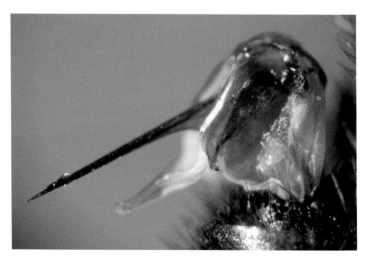

A honeybee sting close up, showing the barbed, lancet-like mechanism for piercing skin, behind which is the venom sac. Both get yanked out and left in the skin when the bee stings – the venom sac continuing to pump out venom all the while.

Bumblebees warm up by basking and shivering and can generate heat chemically to reach the right temperature for flight – important on cold spring days. A furry body also helps.

Honeybees gather pollen, but they also get covered in it, and when they move to another flower, they leave some of it behind, resulting in pollination.

The social whirl

Bees and wasps have a life cycle similar to that of butterflies and moths: They have an egg, a soft fleshy larva, a pupa, and, in some cases, a winged adult stage. The pupa is a rather untidy affair compared with that of a butterfly, with lots of bits such as legs, antennae, and wings sticking out of the cocoon. The other major difference is that we tend to see only the adult insects, as the other stages are usually locked up inside the nest chambers, cells, or combs.

There are two common sorts of social bees that buzz around our gardens – the bumblebees (*Bombus* spp.) and the honeybees (*Apis melifera*). Bumblebees are the round, cuddly ones, brightly striped in yellow and black, and all the more noticeable because they tend to appear in early spring before many other flying insects. The honeybee is slimmer and the stripes are less bold. Throughout the world they gather nectar from which they manufacture honey and pollen, pollinating our flowering plants in the process and therefore playing a key role in life on Earth as we know it.

Unlike bee larvae, which feed on pollen and nectar, young wasps are carnivores – and as such, very useful in the garden, as their favorite foods are all the things that gardeners hate – greenfly, caterpillars, and other insects that munch their way along the herbaceous border. Adult wasps, like most of the Hymenoptera, develop a sweet tooth, which has the downside that they are always keen to have a lick of your ice cream when you are out in the park on a sunny day. On the other hand, the benefit is all the pollinating services that we normally associate with bees. Don't write the wasps off as nature's bad guys – they perform vital services, too.

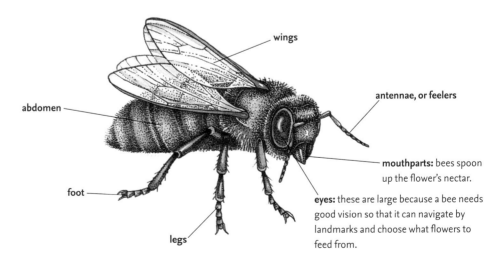

wings

antennae, or feelers

abdomen

mouthparts: bees spoon up the flower's nectar.

foot

eyes: these are large because a bee needs good vision so that it can navigate by landmarks and choose what flowers to feed from.

legs

Honey bee workers

Communal living

Bumblebees and honeybees have somewhat different lifestyles, but both live in a community that revolves around a queen who is little more than a highly efficient egg-laying machine. There may be anything from 20,000 to 80,000 bees in a colony and they are all the offspring of one queen. Some of the members of the colony are males, known as drones, whose function is to mate with any virgin queens they find while out flying in the sunshine; having done this they die. But the vast majority are workers, infertile females who look after the hive and the larvae, producing the royal jelly on which the young are fed for the first three days and foraging for the pollen and nectar most larvae will eat after that. Those larvae designated as future queens will continue to be fed on the protein-rich jelly. When they are large enough, they will leave the hive, mate with males from other colonies, seek out suitable nest sites, and start secreting the wax from which they will make the cells that form the honeycomb. Then the new queen lays her eggs and the process begins again.

Attracting bees

Because bumblebees are so useful to have around the garden, you can encourage them to take up residence by re-creating the conditions found in rodent burrows, one of the favorite places for many species to nest (see p. 224).

Or you can build something that looks like a garden feature but is really a useful bee-nesting site. Heap soil up into a bank in a position that will get sun for most of the day. The soil needs to be what gardeners call free draining, so if yours is a bit muddy, mix it with sand or gravel to coarsen it up. Weed at least some of the bank so that bees don't have to fight their way through the vegetation, and you will soon see them starting to excavate burrows. A pile of logs stacked on top of the bank, with holes of different sizes drilled into the ends and sides, will be an added attraction to those species that like to live in wood.

Quest for the queen

If you look carefully around your home and garden at the beginning of winter, you may be lucky enough to find a lonesome royal, hiding away for the duration. Look in sheds, lofts, garages, wood piles, and among the flowerpots in the greenhouse. She will be there somewhere.

When hibernating, a queen wasp takes on a very distinctive posture, with legs and wings folded up and sitting in a groove along the side of her body. She may also be gripping on with her jaws to wherever she has chosen to overwinter. It is strange to find a living wasp sitting so still, but at this time of year the queen no longer has a workforce to manipulate the conditions for her. Instead she has to judge for herself, choosing somewhere where it is too cold to move but not so cold that she'll die. Once you have had a look, replace her and wish her luck, because most of these insects do not make it to being a queen mum. Lots die of exposure or starvation, or are eaten by birds, rodents, and spiders.

A queen wasp hibernating

Bee happy

Timing is of the essence here: Those first bumblebees that you see cruising around in early spring are the new queens, who will soon be looking for a suitable hole or crevice in which to nest. It's your aim to impress them. The more nest boxes you build, the more likely you are to succeed. A cautionary note: Don't use cotton wool as an easy option for your stuffing material – bees get caught up in it.

Step 1

For each nest you will need:
- a small flowerpot with a single drainage hole in the bottom
- some fine chicken wire
- 4 corks or similar-size stones
- a piece of wood or an old roof tile or slate
- sawdust, hay, and kapok for stuffing
- a trowel

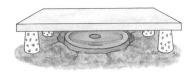

Step 2

1 Start by digging a hole in your herbaceous border, at the edge of the vegetable plot or even on the edge of the lawn where it isn't going to be disturbed by a lawn mower. The hole should be broad enough to accommodate your flowerpot, and a little deeper.

2 Place a pad of bent-up chicken wire in the bottom of the hole to help air circulate around the nest chamber. On top of this put a mixture of the stuffing materials, about enough to fill the flowerpot.

3 Place the pot upside down over the contents of the hole – the bottom should be more or less flush with the surface of the soil. Now cover the drainage hole (which is going to be the entrance to the nest) with the tile, slate, or piece of wood, balancing it at the four corners on the corks or stones.

Step 3

4 Watch for bees coming and going as a sign that you have lodgers.

5 At the end of the year, when all activity has ceased, gently lift the flowerpot and you should see the remains of the wax cells made by the bees. You may even find a new queen or two, sitting out the winter in your cozy nest. If you do, keep disturbance to a minimum, put everything back in position, and you may well have a repeat next year.

Making a bee box

A bee box is a perfect home for solitary bees and wasps, who love to move into hollow stems and excavations made by other insects such as wood-boring beetles. Position your "nest" in a location where it will get plenty of sun. This exercise can be a bit discouraging, as solitary bees and wasps know exactly what they want and can be really fussy, so increase your chances of success by making a number of boxes and set them up in different parts of the garden. Having said that, I have had the poshest-looking professional bee box in my garden for some years – short of providing an en suite bathroom, I don't know what else I could do to attract them – and nothing but spiders, earwigs, and a few beetles ever uses it. I also have a version I made myself from an old catering-size coffee tin and a bunch of old buddleia and elder stems, and it's a positive "hive" of activity.

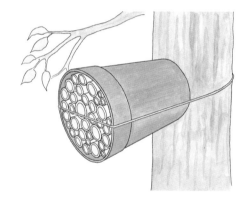

Steps **1-2**

You will need:
- hollow twigs and plant stems of different diameters. Hogweed, buddleia, elder, and some grasses and reeds have hollow stems, and you can supplement your collection with bamboo canes and paper drinking straws
- a plastic flowerpot, coffee jar, or similar container
- scissors
- string, wire, or twine

1 fill the flowerpot or whatever with a selection of stems, trimming them to the height of the container.

2 Attach it to the stem of a shrub, tree trunk, or, if you think you may want to move it for any reason, a garden cane. Make sure the entrance is sloping down slightly, so that it doesn't get waterlogged when it rains.

3 If your housing is approved, you will soon see lots of insects coming and going with building materials. Watch and enjoy.

Ants

a great success story

There are a lot of them – some 14,000 different species, with more being discovered all the time. They have been around for an impressive 80 million years and they are probably the most successful living creatures in the world today. They are basically wingless wasps, and unless you have a trained eye and a good microscope, many of them look very much the same.

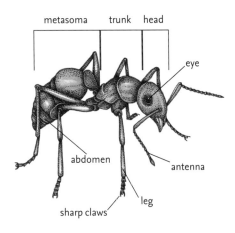

So what makes the ants so successful? Well, their small size is one factor, but the other is that they are highly social and live in huge, terrifyingly efficient colonies. These colonies are ruled over by one or more queens, depending on the species. In addition to laying all the eggs, the queen exudes chemicals called pheromones that are passed from ant to ant in the food they share and in the meeting and greeting process that they indulge in, including lots of licking and stroking with their antennae. These pheromones control the colony, sending out the queen's instructions about defense, foraging parties, and other vital activities. The inhabitants of a colony are all the queen's daughters, who do not breed themselves but devote their energies to servicing the queen and the community – they feed the larvae on nectar and insect grubs, moving them from room to room in the colony as they grow; when the larvae pupate the workers move them to the top of the nest where the warmth of the sun will help them mature quickly; and they go out in huge parties to search for food.

The mating of ants is a strange business. When the time is right, the reigning queen releases special hormones that allow her eggs to produce virgin queens and males instead of the constant stream of female workers. One hot sunny afternoon in the middle of summer, something – it may be temperature, day length, or humidity, no one really knows – triggers a colony to send its potential new queens into a glorious nuptial flight. Mating takes place in the air, the males – having served their purpose – die, and a newly fertilized queen either returns to her former colony or, more usually, sets out to find a suitable site in which to found her own. She immediately starts laying eggs, living off her fat reserves until the first clutch hatches into workers ready to start feeding her again. She uses her jaws to pull her wings off – they too have served their purpose; she will never fly again, and will literally spend the rest of her life laying eggs.

A column of Matabele ants (*Megaponera foetens*) carrying termites back to their colony

Ant town
making a formicarium

Ants do most of their social living underground, so building an ant city is the best way to observe them in action. To collect your ants, look for nests under stones, tin, and wood. Early spring is the best time, as the ants cluster together and you can easily gather a scoopful, which makes it more likely that you will harvest a queen and a good selection of workers, eggs, and pupae.

Step **1**

You will need:
- a piece of plywood 30 cm (12 in) square for the base
- 6 strips of wood about 2 cm (1 in) square in cross section for the frame : 1 x 28 cm (11 in) long, 2 x 24 cm (9 in) long, and 3 x 10 cm (4 in) long
- modeling clay
- a piece of clear rubber tubing at least 30 cm (12 in) long
- a sheet of hard, clear plastic 28 cm (11 in) square
- plaster of paris
- well-drained soil from the garden
- a jam jar with a lid
- enough black cloth or paper to cover the formicarium

1 Screw the wood strips to the base to make a frame. The longest piece is the back, the two medium-size pieces are the sides, and two of the short pieces make the front, leaving a gap. Put the final short piece of wood inside the frame, parallel to the front, but don't screw it down.

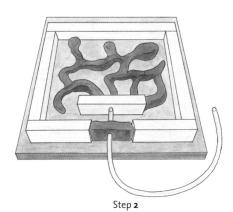

Step **2**

2 Use the modeling clay to form tunnels and chambers the same depth as the frame. Lay the sheet of plastic over the top to test this – if the clay squishes against the plastic, you have built your ant city too high. Make sure the clay snakes around the loose piece of wood. fill the entrance with more clay, and push one end of the rubber tubing through it, butting it up to the loose wood.

3 Mix a runny solution of plaster of paris (see p. 85) and pour it into the gaps not filled by the modeling clay. Leave to set for a day or so, then pull out the clay and the loose piece of wood to leave a series of tunnels in the plaster of paris. Fill the cavities left by the clay and wood with soil.

4 Make a hole in the lid of the jam jar and attach the end of the rubber tubing to it, making sure it is flush with the inside of the lid and sealing any gaps with modeling clay.

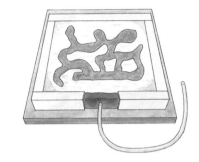

Step **3**

5 Before introducing the ants, place your formicarium in a warm location out of direct sunlight and cover it with the black card or cloth. Now put the ants into the jam jar (which should remain exposed to the light), add a little cotton wool, and soak it in weak sugar solution. Put the lid on firmly and secure it with tape to make it completely antproof.

6 After a brief period of chaos, the ants will get their act together and move into the formicarium. Leave them for a few days to settle down, then start putting different types of food into the jar and watch as the ants march back and forth to collect it. They need sugar, water, and protein, which you can provide with honey, damp cotton wool, insects (alive or dead – a neglected window sill is a good source of these), and seeds. Replace the jam jar with another one whenever you need to clean it out and replenish supplies.

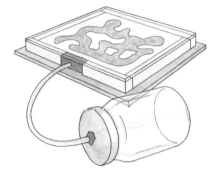

Step **4**

If the ants you collected included a healthy queen, the numbers in your colony will soon start to increase as she lays more eggs and the workers rear more recruits.

Step **5**

Bugs
not just any old insect

To the uninitiated or casual, all invertebrates are bugs. But what entomologists refer to as the true bugs comprise an amazing array of crawling, hopping, or flying beasts that come in a dazzling array of colors. True bugs belong to the family Hemiptera, which means "half wing," so-called because lots of them, such as shield bugs and stink bugs, have half leathery and half delicate wings. Unfortunately some of those that don't have the distinctive bug wings look at first glance very like beetles. A more sure-fire way of telling bugs from anything else in the insect world is the needle-like mouth parts or rostrum. These vary in size, but all have a proboscis that contains two sharp tubes, or stylets, that are pushed into food. One of the stylets injects saliva while the other sucks up liquid food, which may be the sap from a succulent plant or the body fluid of animal prey.

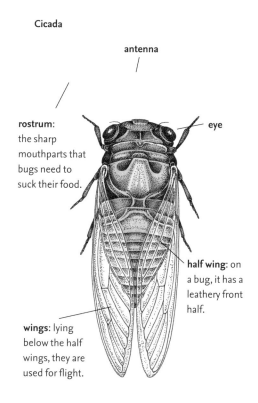

Cicada

antenna

rostrum:
the sharp
mouthparts that
bugs need to
suck their food.

eye

half wing: on
a bug, it has a
leathery front
half.

wings: lying
below the half
wings, they are
used for flight.

Aphids

Although most of us know aphids as garden menaces, very few of the 500 or so species found in the U.K. are actually pests. They are almost all very specialized, feeding on only one or two host plants, but many feed on roots and spend their lives quietly underground, not bothering gardeners or anybody else.

Aphids may be small, but what they lack in size, they more than make up for in numbers. Anywhere that there are plants, there are likely to be aphids. It is thought that in a rich, balanced plant community you could, if you fancied turning over every leaf and looking at every root, every crack in the bark, and every flower bud, find as many as 5,000 million aphids per hectare (that's 2,000 million per acre). They feed on plant sap, which is sugar-rich but protein-poor. This is unfortunate for the aphids, because protein is what they need to make them grow. So they have to drink lots and lots of sap in order to keep the protein intake up. This vast quantity of liquid produces the sticky "honeydew" excretions that keep the ants in the area happy throughout the summer.

One of the reasons there are so many aphids about is that they reproduce at an incredible rate and in a pretty incredible way. To demonstrate this, take a stem of a plant with a few (and I mean just a few) greenfly or blackfly on it into the house in midsummer, making sure that you have at least one large specimen, which will be an adult female. Place the stem in a vase of water and put a high-powered magnifying lens over the bug's behind to watch what happens. In among the dollops of honeydew that the female excretes, the occasional baby will appear too. No flashy displays to persuade a female that this is the best mate, no mates at all in fact, no gestation period, just clone upon clone of baby aphids. Some species can produce ten young a day in this way, and not only that, but each of these young is born with the fully developed embryos of more young inside her. The arithmetic is mind-boggling, but the bottom line is that, if they all survived, a single female could have six million descendants in a two-month period. Thank goodness for ladybugs and the like, which ensure that by no means all of them do survive.

As if that wasn't enough, the truly amazing thing about aphids is that the form of virgin birth or parthenogenesis I have just described is not the only way they reproduce. Like grasshoppers and crickets, most true bugs go through the process of incomplete metamorphosis – they start life in an egg; when they hatch they look like miniature wingless versions of their parents; and then they go through various molting stages before reaching adult size and developing wings.

Given the extraordinary reproduction rate and style of aphids, it's lucky that most ladybugs are voracious consumers of them. Different ladybugs eat different aphid species.

Aphids just have to be different, though. It is because of their bizarre life cycle that they are able to outcompete the gardener with all his tricks and sprays. Different aphids have different ways of doing things, but the common blackfly (*Simulium* spp.) is a good example of their cunning. It spends the winter as an egg, hidden in a crack in the bark of a tree such as a spindle tree (*Euonymus europaeus*) or guelder rose (*Viburnum opulus*).

Come the spring, the eggs hatch, the young blackfly latch onto the unfurling shoots of their host plants, and, four molts later, become plump little females. They start producing wingless clones of themselves – a process that speeds up as the season advances and temperatures rise – until the plant is covered in blackfly. Then something warns them that this is getting out of hand and that they are in danger of drinking their host plant dry and starving if some of them don't leave. So the next generation is born not only with wings but with different tastes – they flutter away from the guelder rose and on to a patch of dock or thistle, or the beans in the vegetable garden.

Settled on to their new host plant, they carry on breeding and feeding, with hundreds upon hundreds of virgin births taking place in the flower beds every day throughout the summer. Then the shortening of the days triggers the birth of another generation of winged females, who fly back to the winter host plants and give birth to egg-laying females, the only ones in the aphid life cycle that need mates. Back on the summer plants, the diminishing numbers alert the females that it is time to produce some males. These too have wings, so they are able to seek out the egg-laying females, mate, and die in the space of a few hours. Back in the guelder rose, the females are poised to lay another clutch of tiny eggs that will see out the winter in a crack in the bark.

Rose aphids (*Macrosiphium rosae*) on a rose stem. The 2-spot ladybug (*Adalia bipunctata*) loves rose aphids.

Getting botanical
plants and allies

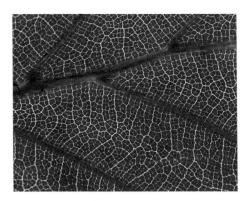

In this chapter we explore the nonanimal kingdoms of life. The most important of these is the plants, but we will also be taking a whistle-stop tour of the moldering masses known as fungi. To any but the most dedicated botanist, this may seem a little dull compared with the living creatures we've been looking at in the rest of the book – it is more of a challenge to get nose to nose with a polar bear than to shove that same nose into the stamens of a buttercup; and the heart may beat out a bossa nova when a tiger turns up, whereas a tiger lily inspires little more than a sigh. Having said that, the biggest living thing on Earth is a plant. The giant redwood (*Sequoiadendron giganteum*), which grows from seeds like pinheads, can weigh 2,145 tons and reach 83 m (272 ft). At the other end of the scale, dead giant club mosses have, over millions of years, formed the world's coal seams, making most of human industry possible. These are the life forms on which all the other, more energetic lives on Earth depend. How can they be dull? So let's see what happens when we look at them a little more closely and apply that greatest of the naturalist's skills, a different perspective.

Above: Beech leaf (detail)
Right: Giant redwood trees

Why care about plants?

At one level, the question of what plant grows where is down to soil type and prevailing weather conditions, but if you look at the bigger picture, plants shape an ecological community; quite simply, they determine the presence of other life.

Rafflesia, or stinking corpse lily (*Rafflesia* spp.), produces the world's largest known flower, measuring about 1 m (3 ft) across. It is a parasitic plant and has no visible leaves, root or stem. When in bloom, it exudes a horrible smell of rotting meat, which attracts insects to pollinate it.

I first realized this when I was eight years old and crazy about insects. Plants hadn't happened to me yet, I hadn't met one that really impressed me, and my eyes hadn't opened to a world that moved at a barely perceivable pace and at a microscopic level. As far as I was concerned, plants were the sorts of things Mum and Dad messed around with – fuchsias and petunias in hanging baskets – and not cool at all.

But the green things were waiting for me just around the corner, and funnily enough, that first awakening came not from the sort of triffid-like plant you might expect to capture a young lad's imagination, but from the very same fuchsias my mother was lovingly cultivating. They were being nibbled by something large and caterpillar-like, and late one night while scrutinizing the herbaceous border with a flashlight I found one of those dream bugs – a finger-size monster elephant hawkmoth caterpillar. It was a beauty, and I collected another and another until I had several jam jars full of fuchsia leaves and big caterpillars. The catch came when Mum showed her displeasure at my caterpillar farming, because I was forever raiding her plants for fresh leaves to feed my captives. The only solution was to cultivate a few fuchsias of my own. I soon became quite a fuchsia expert and enjoyed watching my plants grow almost as much as I enjoyed watching the caterpillars eat them.

As my career as an entomologist continued to blossom, I realized that an understanding of the food plants on which various butterflies and moths depended at different stages of their lives was critical to an understanding of the animals themselves – not only how the plants affected the distribution of a species, but also how the intricacies of the plant's life cycles fitted into the lives of the animals. Now that really pushed my buttons. Much later, when I worked in butterfly houses and farms, and also as a field biologist studying the ecological requirements of threatened fritillary butterflies, the majority of my work became botanical. It doesn't end there, either – as a naturalist you soon find out that some birds roost only in certain trees, some bats feed on specific fruits and flowers, some beetles eat the bark of only one species of tree. And so it goes on.

Assam moth larva (*Antheraea pernyi*). Knowing what the plant is can often help you name the caterpillar feeding on it.

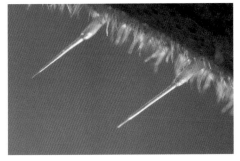

The poison sacs and hypodermic needles of a plain old English stinging nettle (*Urtica dioica*)

I guess what I'm trying to say is, whether you like it or not, plants will affect your life, especially if you plan to spend any time in the great outdoors. In South America, knowing the subtle distinguishing features of regular grass species and razor grass (*Scleria scindens*) can mean the difference between a comfortable day in the field and looking as if you have been in a fight with a jaguar. The same goes for an unfortunate incident when one of my wife's colleagues mistakenly used the leaf of a potently poisonous plant as toilet paper – you can guess the rest. In Australia there is an infamous plant called the stinging tree (*Dendrocnide moroides*) which leaves all those who come into contact with it in no doubt as to how it got its name; for several days, every time you bathe or otherwise get the irritation wet, you are reminded of the full intensity of the original contact. I have even heard of a guy dying having swum in a jungle pool full of dropped stinging-tree leaves! So it makes sense to learn something about them.

Plants...what are they?

Plants can be divided into two main groups. The first and more primitive are the nonvascular plants, which have no special water-carrying vessels within their tissues; they include 14,000 species of moss, 9,000 species of liverwort, and 25,000 species of algae. These plants are examples of some of the earliest to have existed. Plants evolved in water, and many of the nonvascular plants, particularly the algae, still grow there; others, including many mosses and liverworts, have moved onto land but retain a connection with moisture and cannot live in dry places.

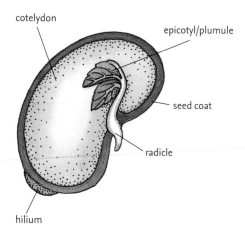

cotelydon

epicotyl/plumule

seed coat

radicle

hilium

You can see cotyledons "in action" if you split a bean into its two white, fleshy halves. Sandwiched between them is a white miniature plant. Look closely, and you will see all the wonderful details of the embryo plant – the leaf structure and lots of tiny perfect veins. It's like looking at a scan of an unborn child.

The second group, the vascular plants, have true leaves and roots and an internal circulatory system of vessels which transport food, water, and other necessary nutrients and chemicals around the plant's tissues.

The vascular plants can be further divided into the ferns, of which there are about 10,000 species, and the most recent and successful of the plant groups, the flowering plants, whose 250,000 species can be further subdivided into the monocotyledons and the dicotyledons. Monocots include grasses, palms, lilies, irises, and orchids and are thought to be more recent in evolution than the dicots, which are more numerous and include all the other flowering plants. The name comes from the food-storage organs in seeds, called cotyledons, and all flowering plants have either one (mono-) or two (di-) These will shrink as the embryo grows, as they power its shoots and roots both upward and downward. The size of the cotyledons varies from plant to plant and gives some idea of a seed's needs – the smaller it is, the nearer the surface it needs to be planted. If a seed is positioned too deeply in the soil, its stores will not have enough energy to push the shoot to the light.

Military orchid – a specialized monocot

Rhododendron – a dicotyledon.

Unassuming little plants
mosses and liverworts

These low-growing plants produce a microclimate all of their own. They exist in spongelike mats that hang on to moisture and tend to become shelter for many smaller moisture-loving creatures. Mosses have little hollow leaves and big cells which act as moisture-storage capsules – a desirable property in species such as sphagnum mosses (*Sphagnum* spp.), used by gardeners to line their hanging baskets and help them retain moisture for their other plants. In the wild you can thrust your hand deep into a sphagnum clump, often up to your elbow, and pull up a plant to see that only the very tip is actually alive, green, and growing – but the rest of the plant, long since left behind down below, keeps on soaking up moisture and providing for the living bit upstairs.

Some mosses have strange, uprising structures that look almost flowery. These contain the plant's sexual organs and require moisture to enable the male cells to swim toward the female organs. Once the female parts are fertilized, they produce thin filaments with a bobble on top – this is the sporing body, and in some species, when it dries out enough, it becomes explosive, blowing up and scattering its contents to the wind. These spores can be cultivated in the same way as ferns and if you scatter them onto damp blotting paper, you can watch them germinating under a microscope.

Liverworts have a similar life cycle but keep an even lower profile than mosses. Look at their leaves and you will see they have cup-and-envelope-like structures from which free-floating buds called gemmae are produced. These often rely on water splashing or flowing over them, and from each one a little liverwort will grow.

These are the fruiting bodies of a moss. The spore capsule at the end will lose its cap and open up to release the tiny spores when it dries out and conditions are right for the spores to blow away.

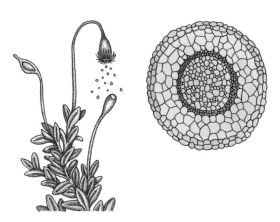

Opened moss capsule and cross section of the moss stem

Simple plants
ferns and their fronds

Fern – young fronds unfolding. Their reproductive parts develop on the leaves.

Look under the fronds of mature fern leaves and you may well see lots of odd little C-shaped brown things. These are the plant's spore capsules (spores are a fern's or fungus's take on seeds), and if you shake the frond when conditions are right, the spores will show themselves as a light dust. To understand the fern's life cycle, harvest some of these spores by shaking them into a petri dish of sterile, moist soil. Cover them and keep them in a light place out of direct sunlight. Eventually the spores will produce a strange, single leaflike disk called a prothallus, which will quickly wither away. Don't lose heart, though, as something else has been happening at a microscopic level. On the surface of the prothallus, egg and sperm cells will have developed and, in damp conditions, the sperm will swim to the eggs and fertilize them. From these female organs a small fern will grow. The sperm's dependence on a film of water to make its way to the egg explains why ferns cannot live far from moisture.

If you start getting a feel for ferns, mosses, and other moisture-loving plants, you can always keep some of your babies and grow them, re-creating the high-humidity environment they need in a bottle garden. Both the club mosses and the horsetails also have a prothallus stage in their life cycle.

Things to do with spores

Ferns need to release their spores only when the environmental conditions are dry and right for "wafting." If you look at a sporing body under a powerful hand lens, you will see that along the edges are thick cells which act as water-sensitive triggers. Shine a torch or some other weak heat source on the spore capsule and you should be able to persuade the fern to snap open and fling out some spores. Drop some water on the plant, and the capsules shut up tight again.

Horsetails also distribute themselves by using spores, but their sporing bodies are tall, freestanding, conelike structures. If you shake out some of the spores and look at them under a microscope, you will see an odd structure with four straps attached to it. These straps act as springs and generate movement, which helps with dispersal. Heat them up and the straps coil up quickly; moisten them, and they uncoil again.

The spore-bearing "cone" stems of the giant horsetail (*Equisetum telmateia*)

The big green life-making machine
photosynthesis

Lie on your back in a deciduous woodland in the springtime and you will feel it. As you gaze up through the backlit tessellations of leaves with the sun dancing over their perfect surfaces, you are looking at a multitude of invisible light-processing machines, an almost magical alchemy that harnesses the sun's rays and gives planet Earth the green mantle that supports everything else upon it. Without it we wouldn't have wildlife to look at – let's face it, we wouldn't even be here to contemplate the fact!

Leaf structure

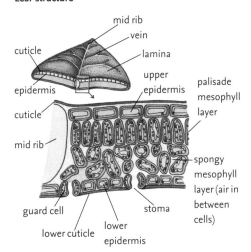

mid rib
vein
cuticle
lamina
upper epidermis
palisade mesophyll layer
epidermis
cuticle
mid rib
spongy mesophyll layer (air in between cells)
guard cell
stoma
lower cuticle
lower epidermis

Chloroplast structure

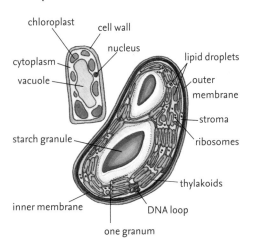

chloroplast
cell wall
nucleus
cytoplasm
lipid droplets
vacuole
outer membrane
stroma
starch granule
ribosomes
inner membrane
thylakoids
DNA loop
one granum

The way we see green plants gives us our first clue to what's important to the life-giving process. We see green because it is the wavelength of the spectrum that the plants use least – it is surplus to their requirements, so is reflected back at us. The reds and blues are snatched away from the rainbow and used to drive the process that turns sunlight, carbon dioxide, and water into the fundamental foods that kick off pretty much every food chain on Earth. That process is called photosynthesis, which means "putting together with light."

When the sun's rays hit our planet, 99 percent of them are absorbed by the land or the sea or even reflected back into space, but the remaining 1 percent is trapped by little green blobs, processing units called chloroplasts that are held within a plant's tissues. Within these is contained, neatly packaged, a chemical called chlorophyll, and this wonderful stuff is the key to life on Earth. The magic that now takes place can be represented by this formula:

$$CO_2 \text{ (carbon dioxide)} + H_2O \text{ (water)} \rightarrow O_2 \text{ (oxygen)} + C_6H_{1206} \text{ (sugar)}$$

What happens in the chloroplast is that various pigments such as chlorophyll B, carotene, and xanthophylls absorb the sunlight and channel it to the other form of chlorophyll, chlorophyll A. Here it releases charged particles called electrons, which are then replaced by the hydrogen atoms in water. The outcome of this part of the process – called the "light reaction" – is that water is split into its component parts, hydrogen and oxygen. The oxygen is released as a gas, while the hydrogen goes on to meet carbon dioxide in the next phase, called "carbon dioxide fixing." Eventually this produces simple sugars such as glucose and fructose (C_6H_{1206}), any excess of which may be stored as starch, or the more complex sugar sucrose ($C_{12}H_{22}O_{11}$). These energy-rich chemicals are stored in the tissues until they are needed, a bit like

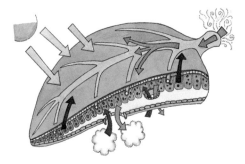

This diagram shows photosynthesis and transpiration in action. The leaf takes in sun and water and produces sugar and oxygen.

a battery pack that the plant uses up when it has to grow or when it is too dark for photosynthesis to take place. The gases involved in photosynthesis enter and leave the plant via little pores called stomata in the leaves and green stems.

While plants are busy building sugar and giving off gases useful to the rest of life on Earth, that very same life on Earth is selfishly taking those sugars and reversing the process by means of something called cellular respiration. This means extracting energy from the sugars by breaking them down, using oxygen and giving off water and CO_2 in the process – exactly the opposite of what happens during photosynthesis. This chemical reaction, which occurs within every green leaf in the world, is the reason why nothing can live without plants; the greenies are inextricably linked to the lives of every breathing thing by that rather dull-looking bunch of numbers and letters printed on this page. It's also the main reason why environmentalists get angry when people start cutting down the biggest concentrations of photosynthesizers on the planet: the rain forests.

Not all plants use photosynthesis to produce all their food. Some, like the mistletoes, are semiparasitic, and although they do photosynthesize, they also feed off their host plant – often an oak tree, in the case of mistletoe. Others have no chlorophyll at all and are totally dependent on their hosts. Examples of this include the toothworts (*Lathraea* spp.), broomrapes (*Orobanche* spp.), and dodders (*Cucusta* spp.), most of which have an odd pinkish hue to their stems and only really exist aboveground as flower spikes.

The pallid flesh color of plants such as broomrape stands out due to the lack of chlorophyll. This is because they are parasites, stealing their living from the roots of others.

Best of both worlds. The semiparasitic mistletoe (*Viscum album*), does a little bit of photosynthesis and a little bit of stealing.

The bubbles of life

All around us plants are producing oxygen as a by-product of photosynthesis – which is handy for the rest of us, as we need oxygen in order to breathe and carry out all of life's processes. We simply cannot get away from the fact that plants are the foundation stone of life on Earth.

Most of the time you obviously can't see a plant produce a clear, colorless gas and release it back into a cocktail of more clear, colorless gases. The exception is when the plant lives underwater, and the following experiment is a great way to witness the production of one of the most useful end products of photosynthesis.

You will need:
- a clear jar
- a funnel
- a test tube
- a handful of pond weed (*Elodea canadensis* is one of the best)
- a long match or wooden splint

1 fill the kitchen sink with water. Fill the jar with water, add the pond weed, and place the funnel upside down over the jar.

2 Immerse the test tube and turn it upside down without breaking the surface of the water, making sure there is no air trapped inside it. Place the test tube over the submerged neck of the funnel.

3 Lift the ensemble out of the sink and place it on a light, sunny windowsill. As the pond weed begins to photosynthesize, you will see small bubbles forming on the surface of the leaves and rising in streams to be collected in the inverted test tube. When the tube is half full (the time this takes depends on how bright the light is and how warm the water), light the match, quickly blow it out again, and, while it is still glowing, lift the tube and thrust the splint into it. The splint should burst back into flame. This is proof that the gas your humble pond weed has produced is life-giving oxygen itself!

Step 1

Step 2

Step 3

Touching the light

"Potato" is just the name we have given to the underground reserve or tuber of a certain kind of plant, and the tuber is the place where this particular plant stashes away vast quantities of energy-rich starch. If you cut into a potato and drop some iodine solution on the exposed tissue, you will notice that it quickly turns from yellow to a blue-black color. That is the test for the presence of starch. Once you are convinced about that, it is time to try an experiment with the living light-processing units on a handy houseplant.

Step 1

You will need:
- a houseplant you don't mind damaging
- a few small sheets of black plastic (tearing up a large trash bag will do nicely) or kitchen foil
- a few clothespins
- 2 petri dishes or saucers
- small quantities of methylated spirit and iodine solution
- a heatproof beaker
- a small saucepan
- a pair of tweezers

Step 2

1 Wrap some but not all of your plant's leaves in the plastic or foil, holding this in position with clothespins so that no light can penetrate to the surface of the leaves. Leave on the windowsill for two days.

2 Take one leaf that has been starved of light and one that has been left as normal. Put some methylated spirit in the beaker, stand this in a pan of water, and heat until the spirit boils. Remove from the heat and, using tweezers, dip each leaf into the hot water for a minute. Then dip them into the spirit and leave until they are almost white.

Step 3

3 Put each leaf in a separate petri dish or saucer, add some iodine, and watch what happens. What you should observe is that only the leaf that was exposed to light turns blue-black, showing that starch, the product of photosynthesis, is present. Only when light could reach the plant's chloroplasts did photosynthesis take place.

Tropism
the way to grow

Plants have never been known for their speed of movement. Although there are exceptions, for the most part they live at a pace at which change is observable only if we film them and speed up the footage. When this is done, they take on whole different personas. A questing bramble stem becomes a serpentine arm reaching out and dragging itself forward on its ratchets of thorns, an unfurling branch of leaves becomes a flapping ballet of salad, and a blooming flower looks like a pyrotechnic display.

The fastest-growing plants in the world are the bamboos, king-size grasses that are capable of reaching for the light at an incredible 1 m (over 3 ft) a day. But even this is not quite fast enough to register with the human eye. Instead we have to rely on indirect evidence of plant growth.

Growth occurs at specific points within the structure of each plant, and different species with different ecologies grow in different ways. To demonstrate this, take a dish of germinating grass seed and one of germinating cress seed. Once they have grown up a few centimeters (an inch or two), take a pair of scissors, give both a buzz cut, and wait to see how the seedlings respond. You will find that the grass picks up where it left off, just as it does when you mow your lawn, but the poor cress will never recover from your barbarity. Why? Well, it's all about the position of growth areas known as meristems. In the grass, the meristem sits in a band of tissue between the roots and the shoot, so when the shoot is trimmed or grazed, the growth cells remain intact. Grasses evolved in ecosystems where they were continually eaten by grazing animals, so this is a vital survival strategy; it also explains why

The fastest-growing plant in the world – bamboo. You can almost see it grow.

These seedlings are leaning to the right – the predominant direction of the light source – a classic example of phototropism.

some members of this huge family provide us with such sumptuous, springy lawns. With the cress, the growth zone is right at the very tip of the shoot; remove this and the shoot is doomed.

Growing plants move toward and away from stimuli, following the lead giving by the part containing the meristem. Directional growth occurs when cells grow and multiply faster on one side of a shoot than on the other, in response to increased levels of growth hormones. This phenomenon is called tropism, from the Greck meaning "a turn," and there are many different kinds. One of the commonest is phototropism, which means it is connected with light. This may be either a positive move, as seen when germinating seedlings grow toward the light, or a negative one, as in the seed heads of ivy-leafed toadflax (*Cymbalaria muralis*), which "self-plants" its own seeds in dark crevices and so grows away from light.

Responding to other stimuli – nastic movements

Movements that are not directional and are not controlled by growth are known as nastics. Examples are the everyday opening and shutting of flowers such as daisies and celandines in response to light intensity and the similar response of crocuses to temperature change. Some of the quickest plant movements are those observed in so-called "sensitive" plants such as *Mimosa* species. On physical contact they will close up their leaves as a way of avoiding looking succulent and being grazed by passing herbivores. Another interesting nastic movement is that exhibited by the carnivorous plant the Venus flytrap (*Dionaea muscipula*), whose scientific name means "mousetrap of Venus." Although they don't actually stretch to consuming mice, they

Some plants such as the Venus flytrap have adapted to nutrient-poor soils by obtaining their protein from the tissues of animals, caught by their ingenious devices.

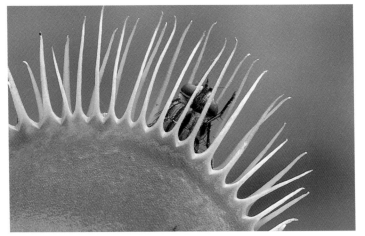

have, like nearly all carnivorous plants, evolved to live in boggy, nutrient-poor habitats and supplement their diet with the bodies of the animals they catch.

Venus flytraps have a pair of specialized leaves that form the famous trap. The surfaces of these two leaves are held open, exposing a red surface and producing sweet nectar, both of which are attractive to insects. On each of these leaves are three hairs, and when an insect lands on them, the pressure on the hairs causes the leaves to snap together.

If you hold a bright light behind a Venus flytrap in a dark room and look along the backlit "jaws," you will see the three trigger hairs on each half. If you touch one of them with a small paintbrush, nothing happens, but touch two at the same time and bang, the trap shuts tight. If you touch the same hair twice within a certain time frame – say 20 seconds – the leaves will also snap closed. This complex mechanism helps the plants to save their energy, as it has to be a fairly big insect to trigger the hairs in such a way. Such an insect's struggles will further stimulate the trap to stay tightly closed. But if the plant is fooled by a small ant or even by a curious naturalist poking it with a paintbrush, the trap will shut only halfway. This allows the insect to escape, as the plant has sensed that the returns it will provide are not worthy of the effort involved in digesting it.

There are many other sorts of carnivorous plants, including pitcher plants (*Napenthes* and *Sarracenia* spp.), sundews (*Drosera* spp.), butterworts (*Pinguicula* spp.), and bladderworts (*Utricularia* spp.). If these fascinate you the way they fascinate me, you are in good company – they were also a great favorite of Charles Darwin! You can experiment to see what stimulates the leaves to curl and release the digestive enzymes by placing various foods on them. Try leaves, grass, sweets, insects, and small pieces of beef. It is the protein itself that gets the juices flowing.

If you come across pitcher plants in the wild, try emptying their contents out into a tray. I am often surprised by the prey items and other residents I find. As well as the partially digested remains of many types of insects, I have decanted the bodies of frogs, lizards, and even a small mouse. The real mind-boggler is that, in some plants, despite what must be strong digestive juices, I have found the living larvae of mosquitoes and other water-dwelling insects. Spiders and tree frogs also sometimes live on the doorstep of death by hiding out in the humid confines.

Even in the heat of noon, the sundew's glandular sticky hairs continue to twinkle with dew – hence its name – luring insects to their death.

Phototropism

You can demonstrate positive phototropism by growing seedlings on a windowsill: The shoots will visibly grow toward the light; turn them around and they grow back the other way. Put little foil hats on some and they will continue to grow upright in response to gravity (see Geotropism), oblivious to the light stimulus the others are following. You can take this to extremes by challenging a germinating seedling to a bit of an obstacle course.

Step 1

You will need:
- a cardboard box with a lid, and extra cardboard to make baffles
- matt black paint
- a planted bean or sunflower seed

1 Insert a couple of baffles into your box and paint all the inside surfaces with matte black paint to absorb any light that might otherwise be reflected.

Step 2

2 Make a small hole at one end of the box with the end of a sharp pencil. Set the box on its side with the hole at the top. In the bottom place your bean or sunflower in a pot of damp soil. Now put the lid on the box.

3 Wait and watch what happens as your seed germinates and the shoot, complete with its light-sensitive cells, goes searching for the pinhole that is letting in the light it needs.

You may wonder how a plant can make all this growth and all these contortions without any light, but remember the seed itself is an energy-storage unit designed for just this sort of exertion. The energy was put there by the parent plant.

Step 3

Geotropism

This is a pattern of growth influenced by gravity. Plants need to know where to put their roots, and the preprogrammed response that allows them to ground themselves firmly in the earth is sensitivity to gravity.

You will need:
- a jam jar with a lid
- a wire support
- a bean
- glue
- cotton wool

Step 1

1 Glue the wire to the inside base of the jar and put the bean on it. Pack some moist cotton wool into the jar and replace the lid.

2 Wait for the bean to start throwing out a shoot and a root. Make a note of the direction of the root's growth.

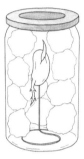

Step 2

3 Then place the jar in the dark and turn it upside down. Watch what happens to the root. Repeat and repeat, and note that whichever way the jar is turned, even in the absence of light, the root will always grow downward.

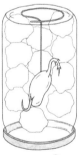

Step 3

Propagules, batteries, and time travel
the secrets of seeds

Seeds really are extraordinary things: They are compact, easily stored, and capable of surviving drought, sub-zero temperatures, even fire; in their dried state they resist attack from mold or bacteria and, despite being energy-packed food sources, they manage to avoid the gaze of many seed-eating animals by strategies such as camouflage. They are full of surprises, too: Some are dynamic – they can fling, ping, pop, and whiz – whereas others are incredibly good at doing nothing at all. The record for any living thing sitting around doing nothing is claimed by the seed of an arctic lupin (*Lupinus arcticus*), which was successfully germinated after more than 10,000 years!

Seeds come in a variety of sizes, from the coconut-like product of the giant fan palm (*Lodoicea maldiva*), which weighs 20 kg (44 lb), to the minute seeds of some species of tropical orchid, with 992.25 million per gram (that's more than 28,000 million per ounce)! But whatever their size, their mission is simple. They have to go forth and find the best place to grow, away from competition, predators, and detrimental climatic conditions. They can do this in a huge variety of exciting ways, and they do it all while they are technically dead, as their cells show no signs of metabolic activity.

Equipped with everything it needs to start a new life, a seed simply sits and waits for the three triggers it requires for germination: the right temperature, enough water, and the right situation, such as the correct soil. Until these things come together, the embryo is held in a state of suspended animation by its dehydrated state – typically less than 2 percent of a seed's weight is water, compared with 95 percent in a thriving herbaceous plant. When all the conditions are right, the seed coat lets the water in, at a rate which varies from species to species. In some species the coat also needs to be digested by bacteria in the soil first, or the seed needs to be subjected to an abrasive action called scarification, caused by passing through the gut of a bird or mammal. This is one reason why some seeds sit inside tasty fruits that advertise their presence to animals in the hope of being eaten, dispersed, and deposited in a ready-to-grow condition in their own little pile of manure!

The seed of a sycamore tree (*Acer* spp.) has a wing that allows it to spin in the wind and travel far from its parent. Here, moisture has triggered germination, and the root, powered by the seed's eneregy store, heads for the dark.

Germination

watching it

We generally get to see only about half of the process of germination, because the other half goes on below the surface of the soil. This is where basic hydroponics comes in handy. Hydroponics is the technical term for growing plants in a liquid medium, and it provides the interested botanist with a window on this stage of a plant's development.

You will need:
- a transparent glass vase or jar
- a sheet of paper
- cotton wool
- a seed (ideally a large one such as a bean, maize, or sunflower)
- chopsticks or a similar long implement (optional)
- graph paper (optional)

1 Place the paper in the vase or jar, fitting it closely to one side. Stuff the rest of the vessel with cotton wool.

2 Push a seed into the gap between the paper and the glass, using the chopsticks if it helps. The seed should stay toward the top of the jar so that you can see a decent amount of root growth; if not, stuff in some more cotton wool.

3 Add enough water to reach the seed but not cover and drown it.

4 If you want to record the daily growth of the roots and the shoot, stick a strip of graph paper to the outside of the vase and mark it each day with a line and a date.

Steps **1-4**

Left: willow herb
(*Epilobium* spp.) attaches
plumes of hairs to its
seeds so they blow away
in the wind.

Agents of dispersal

To prove how good seeds are at their job description, look at your
dog's coat or your own socks next time you have been out for a walk
through long vegetation. Many plants were using what we proudly call
space-age technology before humans had worked out how to carve a
wooden club. Velcro was not a product of space exploration, it was
invented by plants – just think how those burrs and grass seeds have
attached themselves to anything that is fluffy or woolly. They use a
multitude of little grappling hooks that vary in design and number but
work on similar principles.

If you're still not impressed, scrape the dirt off the bottom of your
shoes and mix it up with water. Then prepare a sterile seed tray with
soil that you have microwaved to kill off any other seeds that might be
there. Pour your shoe mix onto the tray and place the whole lot in a
clear plastic bag. Leave it on a windowsill and watch what happens.

Cleavers, or goose grass
(*Galium aparine*), uses the
Velcro technique.

Dandelion (*Taraxacum
officinale*) parachute hairs
open out in dry weather
for wind liftoff.

Suck it up and see: transpiration

Even though vascular plants have a circulatory system that superficially resembles ours, they have no pumping equivalent of the human heart to force their life blood through their veins. Instead they rely on transpiration. This entails losing water, usually through the stomata, and although this may sound like a bad thing, it is actually a very useful "suction pump" process that keeps the plant alive.

A lone water molecule is a rare thing in nature – their natural affinity means that one always attracts another. So as water molecules evaporate from the surface of a leaf, others move in from neighboring cells to take their place; then others move in from the next cells along, and so on and so forth until you get to the source of the water – a feat of micro-plumbing called the xylem vessels, which link the leaves to the roots, where the water enters the plant, and in which water exists as a very long chain of molecules. As these are pulled out of the top, they drag others in the chain up behind them, and with the water move the minerals, vitamins, and all manner of other substances necessary to the plant's health and survival.

In addition to trying the experiment below, you can measure the rate of transpiration by putting the stem of a cut plant in a jar containing a measured amount of water and adding a thin layer of cooking oil, which forms a seal and prevents any water being lost by evaporation. Water will therefore be lost only through the stomata, so any decrease in the water level will be down to transpiration alone. By timing the experiment and marking the water line on the side of the jar, you can measure not only the volume but also the rate of water lost.

If, when the experiment is finished, you put the leaves on a piece of graph paper and draw around them, you can even work out the rate of water lost per square centimeter or square inch of leaf. Warming up the room or standing the experimental setup in front of a fan will enable you to assess how temperature and air movement (wind) affect the rate of transpiration.

An experiment with transpiration

Although transpiration is invisible because it operates at a molecular level, its influences are often felt – it is the end result of transpiration that forms clouds and leads to daily deluges of rain above the tropical forests, for instance. An average 15 m (50 ft) broad-leaved tree can transpire up to 260 liters (58 gal) of water an hour! On a more accessible level, the effects of the same process can be witnessed on your own windowsill. Try this:

You will need:
- 2 glasses
- a few drops of food dye
- a long-stemmed, pale-colored flower such as a carnation
- a sharp knife or scissors
- sticky tape

Step **2**

Step **3**

1 fill the glasses with water and put the dye in one of them.

2 Using the knife or scissors, split the stem of your flower up the middle to about the halfway point. Wind a little tape around the top of the split to hold it together.

3 Place each half of the split stem in a glass of water, move the whole setup on to a windowsill, and leave for a few hours. (The sunnier and hotter it is, the faster the water will evaporate from the petals and leaves and give you a result.)

4 When you return, you should see that the half of the flower whose stem is in the colored water has turned the same color as the dye, demonstrating that the water that has been sucked up as the plant loses water from its petals is directly connected with the bottom of the stem.

5 For an even simpler demonstration, put a humble white daisy in a pot of watered-down blue ink for a few hours and watch it turn blue.

Sun catchers
leaves

It's funny how we all notice leaves as soon as they drop off the tree and start clogging up drains and blowing around the garden. But how good are you at telling different types of tree apart by looking at their leaves? Why not start a collection? Press leaves between the pages of heavy books (see p. 270), make prints by pressing them into the surface of modeling clay, or turn them into lacy skeletons. Impressions of leaves can be made in a variety of ways: If you simply brush a leaf with shoe polish, making sure you work it well into all the leaf surface, then place it on a piece of paper oily side down, cover with another sheet of paper, and rub firmly all over the surface with your finger or a sponge, you should get a good imprint. This works best with older leaves that have fallen from the tree, as they tend to have more prominent vein structures.

Another excellent way of achieving an image for your records is to make a leaf skeleton (see below) and then hijack a photographer's darkroom. Place the skeleton on a piece of a photographic paper below a table lamp, turn the lamp on for five seconds, remove the leaf and place the paper in developer for three minutes, soak in a water bath for an hour, and hang up to dry. You should now have a stunning photographic image of your leaf's veins on a black background.

Autumn color

It's not called "the fall" for nothing. The most obvious feature of this season is that the leaves of deciduous trees drop off. Millions upon millions of leaves that have served their purpose in the spring and summer, attracting the sunlight and housing the chlorophyll that are essential to photosynthesis, must now be dispensed with. During a harsh winter, when it is difficult for a tree's roots to obtain enough moisture from the cold soil, it can't afford to lose too much water through transpiration. So the leaves have to go.

They don't go quietly, though. Their parting gesture is the most flamboyant display of their lives. The key factor in producing the reds, golds, oranges, and even purples that people cross continents to see is decreasing day length. This triggers the plant cells to produce a hormone called abscissic acid, which in turn forms a corky layer of cells (the abscission layer) at the base of the leaf, where it joins the twig. This acts as a seal across the vascular tissue that normally carries water and nutrients into the leaf and takes waste products away. As a result, the leaf effectively starves, the stem that holds it to the plant weakens, and it is eventually carried away by a gust of wind.

A leaf print shows off to perfection a leaf's "micro-plumbing" - its characteristic vein pattern and shape.

This may sound like an unhappy ending, but before the final curtain, the leaf makes a fantastic exit. Because it isn't getting the nutrients it requires, it stops manufacturing chlorophyll. In fact, chlorophyll is an unstable substance that breaks down and needs to be replaced all year round, but cooling autumn temperatures speed up the decomposition, replacement chlorophyll isn't produced, and the green color that has covered the landscape for the past six months fades away.

In its place appear more stable pigments – the carotenes, which can be further divided into the xanthophylls and the carotenoids. These are responsible, respectively, for the yellows and the reds and oranges which have been waiting in the wings while chlorophyll has been stealing the show, and which now take center stage. Another group of chemicals, the xanthocyanins, which produce the rich crimsons and purples, are created by the last late-seasonal gasps of photosynthesis, but trapped in the leaf by the abscission layer as it firms up. The maples (*Acer* spp.) which cover New England are the most spectacular examples of this, but British natives such as dogwood (*Cornus* spp.) and wild cherry (*Prunus avium*) may steal a last curtain call. The production of xanthocyanins is encouraged by dry, sunny days and cool, crisp nights, so we enjoy the most spectacular autumn color under these weather conditions.

Pigments on display, revealed by the death of chlorophyll

Plant plumbing

These lacy skeletons are a great way of showing off how the leaf works. The skeleton consists of the "plumbing" used to supply the leaf with water and to transport the sugars made in the leaf cells during the summer to the rest of the tree.

You will need:
- leaves
- washing soda at the concentration of approximately 40 g per liter (6 oz per gal)
- a pair of tweezers
- a paintbrush

1 Heat the soda mixture until it nearly boils, take it off the heat, and soak your leaves in it for 30 minutes.

2 Using tweezers, carefully remove the leaves and gently wash them under a tap. The soft parts will fall away (this can be further encouraged by teasing them with a paintbrush).

Step **1-2**

The rude bits
flowers

We give them to our loved ones, wallow in their scent, and select them for our gardens because of their color and aesthetic appeal, but flowers do not exist for our benefit. They are the sexual organs of flowering plants, and the ones we notice most are those used as billboards to catch the attention of passing insects, birds, and to a lesser extent mammals such as bats, who have a very serious job to do. The plants use all sorts of lures such as gaudy colors, flamboyant petals, and enticing perfume, and as if that were not enough, some species offer a little gift in return, in the form of energy-rich sugary nectar.

Busy bees: this bumblebee is working hard collecting pollen and nectar from this flower, and no wonder – it has to visit up to 64 million flowers to make 1 kg (2.2 lb) of honey.

This is all about the flying animals collecting the flowers' sexual packages of pollen and transferring them to another plant so that it is fertilized. Some flowers – certain species of orchid, for example – are just a big con act; they look like a sexy example of a female insect, tricking the poor males into trying to mate with them. Before the males give up frustrated, they will have done just what the flower wants, in return for zilch!

From the naturalist's point of view, flowers are also useful ways of identifying the plant that is producing them. When studying them, look at the structure of the flower and at the size, color, and number of the petals and internal organs. Bear in mind that even though many flowers contain both male and female parts, some flowers are only male, others only female.

Stapelia are a group of stem succulents, with large attractive, star-shaped flowers that are often colorful and have interesting patterns. Like the Rafflesia (p. 234), most species produce a smell of rotting flesh to attract insects for pollination.

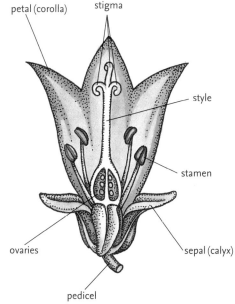

petal (corolla)

stigma

style

stamen

ovaries

sepal (calyx)

pedicel

The flowers of common bent grass (*Agrostis capillaries*) release a lot of light, small pollen grains that are easily carried away on the wind. Wind pollinators need to produce a huge amount of pollen to ensure the success of at least some pollen grains reaching the stigmas on nearby flowers. The diagram below shows a cross section of a grass flower.

We tend to overlook some other forms of flower, such as those of certain species of tree and grass, because they don't need to be showy. They are simply launching pads for the pollen, which is cast out to the mercy of the winds in the hope that it will find another plant to fertilize. The odds in this game of botanical roulette are skewed back in the plants' favor by the production of millions upon millions of tiny, windborne pollen grains, the stuff of hay-fever sufferers' nightmares!

So how do you tell an insect-pollinated flower from a wind-pollinated one? Well, the insect-pollinated flowers are likely to be large, showy, and brightly colored. The anthers (the part of the stamen – the plant's male reproductive organ – in which the pollen ripens) are often hidden within the flower in a way that facilitates contact with the insect or other pollinating agent. These flowers generally produce fewer pollen grains, whose structure tends to be spiky and complex, so that they will stick to the pollinator and be carried away to be deposited on another flower. The stigmas (female sexual organs) of these flowers, which need to receive the incoming pollen, also tend to be strategically positioned inside the flower, to ensure maximum contact with the pollen-dusted pollinating agent.

Wind-pollinated flowers are often inconspicuous, with green petals and no obvious scent. The anthers are large and only loosely attached to the flower, so that the slightest breeze shakes the pollen free. The flowers often dangle, with the sexual parts exposed; the stigmas are feathery to maximise the surface area that will catch pollen. These plants produce large quantities of smooth, light, easily wind-borne pollen grains.

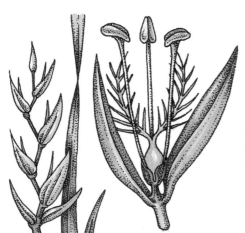

Some trees produce male and female flowers. The male flowers, or catkins, all hang in a group, like lambs' tails. One catkin can release millions of pollen grains, which are transported by the wind. Some will, with luck, land on the stigmas of a female flower of another plant.

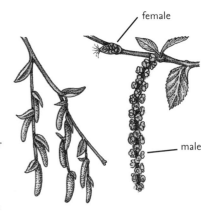

female

male

Trees
the oldies

Trees are arguably the oldest living things on the planet, the record being held by a species of bristlecone pine (*Pinus longaeva*) in California whose estimated age is between 4,000 and 5,000 years! The high altitude and cool conditions they grow under contribute to this longevity, but even in less favored parts, trees are some of the oldest living features of nearly all landscapes, and there are a few tricks that a naturalist can use to calculate their age.

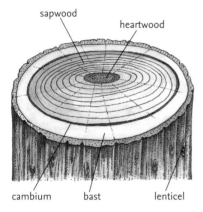

sapwood
heartwood
cambium
bast
lenticel

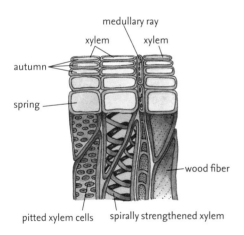

medullary ray
xylem
xylem
autumn
spring
wood fiber
pitted xylem cells
spirally strengthened xylem

The best known way of aging a tree is called dendrochronology and unfortunately involves taking a saw to it and cutting it down! Looking at a cross section of a tree which has been smoothly cut can reveal a number of interesting growth features. The patterns of rings and lines seen are the direct result of how the plant has grown. Just beneath the bark is a layer called the cambium, the cells of which retain the ability to keep dividing in three different directions: inward to form xylem vessels that become the "wood" cells, outward to form the phloem cells essential for food transportation, and sideways to increase the circumference of the tree. (If you think about it you will realize that trees have to grow out as well as up, otherwise they would eventually become top-heavy, unstable, and fall over.)

Each year during the growth period of the tree, the cambium cells multiply and add a new layer. It is these layers that produce the concentric circles or rings. Count these and you will have a pretty good idea of how old the tree was before it was cut down. Other features of interest are the medullary rays – spars of tissue that connect the inner and outer layers of the trunk, enabling waste material from the outer layers to be dumped in the center dead wood and adding further support to the plant in much the same way as the iron ties used by builders shore up and add strength to walls.

As the tree grows outward, the cells in the center die off and become impregnated with a hard, tough substance called lignin. These dead cells are far from useless to the tree, for they are what gives the trunk its strength. The very center of a tree trunk is known as the heartwood. Occasionally a weakness in the tree, such as an injury or a lost limb, allows fungi and other decomposing organisms to gain entry to the dead tissues. This can have mixed results, for although eating away at the heart is obviously bad news for the tree, it also forms cavities which are then colonized by bats or nesting birds and are in themselves ecologically very important.

Estimating a tree's height

There are a number of ways of estimating the height of a tree that are easier and quicker than shinning up it with a tape measure. The first relies on comparing the tree with something whose height you know – in this case, a friend.

The friend, stick, and pencil method

1 Measure your friend's height, then ask him/her to stand at the base of the tree in question.

2 Hold a measuring stick out at arm's length and line the top of it up with your friend's head. Mark a line on the stick that coincides with the position of your friend's feet at the base of the tree.

3 Without moving, raise the stick so that the top lines up with the top of the tree, remembering to keep your arm locked out in front of you. Make a mark on the stick that relates to the position of the bottom of the tree.

4 These two marks give you a comparison between the height of the tree and the height of your friend. Dividing the larger figure by the smaller shows you how many times higher than your companion the tree is. So if the tree is 18 times the height of your friend and he/she is around 1.75 m (5 ft 9 in) tall, the height of the tree is approximately 31.5 m (103 ft).

The belly method

This only really works with smallish trees. You need an obliging friend and a stick that is about 2 m (6 ft 6 in) tall.

1 From the base of the tree, pace out 27 paces of equal length, then push your stick in the ground. Take another three paces and mark this spot.

2 Lie down at this spot with your eye as close to the ground as you can get it and ask your friend to move his/her finger up and down the stick until the finger lines up with the top of the tree from where you are lying. Mark this position on the stick.

3 Because the tree is ten times farther away from you than the stick, multiply the distance from the bottom of the stick to the fingermark by ten, and you have your estimate of height.

The pencil method

Probably the easiest of all. You need a pencil, a tape measure, and a cooperative person.

1 Hold the pencil up at arm's length and walk to a position where the bottom and the top of the tree correspond to the top and bottom of the pencil.

2 Rotate the pencil through 90° so that it is parallel with the ground, keeping the bottom of the pencil lined up with the base of the tree

3 Get your assistant to walk away from the tree at right angles to your position, stopping when he/she reaches a point that lines up with the end of your pencil. The distance between your assistant and the base of the tree will equal the height of the tree.

The tangents and protractors method

This is the most complicated but also the most accurate, as long as your tree is growing on level ground.

1 Make a simple clinometer by attaching a length of wood to a protractor, suspending a plumb line from the center of the wood so it dangles across the protractor, then sticking a nail or screw into the wood at either end of the protractor to act as sights, as on a rifle.

2 If you want to keep the math simple, walk away from the tree until, by lining up the two sights with the top of the tree, you get a plumb line reading of 45°. The distance from you to the tree plus your own height above the ground equals the height of the tree.

3 If you have a head for numbers, you can use the following formula to work out the height of the tree from any distance. If *a* is the distance from observer to tree and *b* is the angle shown on the clinometer, then the height of the tree = *a* x the tangent of *b*. The tangent of the angle *b* can be found from basic mathematical tables. The reason we use 45° to keep it simple is that the tangent of 45° is 1. But sometimes other vegetation may obstruct the view of your treetop at the desired distance, so being able to do the math gives you more flexibility!

Another way of estimating a tree's age that doesn't involve taking a chain saw to it is based on an observation by tree scientists that, no matter what the species, all trees in a temperate locality grow at around the same rate – approximately 2.5 cm (1 in) in circumference every year. So measuring the circumference of the tree in centimeters and dividing by 2.5 will give you an estimate of its age in years. (If you are measuring in inches, then the number of inches = the number of years.)

Measuring tree canopies

Mapping the shape of tree canopies is an excellent way to add more information to a tree study – it helps to assess how much sunlight is reaching the forest floor, the density of tree growth in relation to other species, and so on. Mark the position of the trunk of the tree on a piece of paper and then pace out the distance to the edge of the canopy in different directions. Note this down on your plan. Repeat this as many times as you like to get an accurate to-scale map.

Tree skin: learning about bark

Just as birds have distinctive plumage and butterflies have species-specific wing markings, so trees have their own unique profiles, leaf shapes, and bark textures. Some have such a distinctive general impression, size, and shape that, as with the "jizz" of birds, you can identify them by profile alone. However, no one tree is exactly like another, and unless it is on its own in a sheltered spot, it is unlikely just to be growing straight up. Even among members of the same species, growth and overall shape are affected to varying extents by environmental factors, such as prevailing wind direction, unique to each location and by competition with neighboring trees.

Leaves are one of the most useful ways of identifying trees, but at certain times of the year, they may be missing, and although there will often be a few withered "hangers on" or even a litter of leaves, seeds, or fruits at its base, this isn't always the case. Similarly, the profile of a tree may not be obvious – when you are close to it in woodland, for example. So you may have to fall back on the texture, color, and patterning of the bark to make an accurate identification.

Tree bark performs a protective function, bearing the brunt of any attack, whether from insect, mammal, bird, fungus, or plant – it is a

The shape of this wind-blown tree indicates the direction of the prevailing wind, which has altered the way the tree has grown over time.

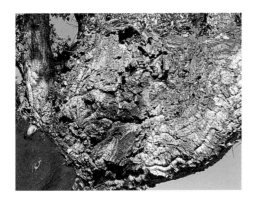

The bark of this cork oak (*Quercus suber*) is such marvelous armor that we have used it for centuries to keep bacteria and the like out of wine.

suit of armor, a flak jacket, and a bumper all in one. In some species it also takes on specialized tasks. Some of the eucalyptus trees in Australia and Indonesia, for example, are pyrotechnicians designed to survive and benefit from forest fires. They produce light, highly flammable, resin-rich bark that burns quickly when a fire sweeps through. This saves the trees from the potentially fatal effects of slow, hot-burning fires and also serves as a trigger for their fire-stimulated seeds, which start germinating when all the competition has been burned away.

Other species – particularly in the tropics, where there is a huge number of lichens, algae, and other potentially harmful epiphytes and parasites, but also familiar temperate trees such as beeches and birches – have developed very smooth bark or bark that is loose and peels off continuously, renewing the surface and making it hard for any other species to get a root hold on their surface.

On top of these protective uses, in young or green-stemmed trees, bark may be another organ of photosynthesis – some species have air holes called lenticels in the bark that work in the same way as the stomata in the leaves. All these roles, in conjunction with characteristic growth features such as fissures, cracks, and branch and leaf scars, combine to form the patterns, textures, and colors that make each species unique.

Even if a tree is dead, removing the bark will probably tear the roof off the homes of many smaller creatures that live underneath it. It is also bulky and messy to store and transport. A much better way to learn about bark is to start a collection of rubbings or molds and use them as the basis of a journal or scrapbook of species characteristics, such as profiles, height, leaf shape, seed, and any other information you can glean. Learn as many of the identification features as you can and test yourself when you are out walking to keep your skills honed.

Mangrove trees that grow in seawater have to protect themselves from salt damage. Some concentrate the salt in the bark or in leaves that are about to peel or drop, or just excrete it through their leaves. Those with special breathing roots that grow up out of the mud have corky, water-resistant bark to protect them from chemicals in the salty mud.

Rubbing it up the right way

Bark rubbing was the activity that started me tree spotting with any accuracy as a kid, although as we speak, I am sitting in a garden in Miami. I have no idea what any of the trees around me are – I may have to start on these now. You see these skills never become stagnant; you can continue applying them throughout life!

Step 1

If you have ever done brass rubbing, then you will be familiar with the simple principle involved in bark rubbing. Traditionally your drawing material would be a ball of a black waxy substance known as a cobbler's heel ball (for blacking the edges of shoe heels), but a wax crayon of a color that contrasts with your paper is a perfectly good substitute. I generally use greaseproof or regular typing paper, at least A4 size (that's about 11 ½ x 8 in) – this allows you to collect a representative section of the bark's pattern – but you may wish to experiment.

Step 2

You will need:
- a piece of thin paper
- strong tape or pins to fix the paper to the tree
- a wax crayon

1 Attach the paper to an interesting piece of bark, ideally one that has no lichens or other growths. Attaching it firmly is critical, as you do not want the paper to move once you have started rubbing.

2 Using the side rather than the tip of your crayon and applying gentle but constant pressure, rub over the paper, always moving in the same direction if possible. The crayon will pick out the higher relief of the bark underneath, and you will get a pattern that represents its textures.

Step 3

3 Make a note of the species name, location, and the height at which you took the rubbing (in some trees the texture of the bark varies with height).

4 You can also make rubbings of leaves and add them to your tree log (no pun intended). You can even frame the best ones as natural artworks.

Making an impression
bark casting

This requires a little more effort than bark rubbing, but the results are spectacular and well worth it, in my opinion.

You will need:
- a large lump of modeling clay
- a robust box
- plaster of paris

Step **2**

1 Knead the clay so that it is malleable, soft, and free of air bubbles. This makes it much easier to work with and gives you a better impression.

2 Firmly press the clay into the bark. Try to maintain a thickness of at least 1–1.5 cm (about ½ in) of clay and don't let the edges taper off. Your mold will be fragile if the clay is too thin.

3 Peel away the clay, which will have the texture of the bark impressed upon it. Place it gently in the box so that you can carry it home undamaged.

Step **4**

4 Back at base, place the mold on a work surface with the textured side uppermost. Using more modelling clay, make a dam around it at least 1.5–2 cm (1 ½–2 in) higher than the mold. You can choose at this point whether to make a curved cast, like the profile of the tree, or a flat section, but a curved one always looks more impressive.

5 Mix up some plaster of paris (see p. 85) and pour it into the mold. Leave to set for a few hours and then carefully lift and peel away the modeling clay to reveal your bark cast, ready for display. If you want to bring out the textures even more, paint the cast with a water-based colored wash. Use bright colors or try to re-create the natural ones, it's up to you.

Step **5**

6 If you are going to make a lot of casts for a collection, it is a good idea to decide on standard dimensions, as it makes them easier to store and/or mount. And why stop at casting bark? You can try making impressions of many things, even leaves and seeds.

Studying plants in situ

Earlier on I mentioned some work I once did on rare butterflies that involved studying the vegetation in their habitats. The following are just a few of the common ways of recording and standardizing our observations – it isn't good enough to walk about and say, well it looks like there are a few violets here and none over there, for example. You need to have some numbers to back up your statements.

The quadrat

This is a simple device that divides the habitat up into manageable chunks – you simply count the number of species represented within the frame and extrapolate over the habitat as a whole. To get a fair representation of a habitat, you should obviously collect as many sample quadrats as possible. For greater accuracy, this needs to be done randomly – which really means throwing your quadrat over your shoulder so that you have no influence on the process and don't bias your data!

Steps **1-2**

You will need:
- 4 pieces of wood 30 cm (12 in) long
- 4 pieces of string
- 8 drawing pins
- nails or screws

1 Nail or screw the wood together to form a crude square frame.

2 Mark the 10 and 20 cm (4 and 8 in) points on each side and pin the string tightly across the frame from each point, dividing your big square into nine smaller, equal squares.

3 This will make a perfectly good quadrat, but if you want something more robust and longer lasting, replace the string with wire and attach it by drilling fixture holes through the wooden frame. Instead of nailing the wood together at the corners, use screws and wing nuts – this allows the frame to be collapsed for easy transportation in your field bag.

Step **3**

You scratch my back
surprising plant relationships

Although the co-evolution of flowers and insects millions of years ago is the plant/animal relationship that most regularly touches our lives – and without it we wouldn't have fruit, seeds, or honey – there are many other examples of animal and plant lives that have become closely intertwined.

Giant ponerine ants (*Paraponera clavata*) feeding on *Heliconia imbricata* plant in a tropical rain forest

Ants and plants have symbiotic relationships that can be a very complicated and beautiful. These plants are known as myrmecophytes or "ant plants" and they belong to a variety of plant families. One ant plant is the bull's horn acacia (*Acacia sphaerocephala*), a thorny bush that lives on the African plains, which come complete with a huge diversity of bush-eating browsing mammals such as antelopes. This sounds like a bad thing for the bushes, but the acacia has come up with its own security force in the shape of some aggressive little ants that live within it. This is no casual arrangement, but a formal binding contract that benefits both parties in many ways. The acacia's thorns have swollen, hollow bases in which ant-colony life occurs. Food is laid on, too, in the form of a supersweet sap that oozes out on demand from extrafloral nectarines on the plant's stems, and protein in the shape of little baglike pouches called mullerian bodies on the tips of the leaves.

In return for this feast, the ants defend the plant. Just try touching, even breathing on it, and out they swarm from holes in the thorns, armed and ready to defend the colony. Believe me, any naturalist who has accidentally bumped into one of these bushes regrets it – they hurt! The ants also do the gardening, cleaning the leaves of any fungus or harmful growths, and they patrol the ground looking for germinating seeds, which may be competition for the parent plant; these are nipped in the bud before they can get off the ground!

Other myrmecophytes include the hydnophytum plants, which have swollen stems that look like footballs. The ant species that live here collect lots of debris as they forage. This is discarded in the chambers, and the plants grow internal roots that tap into this source of compost. The same principle goes for the *dischidia* species, which have hollow, beanlike leaves instead.

Studying plants at home

Before we get carried away with the idea of studying and preserving plant specimens, it is important to remember that plants are just as vulnerable to overcollecting and damage as animals. Many are protected by law. I realize that many lifelong passions for plants have been born from collecting a fistful of flowers for Mum, but the responsible naturalist should always collect as few reference specimens as possible. Digital photography is an excellent alternative that will enable you to identify many species without even touching the plant.

Having just sung the praises of the technological revolution, I have to say I'm a stickler for the old methods. Getting your hands dirty, touching, smelling, and even being stung makes each experience unique and more likely to stand out in your memory, which serves you a lot better than simply pressing a button. On a more practical level, if the plants you are looking at can only be identified by counting the flower bracts, measuring the stamens, or observing subtle details such as how hairy the undersides of its leaves are, you really need a specimen. Look at the diversity of grass species in the average meadow and try working them out with nothing but a **camera**! Traditional skills will also stand you in good stead as a backup when it is bucketing down with rain and you cannot use your camera, the batteries are dead, or you haven't brought the camera with you.

At any time in the field you may stumble across a plant that you have never seen before or that looks a little different. You don't have your field guides with you, so what do you do? You could pick a leaf or flower and pop it into a pocket, but it may get damaged and especially in hot weather, will soon wilt and wither to a pathetic, floppy, unrecognizable mass that is no good for anything other than compost. The secret to getting the most out of your plant specimens lies in keeping them fresh for as long as possible. That is why every botanist worth his or her salt always carries a **plastic bag**. It not only protects the specimen, it also slows down water loss (which is what makes the plant floppy in the first place – see Transpiration, p. 252), and you can write notes on the bag itself with an indelible pen for later reference.

Traditionally, field biologists would go one step further by carrying a slightly bulkier and less crushable item of equipment known as a **vasculum**. This is a rigid box lined with layers of blotting paper or plastic between which you sandwich your various samples. You can buy them from scientific suppliers, or make your own from a plastic freezer bag or the sort of box that Chinese takeout comes in.

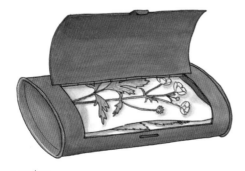

vasculum

Tips on preparation

It's important to keep specimens fresh until the last minute before you work with them or preserve them. On returning home from an expedition, the busy naturalist may have a number of urgent matters to attend to, so the less demanding plants tucked away in their plastic bags and vasculums may be overlooked. The trick is to buy yourself time. The moment you get home, take the plants out of their containers, rinse them in water, and pop them in a vase until you are ready to look at them properly. Transpiration continues after the stem has been cut, so water is drawn up the vessels, leaving nothing but air behind. Even if with every good intention you thrust the stems into water, a bubble of air will eventually block the way, forming an air lock and killing the plant's tissues. If, on the other hand, you remove a section from the bottom of the stem, you hopefully chop away that upwardly mobile air bubble and transpiration can continue unhindered. In other words, your plants stay fresh!

If you are going to dry or press your plants (see below), ensure that they are clean and free from debris and insects (a large, well-camouflaged fleshy caterpillar can really mess up a pressing, and the process isn't very pleasant for the insect either). Remove as much moisture as possible by dabbing and blotting the specimen.

Sometimes it is necessary to put the water back into a plant in order to observe a structure or even to take a section to view under a microscope. This can be done with varying degrees of success by placing it in hot water. Leaving a soft, delicate succulent in warm water for a few minutes will probably do the trick, whereas tougher characters may require a gentle simmer for half an hour or so. The emphasis is on simmer, as a vigorous boil will turn your specimen into soup!

The big squeeze – pressing plants

The traditional way to preserve botanical specimens is in a flower press. Despite the name, these are useful for squishing and preserving all but the most robust parts of a plant. They come in different sizes and are basically pieces of thin but stout wooden board with blotting paper between to absorb moisture. It is this that dries the plants out and is the principle behind their preservation. The press is clamped shut by numerous threaded screws and wing nuts or straps.

You can purchase the real deal from any biological or scientific

Pressing plants

supplier, but sandwiching your plants between sheets of blotting paper and wedging these between the pages of heavy books works well. If you are using books, do try to remember which ones you put your plants in. I am still coming across plant pressings that have been waiting to be discovered for 20 years or so between the pages of *Encyclopedia Britannica*!

Pressing plants does have a couple of limitations. The specimens can lose their original form and become distorted; they will also fade to a greater or lesser extent, depending on what color they were to start with – green is the most unstable and therefore the worst offender – and how fast they are dried out in the press. Drying is best done quickly, so speed things up by keeping the room dry as possible and changing the blotting paper every couple of days, to ferry away the moisture. The fleshier the specimen, the more water it will contain, so the more frequently you should change the paper. As a rough guide, most plants will be dry in two to four weeks.

It may seem a little extreme, but that handy kitchen tool the microwave oven is also useful for drying plants. Make a small press without any metal parts and pop this in the oven for a couple of minutes on a medium setting, being careful not to let everything overheat. Remove the blotting paper, check how it's going, and repeat with fresh paper until you have a satisfactory specimen.

You can mount dry and flat plant specimens in numerous ways, but you should always add data such as date and location. Given the limitations mentioned above, photos, drawings and notes on the colors of the living plant are also very useful additions to your record.

A flotation tank

Specimens that have become floppy and soft, or delicate aquatic plants such as seaweeds and pond weeds, can be preserved too, but getting their position correct without the support of the water they grow in can be tricky. So the clever naturalist uses just that – water. Plop your plant into a tray of water and slide a sheet of stout cardboard into the water under the plant. Slowly lift the cardboard until the plant is lying in shallow water, then use a paintbrush or needle to slide it around until you are satisfied with the arrangement. Carefully lift the cardboard out of the water. Your specimen should now be in its final resting place. Allow it to dry for an hour or so and then gently place it in a press with a layer of absorbent paper on top. Keep pressure to a minimum, and the specimen should not shift its position.

Fungi

Wander through a deciduous wood in the autumn and you will be trudging through a carpet of leaf litter, the home of one of the most extraordinary groups of organisms in the living world. Turn over a handful of leaf litter and you will find fluffy but frail strands of lace; look at the bark of trees and you may see tough, corky layers of bracket fungus; and of course glance in dark damp corners and you will find them alive with the fruiting bodies that we call mushrooms and toadstools. These are all forms of fungus, and I call them organisms because they are so weird that experts can't even agree as to whether or not they are plants – some say they belong to their own unique kingdom.

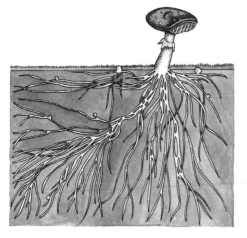

The hyphae form an underground network so vast that there are several tonnes of them per hectare or acre.

Fungi can be split into two classes – the familiar kind that I have just described are the basidiomycetes, while the others are the "saclike" fungi or ascomycetes. These include the yeasts that make so much of baking and brewing possible, and those that feed on human skin and cause such afflictions as athlete's foot. One thing they all have in common is an inability to photosynthesize and produce their own food. So all fungi feed on either living or dead organic material. If it is dead they are described as saprophytes; if it is living, they are parasites.

Whether they are categorized as plants or not, fungi do not have cells like a plant. Their smallest units are elongated, enzyme-oozing tentacles called hyphae, which infiltrate the food substance and form a netlike arrangement called a mycelium. Hyphae vary in thickness, with the smallest less than a millimeter ($\frac{1}{25}$ in) in diameter. But what they lack in stature, they make up for in numbers – there may be 70,000 million of them in a single gram of soil (about 1,200 million in an ounce), amounting to several tons per hectare or acre. The hyphae's task is to move through the cells of their host plant, breaking down

Like many fungi, the fly agaric (*Amanita musearia*) has a relationship with trees, in this case birch (*Befula* spp.), providing certain nutrients for the soil in exchange for carbon from the tree's roots. Find a birch and you might just find the fly agaric.

This large collection of fruiting bodies of this velvet fungus means that there is a huge network of hyphae within the tree helping itself to nutrients.

tough material, collecting nutrients, and turning the onetime stars of the ecosystem into nothing more than fungus fodder. If they weren't around to digest the vast quantity of detritus that Mother Nature produces, the place would be a mess.

To cap it all: fungus reproduction

What we call mushrooms and toadstools may be just the visible fruiting bodies of the fungus, but what a variety there is – something like 6,000 species in the U.K. alone. You simply cannot get bored with fungi. Don't get sidetracked by worrying whether or not you can eat them. Just revel in the eerie black bootlaces of honey fungus (*Armillaria mellea*), the massive giant puffball (*Calvatia gigantea*), which can grow to 60 cm (2 ft) across, the suggestive form of the stinkhorn (*Phallus impudicus*), which one early mycologist found so offensive that he coyly drew it upside down. And remember that what you are seeing is only the reproductive part of a massive subterranean being. Under that dead tree stump there may be 15 hectares (37 acres) of mycelia, which may weigh 100 tons and be 1,500 years old!

The role of these fruiting bodies is to reproduce by means of scattering tiny, lightweight capsules of genetic material called spores. Autumn is the high season for this, because fungi, both above and below the ground, need lots of moisture in order to grow. For most of the year they lurk out of sight in whatever wet areas they can find, but when water becomes abundant, they are out there ready to breed.

The gills of a wax cap fungus (*Hygrocybe* spp.) from which will fall millions of spores

Once the spores of the shaggy ink cap (*Coprinus cornatus*) have been released, the gill tissue undergoes auto-digestion to form a black liquid that you can actually write with.

Right: Rain falling on the springy wall of the fruiting body of the giant puffball (*Langermannia gigantea*) puffs up to seven million spores into the air.

Part of the secret of fungal success lies in their particularly efficient way of distributing themselves around the place. All species, from the tiny molds to the giant puffball produce spores, which, being so small, get everywhere. Your average mushroom can produce a staggering 30 million spores (these are what makes up the "dust" that is visible when you make a spore print, see p. 277), while a 30 cm (1 ft) giant puffball really does throw its numbers to the wind, producing a mind-blowing 7,000,000,000,000 spores! Fortunately, only a minute percentage of these win the lottery of life, otherwise we would all be living on Planet Puffball.

The most familiar way of releasing spores is via a mushroom-like arrangement. The characteristic "cap" is the fungus's way of pushing its body up out of the dark into the air, giving its spores the best chance of catching the wind and being dispersed far and wide. The umbrella shape is no accident, protecting this living dust from the elements. Puffballs are an exception to this rule – they expose themselves to heavy raindrops and wind, as these are what makes a ripe sporing body "puff." That cloud of smoke so enjoyed by many children is actually a puff of spores. Many species of lichen and bird's nest fungus (*Cyathus* and *Crucibulum* spp.) use similarly explosive means of distributing their spores skyward.

Other fungi use insects, particularly those that are attracted to the smell of decay. Cage fungus (*Ileodictyon* spp.) and stinkhorns (*Phallus* spp.) generate a disgusting, sickly sweet stench for the benefit of carrion-feeding flies that walk all over the moist spores, transferring them on to their bodies and from there to everything else with which they make contact. What they lack in olfactory appeal to us they make up for in their incredibly weird forms, personal architecture and structure.

To demonstrate how good these spores are at doing what they do, leave a piece of bread or fruit outside. Within days it will be showing a bloom of furry fungus that will eventually produce little black dots of sporing bodies. These are the "pins" that give these lower forms of fungi the name pin molds. What they are doing is simply colonizing a resource and recycling it, breaking the food down into its component parts. It was a similar incidence of spores getting into places where they weren't supposed to be that led to the greatest accident in medical history. Alexander Fleming was growing bacteria in a petri dish when he noticed that a fungus had contaminated one of them and killed all the bacteria. That fungus, penicillium, was later to become the source of one of the greatest antibiotics, penicillin.

Bake your boletus
dry-preserving your fungi

Life requires water, and the tiniest amount of water can create life in places where you might not want it, such as your specimen collection. Even in a mildly humid atmosphere a spore can germinate and turn meadowsweet into a moldering mess, or a bacterium can breed and reduce a boletus to a blob. So it's best to keep things dry.

Preserving fungi presents its own set of problems – many will dissolve almost as soon as you look at them, others are juicy and more solid, and yet others have such fantastically complex and detailed structures that pressing will simply end in a nasty mess. For such specimens – and this works well with certain plant structures too – the best bet is to use a sand bath. The finer the sand, the better.

You will need:
- an ovenproof metal baking dish
- a baking tray and enough fine sand to cover it generously
- a fungus

1 Turn your oven to its highest setting, fill the baking dish with sand, and bake it until it is as hot as you can make it – about half an hour. Carefully remove the tray using oven gloves.

Step **1**

2 Pour a layer of hot sand on to a baking tray, place your fungus on top of it, and then pour in the rest of the sand, carefully brushing it into all crevices until the fungus is immersed in very hot sand.

3 Leave for a day before exhuming. If the fungus is not totally dry, repeat until it is. It is then ready for storage or presenting. Most specimens will be fine as they are, but to be on the safe side, store them in an airtight container with packets of desiccants such as silica gel, which can be purchased from electrical and photographic shops.

Step **2**

Spore prints

This is a rather fun way to see microscopic spores without a microscope and at the same time produce a beautiful representation of the elegant shapes of the gills and pores that release them from under the cap of a regular mushroom or toadstool.

You will need:
- a mushroom or toadstool
- a sharp knife
- a piece of black cardboard
- a bowl large enough to fit over the top of the fungus

Step 1

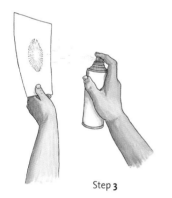

Step 2

Step 3

1 Cut the stem of the fungus off flush with the cap. Do this very gently and without touching the underside of the cap, as you might damage the fragile spore-releasing structures. Turn the cap the right way up and lay it, sporing surfaces down, on the cardboard.

2 To stop air movements interfering with what you are trying to achieve, place a bowl over the mushroom – remember that spores are designed to be wafted by even the slightest breeze, and this will result in a less sharp impression.

3 Leave for a day or so before carefully lifting first the bowl and then the fungus cap off the paper. You should be left with the pattern of the gills or pores, made by the millions of microscopic spores that have lain exactly where they have fallen. The pattern will soon be disrupted as the spores blow around, so if you want to preserve what you see, spray the print with fixative (available from art suppliers) or hairspray. This acts as a light glue, sticking everything together.

Going further

I hope that this book will have sparked your interest and that you'll want to go on to find out more information. One of the best ways of doing this is to contact some of the specialist societies. They usually have good websites with all sorts of links and information, and many produce leaflets and booklets, run conservation projects, and will be able to tell you about events happening in your area. Joining a society can give you a chance to go on outings with experts in the area, and to receive useful information and newsletters. As well as the organizations listed here, remember there is probably a local natural history society or field club in your area.

American Bird Conservancy
P.O. Box 249
The Plains, VA 20198
Phone: (540) 253-5780
Fax: (540) 253-5782
Email: abc@abcbirds.org
www.abcbirds.org/

American Forests
734 15th Street NW
Suite 800
Washington, DC 20005
Phone: (202) 955-4500
Fax: (202) 955-4588
Email: info@amfor.org
www.americanforests.org/

Bat Conservation International
P.O. Box 162603
Austin, TX 78716
Phone: (512) 327-9721
Fax: (512) 327-9724
www.batcon.org/

California Bat Conservation Fund
3053 Fillmore Street, #239
San Francisco, CA 94123
www.californiabats.com/

Canadian Wildlife Federation
350 Michael Cowpland Dr.
Kanata, Ontario K2M 2W1
Phone: (800) 563-WILD
Fax: (613) 599-4428
Email: info@cwf-fcf.org
www.cwf-fcf.org
www.wildeducation.org
www.spaceforspecies.ca

Carnivore Preservation Trust
1940 Hanks Chapel Road
Pittsboro, NC 27312
Phone: (919) 542-4684
www.cptigers.org/

Center for Plant Conservation
P.O. Box 299
St. Louis, MO 63166
Phone: (314) 577-9450
Fax: (314) 577-9465
Email: cpc@mobot.org
www.centerforplantconservation.org/

Children's International Wildlife Sanctuary
PO Box 379
Saratoga, NY 12866-0379
Email: webperson@ciws.org
www.ciws.org/

Cornell Laboratory of Ornithology
159 Sapsucker Woods Rd.
Ithaca, NY 14850
Phone: (800) 843-BIRD
or (607) 254-BIRD
Email: cornellbirds@cornell.edu
birds.cornell.edu/

Defenders of Wildlife National Headquarters
1130 17th Street NW
Washington, DC 20036
Phone: (202) 682-9400
Email: info@defenders.org
www.defenders.org/

The "Ding" Darling Wildlife Society
Email: dingdarling@iline.com
dingdarlingsociety.org/index.html

Durrell Wildlife Conservation Trust
Les Augres Manor
La Profonde Rue
Trinity, Jersey je3 5bp
English Channel Islands
Phone: 01534 860000
Fax: 01534 860001
www.durrellwildlife.org

Environmental Protection Information Center
P. O. Box 397
Garberville, CA 95542
Phone: (707) 923-2931
Fax: (707) 923-4210
www.wildcalifornia.org/

EPA Wetlands Helpline c/o Water Resource Center
Mail Code RC-4100
1200 Pa. Ave. NW
Washington DC 20460
Phone:(800) 832-7828
Fax: (202) 260-6029
Email: wetlands.helpline@epa.gov
www.epa.gov/owow/birds/

Fauna & Flora International, Inc.
P.O. Box 42575
Washington, DC
20015-0575
Phone: (202) 329 1672
Email: ffi-usa@fauna-flora.org
www.fauna-flora.org/

Florida Defenders of the Environment
4424 NW 13 Street,
Ste. C-8, Gainesville, FL
32609-1885
Phone: (352) 378-8465
Email: fde@fladefenders.org
www.fladefenders.org/index2.html

The Hummingbird Society
249 E. Main St., Bldg 2,
Suite 9
P.O. Box 394
Newark, DE 19715

Phone: (800) 529-3699
Fax: (302) 369-1816
www.hummingbird.org/

IUCN Canada Office
555 René Lévesque Bl. W.
Suite #500
Montréal, Quebec
H2Z 1B1 Canada
Phone: (514) 287-9704
Fax: (514) 287-9687
Email: canada@iucn.org
www.iucn.org/places
/canada/
USA Multilateral Office
1630 Connecticut Ave. NW
3rd Floor
Washington, DC 20009
Phone: (202) 387-4826
Fax: (202) 387-4823
postmaster@iucnus.org
www.iucn.org/places/usa/

Intl. Wildlife Coalition
70 East Falmouth Hwy
East Falmouth, MA
02536 USA
Phone: (508) 548-8328
Fax: (508) 457-1988
Email: iwchq@iwc.org
www.iwc.org/

The Jane Goodall Institute
USA Headquarters
8700 Georgia Ave Ste. 500
Silver Spring, MD 20910
Phone: (240) 645-4000
Fax: (301) 565-3188
www.janegoodall.org/
default.asp

The John Muir Trust
Email:admin@jmt.org
www.jmt.org/

The League of
Conservation Voters, Inc.
1920 L Street NW
Suite 800
Washington, DC 20036
Phone: (202) 785-8683
Fax: (202) 835-0491
www.lcv.org/

Migratory Bird
Conservancy
http://www.conservebirds.
org/about_us.htm

The Minnesota
Ornithologists' Union
10 Church Street S.E.
Minneapolis, MN
55455-0104
Email: mou@biosci.
umn.edu
biosci.cbs.umn.edu
/~mou/

National Audubon Society
700 Broadway
New York, NY 10003
Phone: (212) 979-3000
Fax: (212) 979-3188
Email: jwells@
audubon.org
www.audubon.org/

National Bird-Feeding
Society
1800 North Kent Street,
Suite 1120
Arlington, VA 22209
Phone: (703) 525-6300
Fax: (703) 525-4610
postmaster@
conservationfund.org
www.birdfeeding.org/
www.conservation
fund.org/

National Fish and
Wildlife Foundation
1120 Connecticut Avenue,
NW Suite 900
Washington, DC 20036
Phone: (202) 857-0166
Fax: (202) 857-0162
www.nfwf.org/

National Parks
Conservation Assoc.
1300 19th Street NW
Suite 300
Washington, DC 20036
Phone: (800) 628-7275
Fax: (202) 659-0650

Email: npca@npca.org
www.npca.org/

Native American Fish
and Wildlife Society
Email: webmaster@
nafws.org
www.nafws.org/

Native Forest Network
P.O. Box 8251
Missoula, MT 59807
Phone: (406) 542-7343
Fax: (406) 542-7347
Email: nfn@
wildrockies.org
www.nativeforest.org/

The Nature Conservancy
4245 North Fairfax Drive,
Suite 100
Arlington, VA 22203-1606
Phone: (703) 841-5300
Email: comment@tnc.org
www.nature.org/

North American
Butterfly Association
NABA-New York
170 West End Ave., #10T
New York, NY 10023
Email: kathleenhowley
@hotmail.com
www.naba.org/

Operation Migration
In Canada:
174 Mary St. Suite 101,
Port Perry, ON., L9L 1B7
In United States.:
P.O. Box 868,
Buffalo, NY, 14207
Phone: (905) 982-1096
or (800) 675-2618
Fax: 905-982-1097
Email:opmig@
durham.net
www.operation
migration.org/

The Organization for
Bat Conservation
39221 Woodward Avenue

Bloomfield Hills, MI 48303
Phone: (248) 645-3232
Email: obcbats@aol.com
www.batconservation.org/

Ornithology.com
4798 Songbird Lane
Chico, CA 95973
www.ornithology.com/

The Peregrine Fund
5668 W Flying Hawk Lane
Boise ID, 83709
Phone: (208) 362-3716
Fax: (208) 362-2376
Email: tpf@peregrine
fund.org
www.peregrinefund.
org/default.asp

Washingtonians for
Wildlife Conservation
www.w4wc.org/

Washington
Ornithological Society
P.O. Box 31783
Seattle, WA 98103-1783
Email: WOSweb@
wos.org.
www.wos.org/

The WILD Foundation
PO Box 1380
Ojai, CA USA 93024
Phone: (805) 640-0390
Fax: (805) 640-0230
Email: info@wild.org
www.wild.org/

The Wildlife Society
5410 Grosvenor Lane
Suite 200
Bethesda, MD 20814-2144
Phone: (301) 897-9770
Fax: (301) 530-2471
www.wildlife.org/

World Wildlife Fund
1250 24th Street, NW
Washington, DC 20037
Phone: (202) 293-4800
www.worldwildlife.org/

Suppliers

I've tried to give you as much information and advice as possible about the practical equipment you need in the field. It is possible to make a lot of the equipment yourself, as I've demonstrated throughout, but for those essential bits you just have to buy (like binoculars) here are a few recommended suppliers.

Foster & Smith's
Wild Bird Store
Drs. Foster & Smith, Inc.
2253 Air Park Road
P.O. Box 100
Rhinelander, WIS 54501
www.drsfostersmith.com

Wild Birds Unlimited, Inc.
11711 N. College Ave.
Suite 146
Carmel, IN 46032
Phone: (317) 571-7100
or (800) 326-4928
www.wbu.com/

Lowe's Home
Improvement Warehouse
For activities supplies
Lowe's Companies, Inc.
P.O. Box 1111
North Wilkesboro,
NC 28656
Phone: (800) 445-6937
www.lowes.com/

eNature.com
1045 Sansome St.
Suite 304

San Francisco, CA 94111
Phone: (415) 732-7000
Fax: (415) 732-7007

Earth Treasures Inc.
Includes: The Telescope Store, Weather Warehouse, MicroscopesRus, BinocShop
12 Maine St.
Keene, NH 03431
Phone: (800) 550-7192

The Good Nature
Company, Inc.
12137 3 1/2 Mile Rd.
Battle Creek, MI 49015
Phone: (269) 979-1151
Fax: (269) 979-1615
Email: jlbeckgood
nature@earthlink.net

Southern States Coop Inc.
southernstates-coop.com

Home Depot, Inc
For activities supplies
www.homedepot.com

Sharper Image
For Binoculars,
Cameras, Optics
Phone: (800) 344-5555
www.sharperimage.com

Ritz Interactive, Inc.
For Binoculars,
Cameras, Telescopes
2010 Main St.
Suite 400
Irvine, CAL 92614
www.ritzinteractive.com

Binoculars.com
30 East Superior St
Duluth, MN 55802
Phone: (800) 246-6285
Fax: (218) 728-7955
www.binoculars.com

Hudson Trail Outfitters
Email: Webmaster@
HudsonTrail.com

L.L. Bean
Phone: (800) 441-5713
www.llbean.com

Further reading

Baker, Nick, *Baker's Bug Book* (New Holland, 2002)

Baker, Nick, *Nick Baker's British Wildlife: A Month by Month Guide* (New Holland, 2003)

Bang, Preben and Preben Dahlstrom, *Animal Tracks and Signs* (Oxford University Press, 2001)

Baughman, Mel (ed.), *National Geographic Reference Atlas to the Birds of North America* (National Geographic Society, 2003)

Baughman, Mel, *Birders Journal to the Birds of North America* (Stackpole Press, 1996)

Burton, Robert and Peter Holden, *RSPB Birdfeeder Guide* (Dorling Kindersley, 2003)

Brown, Vinson, *The Amateur Naturalist's Diary* (Penguin, 1992)

Brown, Vinson, *The Amateur Naturalist's Handbook* (Prentice Hall, 1980)

Cave, Godfrey, *The Complete Amateur Naturalist* (Penguin, 1992)

Falkus, Hugh, *Nature Detective* (Penguin, 1980)

Gilbert, Carter Rowell and James D. Williams, *National Audubon Society Field Guide to Fishes: North America* (Knopf, 2002)

Harding, Patrick, *How to Identify Edible Mushrooms* (Collins, 1996)

Hayward, Peter et al., *Pocket Guide Seashore* (Collins, 1996)

Macdonald, David W. and Priscilla Barrett, *Collins Field Guide Mammals of Britain and Europe* (Collins, 1993)

Miller, Peter and Mick Loates, *Pocket Guide Fish* (Collins, 1997)

More, David and Owen Johnson, *Collins Tree Guide* (Collins, 2004)

Murphy, Frances, *Keeping Spiders, Insects and Other Land Invertebrates in Captivity* (Bartholomew, 1980)

Nancarrow, Loren and Janet Hogan Taylor, *The Worm Book* (Ten Speed Press, 1998)

National Audubon Society Field Guide to North American Reptiles and Amphibians (Knopf, 1979)

National Geographic The Curious Naturalist (National Geographic Society, 1991)

National Geographic Field Guide to the Birds of North America, 4th Edition (National Geographic Society, 2002)

North, Ray, *Ants* (Whittet Books, 1996)

O'Toole, Christopher ed., *The New Encyclopedia of Insects and Their Allies* (Oxford University Press, 2002)

Oxford, R.., *Minibeast Magic – Kind-hearted Capture Techniques for Invertebrates* (Yorkshire Wildlife Trust, 1999)

Pakenham, Thomas, *Remarkable Trees of the World* (W.W. Norton & Co., 2002)

Pyle, Robert Michael, *National Audubon Society Field Guide to North American Butterflies* (Knopf, 1981)

Rezendes, Paul, *Tracking and the Art of Seeing* (HarperCollins, 1999)

Sample, Geoff, *Collins Field Guide: Bird Songs and Calls of Britain and Northern Europe* (Contains 2 accompanying CDs) (Collins, 1996)

Stachan, Rob, *Mammal Detective* (Whittet Books, 1995)

Thieret, John, *National Audubon Society Field Guide to Wildflowers: Eastern Region* (Knopf, 2001)

Whitaker, John O., *National Audubon Society Field Guide to North American Mammals* (Knopf, 1996)

White, Mel, *National Geographic Guide to Birdwatching Sites, Eastern U.S.* (National Geographic, 1999)

White, Mel, *National Geographic Guide to Birdwatching Sites, Western U.S.* (National Geographic, 1999)

Index

Note: page numbers in *italics* refer to pictures and information contained in captions.

Acknowledgements

The publishers would like to thank The London Wetland Centre, Alana Ecology, Swarovski Optics, and Watkins and Doncaster for their help in this project.

Illustrations

p.20, p.22, p.30, p.31, p.35, p.36, p.42, p.43, p.44, p.45, p.46, p.82, p.89, p.91, p.95, p.97, p.99, p.116, p.118, p.126, p.133, p.134, p.149, p.151, p.158, p.167, p.173, p.175, p.183, p.194, p.200, p.208, p.209, p.218, p.221, p.226, p.229, p.236, p.237, p.239, p.254, p.256, p.257, p.258, p.259, © Lizzie Harper

p.142, p.143, p.145, p.146, p.159, p.260, p.261, p.264, p.265, p.267, p.269 © Sue Hagerty

p.85, p.86, p.101, p.105, p.129, p.135, p.137 © Victoria Edwards

p.59, p.65, p.66, p.156, p.172, p.174, p.196, p.212, p.213, p.217, p.227, p.228, p.241, p.242, p.246, p.247, p.249, p. 253 © 'Ome Design

Photography

p.108 © Alana Ecology; p.27 (bottom), p.37, p.80, p.87, p.102, p.103, p.115, p.132, p.133, p.136, p.162, p.170, p.175, p.181 © Nick Baker; p.49 © Preben Bang; p.64 © Ernest Charles; p.60 © C J Wildbird Foods; p.21, p.70, p.150 (top), p.160 © Corbis; p.54t, p.54b, p.55, p.140 © David Cottridge; p.103 © FLPA; back cover, p.20, p.22, p.25, p.27 (top), p.29, p.31, p.32 (bottom), p.33, p.37, p.38 (top), p.39, p.201 © HarperCollins; p.7 © James Morgan; p.30, p.123t, p.123b, p.195, p.215, p.268 © Nature PL; p. 98 © NHM PhotoStudio; p.32t, p.139, p.151, p.211, p.219, p.244 © Science Photo; front cover, p.8, p.12, p.13, p.15, p.16, p.28, p.34, p.38 (bottom), p.134, p.266 © Amelia Troubridge

The following pictures were supplied by NHPA: p.110, p.244b © Ant Photo Library/NHPA; p.114, 2ndb © Pete Atkinson/NHPA; p.165 2nd © Jim Bain/NHPA; p.165b, p.188 © Matt Bain/NHPA; p.112, p.113, p.168t, p.169, p.176, p.226, p.230, p.231 © Anthony Bannister/NHPA; p.68, p.122, p.155, p.184t, p.192m, p.192b, p.199, p.204, p.223, p.232, p.262 © George Bernard/NHPA; p.125b © Joe Blossom/NHPA; p.119, p.234 © Mark Bowler/NHPA; p.52bl © John & Sue Buckingham/NHPA; p.184b, p.214, p.221t, p.221b © N. A. Callow/NHPA; p.6, p.81, p.90, p.170, p.157b, p.190, p.203r, p.219, p.236b, p.240r, p.251t, p.272, p.273t, p.273b © Laurie Campbell/NHPA; p.76, p.150b, p.178, p.206b, p.240l, p.248 © Gerry Cambridge/NHPA; p.114bl, p.116, p.120, p.163,

p.165t, p.167 © James Carmichael Jnr/NHPA; p.114, 2ndl © Jordi Bas Casas/NHPA; p.40, p.131, p.189 © Bill Coster/NHPA; p.50, p.58bl, p.79, p.92, p.107, p.125t, p.128, p.168b, p.183, p.187, p.192t, p.193b, p.207t, p.207b, p.222, p.235t, p.235b, p.237b, p.250, p.251b, p..258, p.275 © Stephen Dalton/NHPA; p.74, p.84bl, p.84br, p.94 © Manfred Danegger/NHPA; p.91 © Nigel J. Dennis/NHPA; p.238t, p.238b, p.274 © Guy Edwardes/NHPA; p.243 © Patrick Fagot/NHPA; p.57, p.257t © Melvin Grey/NHPA; p.93 © Dan Griggs/NHPA; p.153 © John Hayward/NHPA; p.71, p.88, p.177 © Martin Harvey/NHPA; p.114tl, p.117, p.127, p.164t, p.164b, p.166, p.263b © Daniel Heuclin/NHPA; p.141, p.220, p.245 © Image Quest 3-D/NHPA; p.165, p.18, p.41, p.63, p.67, p.96, p.121, p.179 © Ernie James/NHPA; p.73t © John Jeffery/NHPA; p.138 © B. Jones & M. Shimlock/NHPA; p.271 © Darek Karp/NHPA; p.61b © Rich Kirchner/NHPA; p.180 p.203l © T. Kitchin & V. Hurst/NHPA; © Stephen Krasemann/NHPA; p.198, p.215br © Yves Lanceau/NHPA; p.104 © Michael Leach/NHPA; p. 147 © Lutra/NHPA; p.185 © Trevor McDonald/NHPA; p.202 © Jean-Louis le Moigne/NHPA; p.184m, p.257b, p.263t © Alberto Nardi/NHPA; p.47t © Haroldo Palo Jnr/NHPA; p.45 © William Paton/NHPA; p.148 © Linda Pitkin/NHPA; p.255 © Rod Planck/NHPA; p.48t, p.58br, p.73b, p.77, p.78, p.84tr, p.111 © Andy Rouse/NHPA; p.114, 3rdl © Jenny Sauvanet/NHPA; p.114, 3rdb, p.144br, p.154 © Kevin Schafer/NHPA; p.84tl, p.216t, p.237t © John Shaw/NHPA; p.4, p.197, p.236t © Eric Soder/NHPA; p.47b, p.216b © R. Sorensen & J.Olsen/NHPA; p.48b, p.233 © Karl Switak/NHPA; p.205 © Robert Thompson/NHPA; p.61t p.72 © Roger Tidman/NHPA; p.62, p.106, p.191 © Ann & Steve Toon/NHPA; p.165 3rd © M. I. Walker/NHPA; p.52br © Alan Williams/NHPA; p.193t © Bill Wood/NHPA; p.186 © Norbert Wu /NHPA;